FLOWERS
ON GRANITE

One Woman's
Odyssey
Through Psychoanalysis

by Dörte von Drigalski, M.D.

TRANSLATED FROM THE GERMAN BY
Anthea Bell and Marianne Loring

FOREWORD BY
Jeffrey Moussaieff Masson

CREATIVE ARTS BOOK COMPANY • BERKELEY • 1986

For information contact the publisher:
Creative Arts Book Company
833 Bancroft Way
Berkeley, California 94710.

Typography by QuadraType, San Francisco.

ISBN 0-88739-013-7

Library of Congress Catalog No. 86-70456

Contents

Foreword

by Jeffrey Moussaieff Masson

When I was in Germany in 1980, I attended a session of the German Psychoanalytic Society. It was a particularly well-attended meeting because the theme of the congress was concentration camp survivors and psychoanalysis. This was the first time, I believe, that German analysts had addressed this topic, and one could expect lively arguments. During a recess I was sitting at a table, having coffee with a number of analysts, when a woman joined us. I immediately noticed a shift in the atmosphere: People became very stiff and formal, and I was puzzled and intrigued. The woman joined the conversation and her first comment was to note the astonishing fact that the very first paper at the congress dealt, not with the suffering of the Jews, but with the traumas suffered by the Germans during the bombing of Dresden. She said, with great passion: "Is this not a curious way to begin a seminar on Germans and concentration camp survivors? Are analysts, like other Germans, going to once again attempt to falsely alleviate their guilt by falsely equating two unequal sufferings?" This comment struck me as so right, so opposite, and so different from the kind of milque-toast, wishy-washy statements made about the congress until then, I thought: She must not be an analyst. When she left our table, I turned to the analyst sitting next to me, one of the leaders of the German Psychoanalytic Society, and asked who she was, saying that I liked her comments. He told me that she had recently been a candidate but had been expelled, and was now practicing medicine, but was no longer involved in psychoanalysis. The other analysts at the table began to speak about her in a curious way: On the one hand, they claimed she had no right to be present at an analytical congress; on the other hand, they all agreed that she had been dropped as an analytic candidate, not for her own failings, but for those of her analyst. Her name, they said, is Dörte Von Drigalski, and she has just written a book: *Blumen auf Granit*, that was very much in the news, especially in psychotherapy circles. Curious, that afternoon I bought the book, and quickly became absorbed in the story of Dr. Drigalski's "failed analysis." The next day, I asked my friend, who was well-informed, what had happened within the analytic society. He explained to me, with a certain cynical sadness, that he knew Drigalski's analyst well, as did other members of the committee that decided to terminate her analytic training. "The man was not right for her, he simply couldn't handle her. Too inexperienced. She had the bad luck to fall into the hands of a young analyst who simply was not sufficiently trained, did not possess enough "clinical wisdom" to know how to deal with her "problems." (Less benign critics of Drigalski, or anyone else, for that matter, who is unhappy with therapy, play a classical trick: They turn the spotlight on her, in a version of victim-blaming, and claim that her choice of an analyst was already an example of her pathology, a piece of typical female masochism!) "So the problem," I said, "was not her, but her analyst?" "Oh yes, absolutely." "But why was the analyst not reprimanded?" "Oh, he was." "But he stayed on?" "Oh yes." "And she was dropped?" "Oh yes." "The matter was a delicate one," he explained, "and we could not risk the reputation of the society for a single patient."

But when I reflected on her book, I realized that this story told only half the truth, and it is one with which analysts, or other therapists, are very comfortable: Whenever they are presented with a remarkable failure, they need not implicate the "patient." They can simply say: This particular analyst (or psychiatrist, or therapist) was no good, or was inadequate. The system per se remains untouched and untouchable. But reading a book like Dr. Drigalski's provides one with a unique opportunity. (I can think of only a small number of other books that do this as well: For example, the remarkable autobiographical account of psychiatric incarceration written by Janet Gotkin: *Too Much Anger, Too Many Tears*.) Her book is so honest, written with so much searing anger, it is so personal, in the best sense, that one is faced with a much larger question: No doubt what happened to Drigalski is true and frightening. But it is not unique, and it is not due to lack of "fit" between analyst and analysand. What Drigalski describes, over and over and over, is the emotional tyranny that begins to reign in psychoanalysis (a comic, but not uncommon example: "Your inability to admire me is an expression of your psychopathology") when the analysand really wishes to go her own way, to see things her own way, not to accept the tired cliches, the routine formulaic interpretations that have become the bread and butter of the average analyst. (And every analyst is an average analyst, though in his own eyes he is always uniquely wise.) A more benign analyst may, perhaps, allow this to happen, ascribe what he sees as stubbornness to a lack of capacity for psychological thinking (rather than simple disagreement—analysts must always label what they do not appreciate) and let it pass as that. But this is really an ideal situation. Rarely, I think, in real life, and in the lives of most people in analysis, does this happen. Too often, the genuine differences in perception turn into a power struggle, and one that is waged between two unequals. Because a person who is in need (whether through suffering or through a desire to be accepted into a profession) is in no position to argue independently and fiercely. Disagreement is dangerous, and carries, always, the covert threat of being dropped (if in training) or abandoned (if in treatment). Drigalski often compares the situation of analysis to a bad marriage, and she is undoubtedly right. (But even after years of marriage, we would hardly claim to genuinely "know" our partner. Why the analyst claims this privilege, often backing it up with a negative diagnosis after only a few sessions, is a mystery.) Moreover, it is a very unequal marriage. In truth, all the real power lies with one side. I think it would make more sense to compare analysis to the marriage of a wife-batterer. The woman may stay, for years, but this is only because her options are so limited.

No doubt many readers will disagree with me, and will know many analyses that are not like that, and many analysts who are not like Drigalski's analyst. I am sure they are right. I have no doubt there are warm, compassionate people who practice psychotherapy. But I think it would be a mistake to write off Drigalski's book as the account of a single failed psychoanalysis. It points to a much larger problem. Drigalski explicitly points out that this defense really doesn't work, that the defects that happened in her analysis happen in many (most? all?) analyses, that there is something in the situation itself, that seems to call it forth. Books like Drigalski's are timely reminders that all is not well in the kingdom of psychotherapy, that the emperor's brilliant clothes are not visible to everybody. She details this so carefully, so fully and so repetitively, that we cannot escape asking the serious questions she asked herself over and over during her analysis: Is this man objective? Are these really defects in me? Can this man be objective? How can these seemingly banal, simple-minded, rote interpretations possibly help me? These are questions that we would do well to ask about any psychotherapy. And Drigalski provides enough specific examples, illustrations of the kinds of tired interpretative efforts that we encounter all the time: The need to castrate, the fear of being castrated, penis envy, etc. These can be applied, thoughtlessly, to every account somebody brings to a therapist. The effect can be devastating. But I believe Drigalski's point is that given the nature of psychotherapy, the training of a psychotherapist, the literature they read, it is bound to happen. When we read Freud's essay on the psychology of women, we realize that what sound to us like absurd notions, are bound, eventually, to be translated into therapeutic procedures. So that when Freud claims that women have less of a sense of justice than men, we know that many women who talk about being unjustly treated by a male colleague will find an interpretation, rather than sympathy, from the analyst well-versed in Freud.

Certain people, who are otherwise very critical of analysis, will not even blame her specific therapist. Thus the highly acclaimed book by Alice Miller, *Thou Shalt not be Aware*, discusses Drigalski's book. Miller, a psychoanalyst at the time, maintains that her analysts and those of other analysands who wrote about their own analyses, "devoted themselves to their patients, tried to understand them, and placed their entire professional knowledge at their patients' disposal" (p. 17). She then writes: "In Drigalski's case, her disappointment with both analyses leads to a rejection of psychoanalysis per se, which is understandable although regrettable, for the case of Cardinal for one demonstrates that psychoanalysis can contribute positively to a person's creative growth." (p 19).

Alice Miller blames analysts for refusing to believe and search out early traumas. I certainly would agree with her. But to ascribe Drigalski's difficulties to this failure is to search too subtly. Surely, there is a much more simple explanation, and this is where I would go even further than Drigalski. She would reject classical psycho-analysis for all the right reasons. But I get the feeling she mistakenly believes that other psychotherapeutic schools would be free of the sins of analysis. Her book, however, raises the distinct possibility that it is not only analysis, but all forms of psychotherapy that are at fault. That the very idea of seeing another person in therapy is fraught with danger, is impossible; in short, is wrong. No form of therapy is free of this taint. They are all bad. It is the very notion of clinical psychotherapy that needs to be re-examined. And it needs to be done on the basis of the kinds of material provided by Drigalski. Her book is an immense service to all people who have begun to question whether they are really "sick" and whether anyone, outside of a friend, has the right to offer them "help."

JEFFREY MOUSSAIEFF MASSON is the author of *The Assault On Truth: Freud's Suppression of the Seduction Theory*, and Editor and Translator of *The Complete Letters of Sigmund Freud to Wilhelm Fliess, 1887-1904*.

FLOWERS ON GRANITE

*One Woman's
Odyssey
Through Psychoanalysis*

One Woman's Odyssey
Through Psychoanalysis

HER CONSULTING ROOM WAS ON THE FOURTH floor, in the main thoroughfare, at the end of a neat, bare corridor in a new building. The furniture had a functional look about it; at nine in the evening the room seemed gloomy and the analyst tired and worn. She sat opposite me, smoking. I felt out of my element: Scrutinized critically, no advance payment in the way of trust offered to me. In this silence, I tried to tell her my biographical details. I wanted her to form a positive opinion of me and then accept me for analysis. However, either what I had to say didn't interest her, or I was saying the wrong things. She said nothing; I felt I was shrinking before her gaze. My voice faltered, became thinner, softer, threadlike. I had to make an effort to say anything at all. There were pauses; I tried to speak firmly, but my voice faded away towards the end of my sentences. Her eyes seemed to express rejection, boredom: I had been weighed in the balance and found wanting. I wasn't getting through to her. Finally, after a pause of some length, she asked a question about my motivation. "I want to be able to love properly . . ." I said something about earlier relationships, but that was of no interest to her either. Her critical silence drained me dry, and it was getting worse and worse; I felt insipid, lacking in vitality. She was not enjoying my company. I was annoyed with myself for being so dull and feeble; I reproached myself; I felt different, alone, bad at making contact. Another pause, during which I tormented myself. At last she put another question to me: Was I ever able to feel really angry? She asked it in neutral tones, but to me it sounded a disparaging, condemnatory, sourish, grating neutrality. I felt basically misunderstood: I'd often felt bad about my tendency to fly into fits of furious temper. But how was I to put that across in this kind of atmosphere, if she didn't herself credit me with the ability, or suspect it in me?

I felt like crying; I was getting nowhere in this wretched atmosphere. Making an effort, I did manage to say, "Yes," but in so crushed and quiet a voice that even I felt the assertion sounded silly and unconvincing.

Anyway, the session came to an end, and she had no objection to my going into analysis. I might have been expected to feel pleased; hers was the third professional opinion I needed, and with it I was admitted to training analysis.

Instead, I felt annihilated and drained, discouraged, disliked. She had not enjoyed my company. I had worn myself out and met with no response; obviously I and my life to date didn't interest this kind of analyst, maybe didn't even seem worth discussing; I was a pathological case, and not a very presentable one. I felt so tormented and disheartened that it was a long time before I could get to sleep. I had learnt new things about myself from both my earlier interviews; they had invigorated and inspired me, filled me with enthusiasm. It had been definitely mortifying to be evaluated yet again, by I knew not what criteria, after all the previous examinations.

The first analyst I saw, a gentle, attractive woman, obviously did like me. She had asked questions with interest; even when she said nothing, I hadn't felt I was under pressure. When I mentioned my earliest memories, of being picked up in masculine arms, she said, with an understanding smile, "Yes, I expect that's something you've missed." I said no, I thought the idea far-fetched; I couldn't remember such longings. But in the face of her keen interest, I came around to suspecting my firm rejection of the idea; I remembered dreams of my father's homecoming, men reported missing, prisoners of war who had come back after all, though after a very long time. She did not press me further, but there was a dent on the surface of my satisfaction in having a virtuous if dead father, instead of a worthless but living Nazi father, like other people. And other questions of hers were working away in my mind, softening me up: Had my home life really been as pleasant, delightful and free of conflict as I said, wouldn't I have had better relationships with men? She thought I was still idealizing the family; she judged me in a very friendly way, but said she didn't quite understand me.

She could see no compelling reason why I should want to go into analysis. She seemed used to seeing vehement suffering.

I had felt good after seeing her, but I too wondered: No, I wouldn't have gone into analysis at this point of my own accord—that is, if I hadn't wanted further training. I was not overwhelmed by my suffering.

It had been said that all who go into training analysis really do so because of their own problems, hoping to solve them in their psychoanalytic training, and that everyone who chooses such a career has substantial reasons for doing so. However, my conscious motivation was good enough for me: I had enjoyed studying medicine, and as with many people of my age, I had come down to earth after my examinations, during my hospital work. The close contact with patients (while learning how to care for them and interning) was dissipated; work became abstract, mechanical, robot-like, dehumanized. There was a certain amount of contact while taking a case history, but what with the pressure of time, and the emphasis on the purely functional aspect, this was often very frustrating; one couldn't go into the emotional background, and the often tear-provoking memories which were stirred up. Not many people were unaffected by questions such as whether their parents and brothers and sisters were alive, when did they die, what had they died of, but the more a doctor disregarded this tangled mass of feelings, refusing to let it detain him, the more efficient he seemed. But this was generally the last moment of human contact; after that, objective procedures went their prescribed way. You got used to it after a while, to some extent, at least. No account was taken of any connection between a patient's sickness and his experiences, feelings and relationships. For instance, asthmatic patients often came during the night; after they had been given what were considered suitable injections, they were sent home again. Nobody stopped to think that they just might be desperately lonely, might be frightened for some reason or other, and that this was one point where therapy might begin. Medicine practised in this way seemed superficial and pointless; I didn't enjoy it.

In any event, I and many of my contemporaries found it a logical development to turn our interest towards psychoanalysis if we wanted to preserve something of our dreams and do more than function like robots.

(When a great many people suddenly express a wish for further training, it probably indicates pathological flaws in conventional medicine rather than a boom in doctors with secret neurotic motivations. Psychoanalysis was considered the best training in this field; and in the light of the demands commonly made on doctors, such as hours on night duty without enough time to catch up on sleep afterwards, an additional four hours' work a week didn't seem excessive.)

Still, unconscious motivation certainly does play a part, just as it does with doctors whose specialized professional interest is in the bones, the urethrae, the posterior or the female genitals. And for years, I've been irritated by the suspicion with which those possible personal problems are regarded; after all, it was a man with a club foot who discovered the first effective operation to help the condition, a fact which didn't detract from the usefulness of the procedure.

(As I hadn't formed any really clear picture of my own motivation, I found—later, anyway—that when I felt doubts, people pointed out to me, with knowing looks, the personality disturbance I myself had shown in deciding to go into analysis: A vicious circle.)

I had certainly wondered why, at the age of twenty-six, I wasn't living in a stable relationship and had no children, but there were ordinary explanations for these things, and women friends of mine from a similar background were in the same situation. I hadn't previously had any really serious difficulties, at school or during my training.

With my increasingly critical attitude toward conventional medicine, I was finding it hard to function well; I became listless, caught an infection, and had plenty of time to read while I was sick. Psychosomatic medicine, then, was something which could renew my enthusiasm, as could the atmosphere and the staff at my new hospital. No one there had to stand at attention, so to speak, to report on such matters as blood sedimentation rate. Everyday relationships bore simply no comparison to what I was used to in hospitals orientated towards organic medicine.

That was why I wanted to go into psychoanalysis. Or so I thought.

I discussed my misgivings and reservations with people who had already been analyzed, and was told that my feelings were quite natural, the product of resistance and anxiety; after all I had known I would be going into analysis with this woman, and had then distanced myself, so as to avoid feelings of too close and positive a nature. I must surely be aware of such reactions in myself and she was always reserved at first, they said. I couldn't think, offhand, of any situation in ordinary life after which I had felt so devastated, but that just went to prove the strength, effectiveness and intensity of psychoanalysis.

The fact that I had been enthusiastic about my first analyst seemed to fit my psychological pattern: I had no husband, only lovers, none of whom lived nearby. She had not posed the threat of any analytical intimacy, so I had been able to feel good.

Stories of my analyst's warm and affectionate nature convinced me; I made my diagnosis and threw my own experience overboard. The explanation that I was afraid of positive feelings was an interesting one too; it showed me I was already beginning the analytical process.

My misgivings did return when I phoned her about the start of my analysis. She asked, in a cool and distant tone, if I *really* wanted to come to her; she was only going to be in this town for a year. I was upset, and felt she was trying to shake me off.

I'd already known what she told me; indeed, we had discussed it at my interview; however, she had been recommended to me in such a way that I had no real choice. Once more, other people reassured me: Laughingly they said that was just her telephone manner, and it didn't mean anything.

A telephone conversation we'd arranged to have a few weeks later made me uneasy again. Its content was similar, but there was an even greater lack of feeling; a distinct rejection. I felt irritated and depressed, and went to someone who knew her and must have the overall picture, saying, "She doesn't want me." He comforted and calmed me; I had another telephone conversation with her, and finally it was decided that I could begin analysis with her after all.

*　　　*　　　*

At the start, I was still in the first flush of my enthusiasm for analysis and my new hospital; I was feeling good. I didn't actually experience those sudden and intense great changes in myself and my environment that I'd expected, but those had been dreams anyway. I was full of facts and data and biographical details I felt I absolutely had to tell her. Our first sessions were thus very full and passed quickly. I didn't even think of talking about any current difficulties; I wanted her to get to know me first. She hardly seemed to react at all during these sessions, but I put that down to the fact that she was listening; obviously everything was important, including myself. After a few sessions, the pressure of information I had to impart slackened off, I became calmer, and there were some pauses. I was not sure if I'd told her enough; I might have forgotten something essential. I asked how we ought to go on: Was this the right way? Perhaps to elucidate the function of pauses and their justification, she said, "Ah, *now* you are presenting affective factors." The atmosphere being rather strained and aloof anyway, I felt this meant that I had shown nothing affective so far, and had not been acquitting myself well. I felt she had not liked our sessions. At any rate, I saw what she said as reproof for what had gone before, and thought her voice bored and disparaging. And yet, so far as I could tell myself, I had not been any more dispassionate or lacking in affects in the earlier sessions. I had been under more pressure at the start. But what really were the right affects? She had asked me about that at our initial interview. Were they, qualitatively speaking, different from what I experienced as my feelings? Did I really have any feelings? How was I constituted, inside myself? Why wasn't she enjoying my company? Had I previously been able to deceive everyone except her? Was she, perhaps, the first to see through me, completely and to destructive effect? Was I, perhaps, like a blind person imagining colors?

I could not summon up any enthusiasm for her at this early stage.

She was not my kind of person: I didn't like her appearance, her way of dressing—aesthetically, they did not seem successful. Yet she obviously took trouble with the way she looked. However, I didn't think she seemed casual enough, not really chic. Her skirts always struck me as unnecessarily long. I thought she lacked glamor. She was carefully groomed, but she didn't really seem to have found her own style. I had problems with her elastic gold watch bracelet.

I didn't like her apartment at first, either. The hall was so tidy, almost as if it had been licked clean. Was she forever putting things in order, vacuuming and cleaning, so that nothing was left lying about, and nobody could see anything in her private life? All this well-organized neatness was foreign to me; even the coatrack was never too full. The furniture was functional but in no way attractive. A small picture on the wall showed a few flowers growing from a fissure in barren rocks; it was all in one color, black and white and grey.

Did I want to keep a distance between us, so I could change less, so that fewer homo-erotic feelings could arise? Was it, maybe, a state of total confusion about my feelings, needs and wishes that made me react so strongly against her personal taste? Was I nothing but resistance personified?

Later on, I liked the view from her couch, one of clouds sailing past in the blue and hazy sky. The structure of the room was important too, with its reliable tidiness, always the same as before; it showed stability, both internal and external. At that point I was glad of her love of order, the speed with which she wrote medical certificates, made out invoices, left nothing undone; that same love of order made her insist on adding any time missed from one session of analysis to a later one. And the regularity of those sessions— appointments almost never and then most reluctantly altered— seemed to exercise a restraining influence on my own disorder.

I was curious to know how she conducted her private life. Inhibitions prevented my actually asking, and anyway, it would disturb the transference. However, I knew she lived alone. Did she like that? Had she nothing better to do in the evenings, or did she get so much pleasure from her profession that that was the reason she had set my initial interview at so late an hour? She had struck me as overworked at the time. She seemed happy enough during our sessions now, under less strain than at the start, but there was a feeling of suffering about her, a certain sense of unhappiness and resignation. Nothing marked, but clear, and always present. I had never seen any such thing in my mother, nor in the first analyst, though I couldn't really judge after my single session with her. Was my analyst's attitude more mature, maybe; did it make her better able to cope with life than my mother? At the time, so far as I knew, she had never written anything, yet she had a keen intelligence. That was obvious, and it appealed to me.

So why, unlike similarly gifted men, had she never published? She deserved a little more social prestige. She didn't seem to have made the most of her life or realized her potential fully. Men I knew wrote, and didn't go around with frustrated talents.

I couldn't get used to her appearance. I found her somehow inhibited, unfulfilled air a constant stumbling block. I would have liked to feel proud of her looks, proud of her when talking to men, not just to fellow analysands who were on her side anyway. I wondered why it was so important to me that she should look good, why I minded what skirts and shoes she wore and how she did her hair. Was she so much a part of me that I couldn't feel I was separate from her, outside her, independent of her? Did I exist only as an entity with her? As I had with my mother?

This could be an unresolved relationship with my mother—a strong umbilical cord that had never been cut. It was still disturbing, though; there were a number of things I just didn't like about her. I tried not to let it loom so large, to see it in a more neutral light.

After all, I made too much of my own appearance, of fashion, and boutiques, and other people; of whether I thought I looked good and felt good or not; my mood was easily influenced by clothes. I bought a good many, and often made the wrong choice. I thought I could feel my mother's taste lurking at the back of my mind; I resisted it, sought other models, and became unsure of myself. I took more notice of what other people said, especially people who'd been analyzed, and tried to orientate myself accordingly.

Was my identity so strongly influenced by my outward appearance? By external factors?

I found a good deal that was negative in me: The fallibility of my own taste, my poor sense of personal identity, my dependence on the judgment of others, my inclination to conform submissively to the style and opinion of other people, a competitive attitude towards fashion, apparently aimed at men but really at women, unacknowledged homosexual feelings transformed into rivalry, and actually accompanied by a lack of interest in men, my mother's mistake in imposing her own taste on me until I had hardly any of my own, and no chance to develop it, the consequent stunting of my personality, as a result of that and of the lack of a father who would always have loved and supported me, the critical and competitive attitude of my brothers toward me, not conducive to erotic development (defense against incestuous feelings), and much else.

I now turned the vehement hostility I had felt for my analyst's appearance against myself. If I was not reproaching myself, I was reproaching my brothers, or my mother, or—in the abstract—the fact that I'd grown up without a father. I felt envious of more fortunate people, furious with those responsible, miserable over the enormous disadvantages from which I suffered.

On one occasion this became too much for my analyst. She asked, in tones of annoyance, what I was really after; I *was* well-dressed.

The sense of well-being I could draw from making myself up, even on my own, trying on my clothes, looking at myself in the mirror was spoiled; it reminded me of my weaknesses. When I passed a mirror during the day I took pains not to look in it, not to touch up my make-up so often, not to rely on reassurance from outside.

*   *   *

During these first weeks, I frequently woke at night, or felt an urgent need to discuss something with my analyst during the day. I began to write these things down and think my way through them on paper; this often resolved my tensions, the problem cleared up, and the matter seemed to be dealt with; I could go back to sleep, or at least, I felt calmer. As I had often been in the habit of writing long, detailed letters if I didn't have enough contact with people, this now came naturally to me. Only they weren't letters these days, more of a supplement to the analysis which took up so little actual time. The pressures and uneasiness with which I sat down were dispersed by the act of writing, and it helped me to cope, inwardly, with many subjects.

Since I had, so to speak, written off the problems, they were no longer acute, and it was a relatively long time before I mentioned the matter. I met with stern intervention. I was acting out, she said, trying to keep something from her; she did not approve and it did my analysis no good. I felt hurt and baffled, and insisted that writing did clarify some things for me; I told her I'd always liked writing letters when there was some difficult question to be formulated.

She was welcome to read what I'd written, but it did do me good. I came up against a firm no. I had never known her so definite before.

All the same, I couldn't see any point in her arguments at first, and I was still determined not to obey her prohibition. After all, she could read what I wrote: It was just that I sometimes had thoughts in the middle of the day, or at night, thoughts like a bubble rising within me which had to come out. So I went on writing for a few days—but her prohibition had its effect. The pages became fewer, my handwriting small and crabbed, my verve was gone; I had lost the playfulness and fluency that brought relief. Nothing much came of my writing now but an objective diary; that way out was closed.

I assumed that the fact I couldn't write any more showed she was right. If I hadn't really wanted to keep something secret I wouldn't have reacted to her intervention like that; only someone with a guilty conscience would be affected.

Children who read a lot are often schizoid, a colleague of mine told me. Perhaps the way for my disturbance had been paved long ago. Sometimes it almost made no difference to me whether I wrote or phoned; if I couldn't reach someone at once by telephone, I just sent a letter. However, I had an idea that I wrote only when I didn't have enough contact with other people. I must either talk or write. Was that a sign of neurosis? Had I already written too much out of myself, instead of investing it in human relationships? Perhaps I didn't notice the difference between myself and other people because this was the only way I knew life.

*   *   *

A woman I knew had large, beautiful breasts; I thought my own were too small—immature and childlike. "You aren't really envious of her," my analyst told me, "you're envious of your mother and competing with her." My mother had had breasts like mine as a girl, but they were much larger when she reached adulthood. Real women, to my mind, were big-breasted.

I was partly relieved to find I wasn't suffering from simple envy of my acquaintance, and it was a biological fact that I would be inferior to my mother in that respect, at least up to the age of puberty.

So my admiration and sense of inferiority weren't my fault. Even if I had in fact felt very envious, that could be laid at my mother's door as well: She might have repressed me, seen me as a rival. One is born into that kind of situation.

I didn't like to feel I was unloading family feelings on my acquaintance. I hoped she didn't notice. But as my envy was directed against my mother anyway, I need not feel ashamed; it wasn't actually real.

All the same, I did think large breasts were prettier and more mature, both before and after this interpretation of my feelings. And now there was something neurotic about my admiration for them; it reminded me of the time when I was at one with my mother. Such a distinct feeling, and all wrong: Carried about with me and transferred to the first appropriate person to come my way. I would do better to be cautious with such feelings; they were not to be relied on. Better not show them at all.

*   *   *

One thing I found very trying was my analyst's way of coughing, and still smoking though her lungs were racked by the cough. In my beginner's conception of things, I felt coughing was something introverted, aggressive, telling somebody off, anger, turned inward, getting rid of something, coughing it up. This, at any rate, was what I had read in textbooks of organic medicine, and I had known patients at the hospital who radiated aggression and torment. Under the microscope, I had seen what the pulmonary alveoli can look like when they have been maltreated and devastated to a point where breathing is almost impossible: They look inelastic, stiff, full of particles of soot and dust.

She was a heavy smoker, and sometimes had fits of stifled, hollow coughing which she attempted to control. These were painful moments. It was some time before I could bring myself to say so, and then my fantasies and anxieties were swiftly countered with the information that she had chronic bronchitis. That was a fact: Had to be accepted as a fact, one must probe no further. However, it alarmed me, and made me feel guilty and anxious. Had I provoked her coughing? Was it her way of reacting when she felt irritated? Was I to blame, or partly to blame, for her inner destruction? Why did she keep on pumping smoke into her ailing lungs? The sound was dreadful. It would have been better to cough it all out, just for once. Why did she suppress her urge to cough, master it, fight it? In itself, it was a healthy urge: the body's appropriate response to injury.

When I was studying for my medical examinations, I had had a particular horror of lung tumors which slowly suffocate the patient, leaving him unable to breathe because the lungs are full of water, and no more oxygen can reach their tiny vessels. How bad was the state of her lungs? Surely she was devastating her own body! Why didn't she stop smoking? Freud, of course, had continued smoking. But I just didn't like the smell of smoke; no one at home had smoked except my stepfather. I had never taken to the habit myself, though once I came near it; I was in a bar, I was feeling short of sleep, under strain and generally ill at ease, and everyone around me was smoking, so I had tried it again. When I inhaled, I felt an aggressive and angry greed; the little flame and the glow growing at the end of the cigarette were attractive, too; I could well imagine becoming addicted. It alarmed me, and I didn't want to get into that kind of mood again. Why did she smoke?

Did people ever have fits of coughing for solely organic reasons, without any psychic factor to set them off? Judging from her reactions, it was not right or reasonable for me to be thinking along these lines in this analytical situation. It did trouble me, all the same. Did she have a dangerous sickness—ought I to be more considerate of her? Why did she accept it so passively? Did that mean there was nothing to be done about it?

On the other hand, I was quite happy with her clear directive not to think about it any more, to accept the neutral explanation of chronic bronchitis as a fact. If there was something really wrong with her, I was not particularly keen to know. After all, our sessions were supposed to be about me, or predominantly about me. I enjoyed seeing myself taken so seriously for once, regarded as so important, having so much attention and interest exclusively concentrated on all the tiny workings of my mind. I liked not feeling I ought to fight off slight dejection, vague feelings of being out of sorts, mild depression and listlessness by means of self control, morning exercise, strong coffee, and forcing myself to be active, or alternately fretting over them; instead, I could take them to be the logical effect of some actual cause, something that was oppressing me. I could see them as an important and meaningful part of myself, in no way fanciful, crazy, or to be condemned. It did me good to understand how I repressed things: For instance, I might have heard bad news, or read something which vaguely reminded me of something else that troubled me, and I then put the whole sad complex out of my mind to such a degree that only a vague and diffuse depression remained. Or the cause could be something that had made me angry the previous day, something said at supper which I had not consciously registered at all. I was classifying my feelings of annoyance or resignation better, and slowly learning how to put up my defenses earlier. All this was good, significant, and interesting.

All the same, I still wasn't at home with the atmosphere in that room; I just did not feel warmth or acceptance there. I listened, helpless and envious to the enthusiastic accounts of other analysands. They all thought her a very warm person; that just was not the way I saw her, though she was certainly clever, confident and independent-minded. Was this a matter of my own defense, my emotional incapacity, inadequacy and inability to love? Was that why I wasn't married? Did my coolness towards her indicate my reason for being in analysis? Who was there in the world that I really liked? Did I genuinely love anyone at all without severe reaction formations, without a strong sense of ambivalence? My rather lukewarm attitude towards her seemed more likely to indicate my own emotional poverty.

I tried hard to feel warmth toward her, but I still felt she liked other people better, they were more her type, and she probably attended to them more closely. One woman told me she'd laughed during their session, something I just could not imagine. When I finally ventured to say so, she pointed to my sibling rivalry and maternal transference.

"Probably," she said, "I had felt as a child that I was not as much loved as my older brothers." Was it perhaps that my mother got on better with men, in this case my brothers? Had she wanted a little girl at all? Was what men said and did, everything about them, worth more to her in general than what women and girls said and did?

In fact, my mother had always wanted a girl, and my father had written to the same effect; my first name was chosen long before my birth.

However, I could think of a number of situations where I had felt younger, weaker, less important, someone to be taken less seriously than my two brothers. My kind grandfather certainly read aloud to me, but he did more serious things with my brothers: Hearing them recite the vocabulary they were learning, for instance. By the time I was old enough for such things myself, he was dead. He had taught me my alphabet, but that was nothing much compared to his conversations with my brothers. Had my mother really been glad to have a daughter? Or had she only told me so, to console herself and me for the fact that I was a girl? What did she really feel for me? Had she not, perhaps, actually thought a good deal more of my brothers? I grew distrustful: Formed suspicions, worried away at the idea, asked questions. I couldn't remember instances of our being treated in any conspicuously different way, or glean anything definite from stories I'd been told. My mother's relationship with my brothers was something so different, they themselves differed from each other, my relationship to her was different again. There could be no comparisons: Qualitative ones, yes, but not in point of intensity. And I could make no credible assessment myself.

Transference, however, made the original situation seem quite clear and unmistakable. My suspicions and feelings in analysis showed what life at home had really been like. Or rather, to be exact, what I had felt it was like. The next question, of course, was whether my perception of it at the time had been neurotically distorted.

This made everything rather more complicated and less clear. It also made me more suspicious: Confused and distrustful. Why was it so hard to pin down and establish the facts of so common, simple and ordinary a state of affairs as the question of discrimination of favoritism in my family? Had our harmful, damaging and pernicious family tendency perhaps been to let things happen unobserved, in secret, so you couldn't actually lay hands on your opponent, who could strike all the harder for that?

I was sure of my feelings in analysis, but they originated with my primal family and belonged there, not here and now. I was experiencing reality falsified and colored by my problems. I could trust my perceptions only to a limited extent, by roundabout ways, through back doors.

One man, hearing I had just started with my analyst, smiled nostalgically: "Ah, you're in the honeymoon period!" I felt ashamed: He was a nice, pleasant person. What kind of relationship had he had with her, and why didn't I have a similar one? What was the matter with me? What poison within me barred me from love: From loving her, and feeling love?

My relationships with my brothers and my mother were undermined by my anger, my suspicion and my probings. I took a number of opportunities to discuss the past, argue about it, complain. They found some of what I said convincing, much of it surprising and alienating. They thought I was being egocentric, difficult, and introverted. I thought this was a typical reaction, showing that something was changing, I was beginning to work free of a repressive family atmosphere.

But I also still had the feeling that my analyst was treating me coolly, keeping her distance. I thought I could sense that quite clearly. This meant, then, that my mother had not really been as fond of children as she claimed. She had certainly always been very good with babies, who would often laugh spontaneously for her, and she had looked after several children in addition to her own for a while. But my feelings in analysis showed her up. I knew more than anyone now. The reliable, loving background provided by what remained of our family was an illusion.

I became cautious over my perceptions; also bitter and agitated. There was a good deal wrong with me: The trouble was hard to reconstruct, but analytically telling. I felt things differently from the way they were; I was surprised by the misconceptions, displacements, reaction formations and repudiations which I found changing my inner world. What was there in myself upon which I could rely? Which of my perceptions? Not those I felt most confidently and vehemently, anyway; vehemence seemed to indicate that I was covering up and defending against a feeling of a different and perhaps diametrically opposite kind. I must be particularly wary of my spontaneous and confident feelings.

When I thought I detected an amorous relationship between two of my friends, back came the uncomfortable question like a shot: How did I feel about the man in the case myself? I remembered a dream in which he had led me into a large room full of men, and I was to sleep with all of them, because that was the best way for people to get to know each other. I found I had to admit to such desires. I wanted to indulge them myself, so I suspected them in others. I felt unhappy with the wavering nature of my sexual desires; I had simply been projecting them.

I wanted a faster engine for my Volkswagen. The variant with the slower engine slowed me down; I felt it chugged along not much faster than my previous and very old Volkswagen model.

"I think we have a displacement here"—i.e., the displacement of original sexual desires, now to be satisfied by speed. And the idea actually had come up at the same time as a new man in my life. Displacement was defense, and not a good thing.

Thus, my sexual anxiety led to my failure to experience this very important feeling correctly, genitally; instead I was offering myself speed as an inferior substitute gratification. I no longer wanted the faster engine; I felt people with fast cars were suspect; I could seldom regard them with tolerance.

I tried to keep myself under great control so that no one could see the bad part of me. I was amazed to see an analyst going about with a cold, just like that, without any concern. Just then I was embarrassed by my visible cold (unimpassioned*—cross*—"having it up to here"—emotional snot trying to get out—telling someone "where to get off"*—trying to elicit affection through illness—viral miasma as a distancing device, etc.).

My physical relationship with a lover I had known for a long time, and with whom I had lived for a while, became difficult; I no longer felt any desire. Or at least, physical clumsiness often entered into things, reviving my guilt feelings. The magic had gone. When I met him I was instantly afraid he would be feeling great desire, while I felt very little or none, and he would notice it again and be sad. I remember my analyst's gruff question, "Have you tried everything?" and following on from that, "Positions which stimulate your clitoris more? Other ways of making love? Have you exhausted all the possibilities?" I could have crawled away into a corner. I felt a fool. Yes, we had tried various things, but not systematically. Perhaps there were other ways I didn't even know?

*Translator's note: All these phrases indicate the idiomatic meaning of the original German terms, all of which denote various cold symptoms.

I forced myself to say, "Yes," and that disposed of the organic, technical side of the matter; what remained must lie within myself.

*   *   *

I sometimes seemed to alienate her. A new lover, who had visited my family with me, took me gently in his arms. "What a way to treat you!" He thought my family regarded me as a child, as neuter, ignoring all that lay below the waist. He thought I had lacked a father who could be relied upon to admire me. He conceived the notion of making an enlargement of a photograph of my lower body and hanging it on the wall. I had felt fine at home when he was there, as if I had more backbone. I too thought that my brothers didn't take me as seriously, as a woman, as I could have wished, for incestuous or for I knew not what other reasons. I thought myself severely undervalued; it seemed an excellent idea to break up their systems with a photograph of my adult, naked genital area. The thought of it made me laugh.

My analyst asked if I was *really* going to do it, in tones of disapproval and surprise. I answered, feebly: "Well, no, of course not, not really." It had just been a good idea. After all, my family knew about erotic and sexual matters, they didn't need any sex education lessons from me. It had just been a joke that had served its purpose. She seemed to feel she had to keep me from some thoughtless and chaotic course of action. What had really mattered to me was my lover's staunch partisanship, the way he understood both me and my situation.

He also thought there was a discrepancy between the lower part and the virginal part of my body, and only laughed when I asked more questions: Yes, it was so, he said, he was sure of it. This was important to me, but my analyst didn't seem to like it. It didn't fit. Perhaps I was just showing off, keeping things on the genital plane so as to deny my basic disturbance, not have to bother with it, and that wasn't the right way for me. She made me feel awkward, like a very young girl who has gone too far.

The better way for me, apparently, was sadness and suffering, and in particular grief for my father. She was right beside me there, feeling for me. I was safe there.

I could not cope with that wound in my history: My boundless longing and vehement grief for my father. My defenselessness and idealization, matters which we had already broached in that initial interview, now collapsed. I could scarcely bear to see a film showing a father picking up his small child, or a man coming home again after a long absence; it was all just too much for me. I spent many sessions of analysis in tears. Once this wound had been exposed, not much changed. It became quite usual for me to weep over it, and I wasn't ashamed to do so, now that I was amongst people who had been analyzed. War films, featuring men in uniform, had a magic about them, an aching romanticism. I went to a war film on my father's birthday; it was set in a submarine, all the characters were men, not a single woman among them, and it was not really a very good production. However, I sat through that film in tears, paying rapt attention to the characters' endurance, their optimism in desperate straits, and left the theater feeling calm, content and exhausted.

I remembered my unrestrained envy of a girl in my class at school whose father was around, had been there, just like that, since 1945, hadn't even been a P.O.W. My stepfather had been around too, but he wasn't what I wanted. I had not called him Father, but "Ather." I had involved him in conversation about my real father and left him in doubt that he himself would eventually have to go. There was a film showing at the local theater put together from various amateur films, which many of my class went to see. If you identified members of your family in it, if you spotted your father, you could win a picture.

That was an idea I had previously entertained which now seemed impossible to me: Having a baby without being married appeared extremely irresponsible, criminal. An offense against the child.

Despite their overwhelming nature, my feelings about my father somehow fortified me; they went down to my roots; this was right, the kind of thing that made life worth living, even if my eyes were swollen with weeping and I felt tense and had headaches. It touched my whole being, not just in a vague, halfhearted way, but affecting my entire body, exhausting it as hard work does.

What else was right about me, besides weeping? I became suspicious and scornful of people who were simply nice to me. I knew one man who liked me very much; I felt his liking me made him stupid, showed that he didn't see through me, my outward appearance had deceived him. I couldn't feel someone so naively trusting counted for much.

I was surprised that my inner vacuum and poor capacity for loving hadn't struck people before. How was it that I'd sometimes made the opposite impression, if anything? Did that mean that I actively provoked positive reactions in others in order to soothe my inner doubts? Does someone who screams need to scream? A person who is constantly motivating others to provide reassurance of his or her good nature may need that reassurance very badly. I heard the opinion that "there's a very great deal in her" voiced by a hyper-aesthetic teacher of German, a man attracted to boys: It was almost a declaration of love from this sensitive man, who was at best neutral in his attitude towards girls. Had I purposely set to work, at the time, to conceal the fact that I felt nothing for him and his concern with Hölderlin's poetry? I had a pleasant memory, too, of the practical nursing part of my course. A patient regarded as difficult, a retired hospital head nurse, offered me her well manicured hands on my last day, for me to cut her nails. She was so reserved that I felt this was a great honor. Had this problem case put me on my mettle? Did I want the positive liking of such a "difficult" person to set against my internal doubts? Did I need constant evidence of love to overcome the voice of honesty within me? Why else had I sometimes set off such excessive reactions?

A nurse on a surgical ward, someone I hardly knew, had said of me that the mother of such a daughter could "think herself lucky," a remark I repeated at home if anyone found fault with me.

But now I saw much I thought suspect. I lost my sense of irony, caricature, the macabre. I was quick to see ill will and aggression wrapped up and disguised as humor. I easily felt hurt and insulted. At home, they had regarded the German teacher's remark as just a joke: Why, to think of a girl's getting through to him for once! I took this as proof of our cool, unloving family relationships. I now complained that my family hadn't believed I could get anywhere with him, hadn't taken the remark seriously, hadn't recognized in me those mental qualities that he suspected. Why did they all have to cut me down to size and castrate me with their laughter? Was humor their way of putting me down, avoiding intellectual and emotional competition? What was it covering up, what vast amount of aggression?

One faithful and reliable friend became important to me. I had always thought of him as clever, intellectually stimulating, but physically neutral and unattractive. It was fortunate, but at the time I simply didn't see him as my type. Reading "On the General Devaluation of Sexual Life," which describes men's division of their women partners into the two categories of mental/spiritual and sensual/sexual (saint and whore) as a matter of unresolved attachment to the mother, I thought of myself and this friend of mine. (A good many people have found themselves suspecting they suffer from any aspect of neuroticism which they happen to read about.) I was still seeking that disturbance in myself that had driven me to analysis. Perhaps this was just where my difficulty lay: An unresolved attachment to the father leading to my inability to feel drawn to one and the same person both sensually and intellectually. I had probably discounted him erotically because of our good intellectual relationship. I had just read that article, and brought my suspicions to the analytic session with me. My analyst's interpretation confirmed my own. "You had no sensual experience with your father, so you can have none with this friend of yours either."

This was bad news. So it was true, and I could apply the principle to all my previous relationships. None of them had been ideal. Anything that I had, none the less, been able to feel and enjoy wasn't worth mentioning: It was not the real, the original thing. In fact I never had touched or felt my father; he had gone to the war before my birth and was dead soon after it. So I was crippled. The important, decisive, formative factor in sexual relationships is probably imprinted on one by one's father; everything else— relationships with my stepfather, my grandfather, with fatherly friends—seemed an unimportant, worthless patchwork.

Can one ever compensate for such a flaw, for a deficiency in one-self not caused by any repression, trauma or conflict, but existing simply because a sensual quality has never been used, never been brought into play? Or at least, not in the "right" way, through contact with one's father, as with almost all other women I knew. Any feeling I might have developed through contact with other men seemed to me as nothing compared with the original, real thing, every daughter's right.

I did have acquaintances who didn't think me so disastrously different, but they were not analysts. My experience was not the real thing, wasn't to be taken seriously, and nor were they if they couldn't see that. I had a woman friend, analytically trained, who described the problems at which I hinted as nonsense, but I didn't much trust her view of the matter. It might be that she just liked me, or perhaps she herself had similar problems which blinded her.

The proposition had a powerful effect on me. I fantasized about the potential for experience that other girls, girls with fathers, girls from complete families, might enjoy—surely did enjoy, if my own feelings were just a faint, inferior copy of something vital, more primal, more powerful. I had no woman friend so close to me that I could frankly compare experiences with her.

So I was much sicker than other women. Crippled and handicapped for life, for love. My problem lay elsewhere; if I was lucky I could make up a bit for what I'd failed to learn and experience, but nothing much was really to be expected in the way of success. It wouldn't be like resolving a failure to work some ordinary problem through. Presumably I would always be inferior in that area.

This interpretation of my problems gnawed away at me; I don't remember ever discussing it with my analyst again. I now knew that my physical experiences were not the real thing. She, as an analyst, had recognized that fact.

In a dream, I saw a man hovering near the ceiling of a square, locked, whitewashed room, a drowned man, but not an unpleasant sight. The corpse moved slowly, gently, rhythmically, as if under water. It was eerie, repulsive yet attractive. I tried to draw some kind of conclusion from the dream. Towards the end of the session my analyst emerged from her state of withdrawn reserve. "Well, if you see the penis as a waterlogged corpse, then nothing surprises me." It was said with some anger and a slightly scornful undertone.

Her interpretation was made quickly, and I couldn't easily reconstruct the situation just then. Her train of thought and the idea itself were foreign to me, but she had found them in my own associations. She was a good analyst. So I saw a penis as something repulsive, rotting; a sickening and stinking object, or anyway, certainly not a thing of beauty in which I could take any pleasure. If I went about with this kind of idea in my head, then my relationships with men had really been cover-up exercises: Their fragility and the quarrels I provoked were both understandable, considering the depth of distaste I must feel towards a waterlogged corpse.

It occurred to me that while I was studying for my examinations, I had had a particular dislike for forensic medicine; it was the one branch of my subject on which I indeed had never attended a lecture. I had been especially revolted by the various stages of decomposition in drowned bodies, which we had to learn by heart; I had gone around citing this as proof of the sickening nature of the subject. For instance, there are marks left when a submerged corpse, initially lying on the bottom, begins to rise slightly once bacteria have caused gases to develop, and is then propelled along by the current, so that the hands and feet—which will be hanging down because they do not offer gas-forming bacteria as good a breeding ground as the trunk—are scraped as they move over the bottom. Thus one can draw conclusions about the date of death, or at least the day on which the corpse went into the water. There were other disgusting details too.

So disgust was my way of resisting an instinctual desire. I must feel a pathological sensual connection between penis—drowned corpse—father—rotting in Stalingrad, perhaps in the melting snow—coitus—possible fathers—sexual partners.

I thought my life history looked rather unfortunate: Full of corpses. My father had died just after my birth; my uncle when I was one and three quarters, my great grandmother when I was two, one grandfather when I was five and the other when I was nine. My maternal grandmother had died before my birth, and my other grandmother before I could really get to know her. Wartime pictures had always held a special attraction for me, particularly when they showed the dead. When I went looking at churches with my grandfather, I had always been particularly fascinated by that type of sculpture which shows two views of the dead man, first intact, in full knightly armor, then as a skeleton consumed by worms and snakes, eaten away, disintegrated, a gruesomely beautiful sight. I used to find representations of Christ on the Cross interesting too. I and a slightly older boy, who had come by a banknote after the currency reform, had bought four crucifixes in ascending order of size. The corpse hanging on the cross excited me: The nails in the hands, the drops of blood running down from the crown of thorns, the starved, emaciated body with its bleeding wounds. No one in my family was religious, and they were surprised. However, we were very pleased with our purchases.

I also remembered reacting to the sight of corpses more strongly than anyone else during our medical training. I was able to control my disgust, distaste and nausea, but I did not have as thick a skin as many other people. I had problems with pathology as well; I did see that the subject, which used logic to seek out the cause of the actual sickness, was very important, but I could never quite shake off my disgust and sense of shock, and view it in a factual, abstract light, when the person concerned was somebody I had known. Demonstrations of dissected corpses, and professional discussions held around those corpses, were always a source of horror to me. I often felt shaken when others had switched over to objective interest. Almost always, a written account would have been enough for me.

I saw my environment and my future in a new light. If I was like this—half rotten, all wrong, neurotic, burdened with unhealthy mental associations—if I connected love and life themselves with death, corruption and decay, then how was I ever to lead a pleasant, contented life, loving and bearing children? Why was I so deformed? Why did something like this have to happen to me? Penis = waterlogged corpse: Whatever was to become of me? Did I have any chance at all of becoming something like a normal woman, capable of feeling and loving? Had I deceived the men who'd been attracted to me? Had I developed charm in order to suppress my basic internal sickness? Yet I'd often appeared, and to conventionally-minded people at that, as the ideal type for a daughter-in-law, remarkably normal, someone who could be expected to bear many children. Had all this been a desperate act of defense, covering chaotic, putrescent neurotic depths? I no longer knew what to think of myself, my relationships, my whole previous life.

At any event, I found my mother's banal, simple faith and belief in me naive and unreal. Hers was the way most people, particularly the highly neurotic, react when they have to see their children as extensions of themselves. Her opinion could certainly be discounted: It was biased and probably arose from her own psychological needs.

There was also a certain fascination in having discovered something so powerful and analytically impressive in myself.

I withdrew, quietly, from the more vital, powerful kind of men I knew, men with the right feelings; they were just the kind who would soon have seen through me. I missed the suggestive fooling around of flirtation almost as if it were a vitamin, but after all, it had been mere show, a Potemkin village.

It seemed analytically correct for me to feel angry with my mother.

After one ghastly dream, I went to my session weeping, totally overcome by pangs of conscience: I had dreamed of an elderly woman being run over and mashed on the railroad tracks when she failed to notice a barrier; at first she was nothing but bloody pulp, and then—for the train was a long one—she dried up and turned to fibrous, dry, colorless dust. She was almost gone. And I had watched it happen; it wasn't actually my fault, but I had just stood by, watching.

The dream in itself seemed horrifying enough, but I saw it as something much worse, relating to my mother and godmother, who had lived with our family and helped to bring me up. Nobody else. My pent-up rage must be murderous. I could barely speak for my tears, my swollen nose and self-condemnation.

I felt a little better when my analyst soothed me; she could well understand that this weighed heavily on me, she said, but as she knew, such dreams did happen, and such feelings were real; a great many people had them. The longer and more firmly one had previously repressed them, the more vehement, brutal and powerful they were. It was a productive sign, indicating change, if I could now allow myself to have dreams like these. I felt comforted. She did not think of me an unspeakable bitch because of my death wishes, she wasn't shocked, she even thought them significant and productive.

Obviously I had grown up in so aggressively inhibited an atmosphere that I was now reacting violently. Had mine perhaps been a terribly restricted, regimented childhood which I did my best to idealize, by dint of strenuous defense, denial, reaction formation? If I had such dreams, then I must be a mass of hatred, rage and destructive urges, kept within bounds only with difficulty.

Her interpretations, and those memories in which I did find hatred and rage, did not bring much relief. The tension remained; I was full of self-condemnation.

One dream left me baffled: My two brothers were chasing me in the jungle, trying to upset me by trying to put snakes on my body; I ran away, they brought down snakes of every size from all the trees. Any associations I could find for this dream were vague; the whole situation seemed too outlandish and exotic. I must have been spending too long over it for her liking, for she said, sounding bored, "But don't you see the sexual content? There's no ambiguity about snakes." I realized my stupidity; I ought to have thought of that myself. Her disparaging tone confirmed me in my belief that I was different from other analysands.

Her reaction to a memory of my stepfather was similar. I sometimes got into the tub with him or sat on his lap while he was on the toilet. "Can't you think of anything else in that context?" No, I had just sat on his lap; I thought he's been reading the newspaper. She pressed the point, asking her question again. I felt quite neutral, couldn't remember anything in particular about the situation, it was just a vague memory with no feelings attached. Finally, with emphasis: "But you were sitting on his *naked* penis." I hadn't seen her point at first. But yes: It must have been a strong sexual stimulus, arousing violent and overwhelming feelings in me. At that age, I had had to repress and deny them. These must have been deeply traumatizing incidents. The fact that I was sensually attracted to men of rather ravaged appearance, with bags under their eyes like my stepfather's and thick lower lips, fitted in with this theory. I tried hard to remember my feelings at the time. The situation was clear in my mind, but had nothing affective about it, which said much for the original violence of my feelings and my strenuous repression of them. I could only draw conclusions and inferences, no longer sense or feel.

I felt horror of the deformity in me; I veered between rage, resignation, disbelief, and a certain respect for my own overwhelming, sick and analytically impressive case.

However—if I really had been thus deformed by my stepfather, there was nothing I could do about it. Why had I had such a stepfather like that anyway, instead of having a real, responsible father? How could something so bad and likely to induce neurosis occur in a family that was nothing out of the ordinary, even if decimated by the war? Where had they been, those whose job it was to see that all was well, those who ought to have looked after me? That was my mother's responsibility. Why did it have to be me who got into such trouble?

*   *   *

The war, my dead father, my stepfather—I hadn't chosen any of those things for myself. It was exceedingly unjust. I gave my anger free rein. I could turn it most easily on my mother; she had wished this kind of situation on me; I also felt angry with the Nazis, with the imbecilic politicians of today, disinclined to put a stop to such things; with my extended family on both sides, who had really had enough money to pay the ransom without which they couldn't emigrate, being considered politically unreliable; they had had it all set up, with a job waiting at an Egyptian hospital. I began to hate my father for his irresponsibility. Why did he have all the wounded flown out of Stalingrad, and not himself? Was it some idiotic sense of honor stemming from the Nibelungs? Was anyone who happened to be wounded more important than him, solely because he was wounded? Was it right to observe so stupid a point of medical honor when you had three small children? I felt sure not all those wounded men had had three children waiting for them. Why hadn't he gone along with the supporters of the Third Reich? Such men had stayed home and survived. The values were all adrift in my head. I might have had an outright super Nazi for a father, I might slowly have come to see his weaknesses, discussed politics with him, disassociated myself from those politics—but at any event these dreadful distortions and idealisations of mine wouldn't have set in. I had heard it said that dead fathers are the strongest. I felt anger against him for that, too.

My conception of values was shaken. My mother had comforted herself for the probable or at least possible loss of her husband with my existence, and in so doing had been responsible for my unhappiness. I was deeply envious of my brothers, who had known our parents' full, loving marriage, and had drawn from it their independence and self-confidence. Indeed, I was deeply envious of anyone who grew up in a family with a father. I viewed other war orphans, including classmates of mine, with retrospective horror, feeling certain they had gone as wrong as I myself, in the same way.

I felt bitter, I thought I was unjustly treated; the pathological condition which made me so different isolated me. So did my envy. I thought my acquaintances' current problems very ordinary; they did not impress me. What was an unhappy love affair, compared to my fundamental flaw?

I no longer knew whom or what to think well of, or how I was to think well of anything. When I looked closely, most things about myself, my family and my environment seemed appalling, mendacious, distorted.

Was there anything in which I could really take pleasure, of which I could be proud? Not my parents, certainly. "No, things aren't altogether easy with such a radiant mother." I had once regarded myself as lucky in my parents: Not any more. But one represses unpleasantness and sadness; as a rule, awful things are the most likely to come to light during analysis. So I had heard and learned. But the process did not seem quite so radical with other people; they did not appear as much affected, as worn down and devitalized as I was. However, those people could see the warmth of my analyst's personality, felt they were in good hands with her. And that was something I could not, absolutely not, feel because of the transference. Or at least, not yet.

My emotional disintegration showed that I had gone into analysis just in time; that I was in great need of it, was considerably more disturbed, sicker, nearer the end of my tether than I had thought, and than those who knew me could have seen. For reasons best known to myself, I had probably gone all out to appear efficient, stable and vital. And now that shell of mine, formed as a defense mechanism, was crumbling away. I could think myself lucky it was happening now, in comparatively well regulated circumstances, and that I wasn't having a breakdown somewhere or other remote from analytic help.

As my awareness of my sickness increased, I invested more hope in my analysis; later, it became my only hope. I became a believer; I could convey belief and confidence in analytic therapy to my patients too.

And I was indeed able to pass on what had done me good, to convincing effect. If I saw someone feeling upset, oppressed, trying to put on a brave face in a well-behaved restrained and resigned manner, becoming monstrously sad and wallowing in depression, feeling an aching longing after separation or loss, I could do some good. If the patient did not take his own wishes, needs and requirements seriously enough, but was keeping himself in a state of starvation, I knew how to deal with that. I drew some comfort from these pleasant therapeutic episodes. My patients did not see me in such a calamitous light as I saw myself.

*   *   *

My lack of self-assurance was a theme frequently discussed. After my last examination, which had assured me the top grade, I had gone home in tears, not in the least proud of myself. At the time, I explained it to myself by thinking that given industry, anyone could master the study of medicine with relative ease, and grades were given arbitrarily anyway, so there was nothing to be proud of. Other possible explanations now emerged: Of those members of my family still alive, no one else had an academic degree; I was the first to take this university examination (given at the end of six years of medical school). My inability to relish the fact could derive from feelings of guilt towards my mother, who had not been able to complete her own medical studies after the war. And perhaps I was avoiding competition with my brothers by not wishing to assume the adult role of a trained and independent doctor of medicine. To my own constraints and anxieties could also be added the fact that their own problems, their desire not to endanger their sense of their own worth, really caused them to reduce me to the status of a poor little wretch who had only just, by a stroke of good luck, managed to pass her exam and wasn't to be taken seriously. They had laughed at my title of "Doctor," and I myself had thought the work I did for it ordinary enough, compared with the courses in other faculties.

It hurt, now, to think that my flat, let down feeling after the examination had not in the main been founded on reality, but was more likely due to my knuckling under and bowing to other people, and to my own neurotic inhibitions. It was just cowardice that made me feel like that, even if I'd caught up with the rest of my family from behind and surpassed them all. Perhaps the very magic that medicine had always held for me during my studies was fed by rivalry: By my efforts to excel, to be recognized as a grown-up person at last.

It was also depressing to find that I couldn't recreate my feelings of the time. I had probably had guilt feelings, I had probably experienced deep inhibition of my aggression, but I couldn't summon up those feelings now. I could deduce them, suspect them; I couldn't feel them. I felt stupid and slow. Everybody I knew had feelings of anger towards members of their families, but there was much I just could not recall.

*   *   *

I thought many of the men I met dull; I could get nothing from them. I wasn't at that time aware that the male model type, the sort to be seen posing in underwear ads, etc., tends to be homosexual and unlikely to feel any attraction to me. I just didn't fancy them at all. On the other hand, I did like the look of certain criminal characters, prison inmates. I'd seen a series of photographs in the local paper of men who had committed murder during robbery; I found them appealing, exciting. "What attracts you to them?" asked my analyst. I thought them handsome in their own way: Self assured, with intent, resolute eyes. They seemed strong, dependable, powerful. In their photographs, they seemed tender, resigned, experienced, knowing. I couldn't express it exactly. "Is it violence that attracts you?" Perhaps, but I was certainly attracted by the expression of beauty and resignation in their eyes.

However, her question, and the wider context, told me what we were getting at: I was looking for violence, desired rape, so as to be spared guilt feelings, wanted to be endangered in a conventionally feminine fashion, because I thought I could experience my sexuality only through punishment. Cruel men would punish me for my instinctual wishes. It was quite safe, because they were behind bars, where they couldn't get at me or I at them. With my fears, the only feelings I could summon were for people in photographs, paper men with whom I'd hardly be likely to come into contact. But there must be such men around in ordinary life too. Why didn't I come across them? The idea that I wanted punishment and violence was new to me, though; it wasn't even quite clear, she'd just suspected it in me, asked me about it. However, the suspicion that I harbored very sick desires stuck.

In many ways, life was actually easier now.

I regarded my slips as significant, phenomena well worth studying. They often showed me something. If I went into the wrong room by mistake, and obeyed an impulse to look around it, I might find what I'd been looking for after all, or something urgent and important. If I couldn't find my car keys, lost my handbag, caught my arm in the lining of my coat and found the sleeve restricting me, I didn't really want to go out. It was an effort not to regard myself as crazy, bad at concentrating, clumsy, inconsistent, and not to feel upset but to regard my impulses as significant and purposeful.

My analyst was surprised by this, but didn't try to stop me. "Well, if you're finding you have that kind of access to your unconscious . . ." That sounded good, astute.

One interpretation of hers really struck me: I was careless with papers and documents, had completely lost two certificates; I hated dealing with my green social insurance card, police registration, invoices and so forth. Once, when I was in the hospital, I discovered that my health insurance had run out because I'd failed to open reminder letters. I always felt cross or weary at the sight of bureaucratic forms, and set about filling them in very awkwardly, and then my failure to deal with the mess depressed me in its turn.

"Why haven't you done it yet? What stopped you?" I couldn't think of an explanation; I felt inadequate. "You really want your mother to do the job for you." After a little while I began to cry. This was bad. My wishes were so childlike; I'd never managed to break with home. Was I so deeply unable to cope with life, unwilling to show competence on my own account? Did I always want others to do the work for me? If I still desired symbiosis with my mother so strongly, all my efforts hitherto were pointless, and it was hardly surprising none of my relationships had led to a more stable connection.

Hurt and defiant, I proceeded to get a few things done, but in principle nothing had changed. I was just making an extra effort to overcome my automatic resistance.

*   *   *

Former acquaintances thought me more irritable than before, more self-centered, less able or willing to adapt to others, run down. One friend who knew me very well was worried; he won-

dered if it was right for me to torment myself thus, become so unsure of myself. My handwriting was getting so small and uncertain. Objectively, I thought he was right. My family said I'd gone
into my shell, I was self-centered, quickly angered, quarrelsome
and egocentric. I thought this was understandable and quite logical; I'd previously refrained too readily from asserting myself, I'd
given in too easily, and the present change in me upset an established order. Other analysands mentioned their similar experiences; mothers, in particular, reacted to analysis with jealousy. My
fatherly friend kept a tolerant but still anxious eye on me. My
Upper Hessian godmother thought I looked "terribly pale," "thin
as a rake," and asked if I was sick? Unanalyzed people couldn't
share my pride in what I was now achieving; an acquaintance said
in some surprise that I'd always been able to make easy contact
when I felt good.

To professionals, I appeared as one does "in the analytic process;" it was normal, such changes might be expected and proper;
many people experienced the same kind of thing. Some liked me
better in this state—near tears, quiet, sub-depressive, unsure of
myself and in need of comfort—than when I was on top of the
world. Perhaps when I did feel good and was in good shape there
was something repulsive, castrating about me? I knew penis envy
and castratory tendencies did show up in analysis. An analyst told
me later that when unhappy I was "closer to myself."

What actually went on around me seemed less important. My
feelings, fantasies, ideas were of analytic value: In particular the
more deformed, distorted and problematic of them. For instance, I
easily explained one woman's hostility to me as the result of my
own latent aggression, the echo of my ambivalent, secretly hostile
attitude toward her. My efforts to get closer to her, explain, express
myself were fruitless and heightened the hostile tension. However,
as it was clear that almost all tension can be relieved if it is
expressed—and that hadn't worked—I knew that her reaction was
provoked by something within myself: For instance, my feelings of
hatred for my mother, fears of contact, homosexual anxieties, feelings of rivalry, etc. I was very ready to attribute great blame to myself. It would have been a primitive approach to account for the
tension by ordinary envy, jealousy and power conflicts. I first took
a good look at myself, and felt an urge to give up entirely: Give up

myself, my values, my usual habits. Behind many of my feelings others lurked, feelings I defended against, unpleasant ones.

I was functioning fairly well at first; I took care to write letters punctually and felt depressed if I didn't. This showed that my ego functions were all right, but there was coercion in it, I wasn't acting easily. There might be a strong superego in the background. "Why are you so troubled? Why can't you just enjoy the evening?" Other people seemed to take things more casually. I haven't heard of such an interpretation in this connection, but it was valid here.

The dictates of my superego were too stern; I ought to soften them. Once, when I had a discharge, I went straight to the dermatology clinic and knew by noon that I didn't have a venereal disease: A good thing in itself, but it seemed typical of the way I faced the affective. It showed how I avoided living out my feelings, letting them develop, how I took active measures to suppress them and put them in order and then forgot them. I hadn't lived out my anxieties, worries and fantasies about the sexual partner who might have infected me, I just took instant practical steps to solve the problem. My mother, certainly, would have condemned procrastination in such a context; it was probably due to her that I acted fast. But I'd also spared myself a nagging worry that might have lasted days, and had had to make myself do it. I had the impression I wasn't treating myself in the best way in allowing my mother's brisk activity to come spontaneously to the fore in me; I might be harming my finer, softer, more sensitive feelings. My similarly indisposed lover laughed. "Well, what are we to do with each other?" He had thought ahead.

*   *   *

I had a few ideas of my own to set against my analyst's interpretations, conjectures and assessments—even if the latter weren't explicitly expressed. I had some awareness of my own in regard to some of her opinions. If she was cooler to me than to others, and I was not wrong to leave this impression, I now found she was justified, considering all I'd come to know about myself.

Once I came to my session animated and excited. Seeing a woman I knew stroke another woman's hair lovingly, tenderly, I'd glimpsed another dimension. "There's something lesbian there!"

She didn't accept this, sounded annoyed, slightly cross. "Oh, you'd see anything as lesbian!" . . . Because of my anxieties, barring me from satisfying relationships with other women. But the act of tenderness had impressed me; I hadn't perceived anything between the two women on this wavelength before, but now it explained their fierce quarrels, heart-to-heart talks and reconciliations. I tried to cling to my perception, but she still rejected it, so I felt stupid.

I felt dissatisfied with my own therapeutic practice at first; I had doubts and felt unsure of myself. I felt I was somewhat megalomanic to undertake intensive treatment so soon, without sufficient theory and experience. I worried whether my goodwill and caution would avert those mistakes that may be expected of a beginner.

Apropos, she asked, "Why must you always compare yourself with older, more experienced people? With your elder siblings?" The fact was that I had always had elder siblings around me who were more advanced than I, who could talk and walk before me and had mastered skills which I still had to learn. Why did I feel so inferior to the more experienced? There would always, or almost always, be more experienced people than me. Why couldn't I be content with what I already could do? Why did I think only the skills and experience of others counted? Why had I no point of reference and scale of values within myself?

I had, in fact always been particularly cross and impatient when I failed to learn, comprehend, grasp something as fast as I'd have liked. I shed tears over learning to knit. One of my brothers liked knitting; I got my own needles damp with sweat, my yarn was taut and grubby. Only with jerky motion could I push the sticky needle through the right stitches. I had certainly had some discouraging early experiences.

On the other hand, if something remained unclear in a therapy session, and I understood it only later, during supervision, it could be too late to make up for the inexperienced reaction in the next session. If psychoanalytical technique was so effective, it was negatively effective too. "Why don't you trust yourself more?" That sounded friendly and encouraging; I was probably all right, for someone of my age. But still, I had less experience than others; comparison with more experienced people was bound to be to my disadvantage, never mind early sibling rivalry.

My self-doubts annoyed me. I must rethink things, reorientate my feelings, treat myself differently. Apart from a vague complaint against life for making me the youngest of the family, I couldn't think of anyone to blame but myself. My present experience was all mixed and muddled up with uncomfortable experiences from the past.

After reading Freud's *Psychopathology of Everyday Life*, I had expected to find myself making fascinating crazy discoveries. I would see amusing, convincing revealing little details which would make the day more vital, full and intriguing. I thought the passage in which he intended to make an offering to the Madonna if something went well and then, involuntarily and against his conscious intentions, broke the Madonna with a well-aimed slipper while singing a tune with appropriate words, was illuminating; also the one where he brought a fellow traveller to express his fears of fatherhood by means of a slip of the tongue.

But so much was wrong with my own psychic world; so much was bad, sick, negative, and must be changed. It was like seeing life through dark glasses. I kept thinking, "This is all I need!" Why did I wallow in *nothing* but unhappy childhood experiences, sickness, neurosis? Why did so little that was cheerful, amusing, encouraging occur to me? The reason must be my disturbance, the equilibrium I so laboriously maintained towards the outer world with my strong defense mechanisms.

Once I arrived for my session in a silly mood, with a tune running through my head. It was a pop song about a woman waggling her little behind. I soon felt the atmosphere in the room was tense, and was startled to find I must have been thinking of her, although she usually wore skirts that were rather too long and full and made a neutral impression; no bottom-waggling could have been seen beneath them. Associations were slow in occurring to me; I soon felt the atmosphere most uneasy. After a long and painful pause, she remarked, "You are trying to make fun of me." She sounded stern, and indeed I had laughed, giggling in a silly way, as if overtired. That particular session was unproductive and short on words. I didn't feel like laughing that way again.

After my first few sessions, I had met a man and the relationship quickly became intense. She remarked, "You've fallen in love at this point to shut yourself off from me, to keep me from getting too close to you." So it was a form of protection, a way of distancing myself from her. However, he was the kind of man I had liked; other people felt enthusiastic about him too. Still, I would probably have flung myself into the intimacy less readily and wouldn't have concentrated on him so hard if I hadn't also been concerned to avoid, or at least delay, forming a close relationship with her. I didn't believe her interpretation at first; I was too enthralled by him. But it gnawed away at me. The fact that for a while I ceased to care about my career, my analysis, my professional future, and had been thinking of children, was an indication of my defense against really throwing myself into the analytic process, surrendering to it. There was much in me that he understood very well, and that, too, seemed to indicate that I wanted to set someone up in competition with her, a father figure, or at least some third person to help me escape the maternal/analytic dominance.

At least a part of my enamored state was resistance: An artificial product.

What did I like about him? I tried to explain; she thought of a quotation from Brecht's Pirate Jenny, about being unable to help it, but I didn't have the text in mind, nor did I like worrying away at the question; it just was so. I liked his lower lip, his energy, his vitality, and his rather large eyes with slight bags under them. My stepfather had had noticeable bags under his eyes. His full lower lip reminded me of a man with whom my mother had been friendly, who had come on the scene when I was two and a quarter years old. I often found his bow legs exciting too. I was surprised to note these characteristics; I must depend on them a lot, and that was another reason why I had fallen for this particular man just now. He was quick to understand me; when he asked, "What does your father do?" and I told him my father had been killed in the war, he took me in his arms, realizing how I felt.

Later, when the relationship had ended, I must have made too much of a fuss. "There are other men in the world, you know . . ." said my analyst. I could tell from her tone of voice, that she meant it was time I stopped thinking about him.

It was a strain when I came to a session in a good mood, enthusiastic over something or other, and then we got down to working on some depressive factor against which I had been defending. Often I didn't want to believe in it, and stubbornly tried to cling to my good mood. But there almost always was something depressing me, something I didn't want to think about, something I'd had good reason to banish to the farthest corner of my mind, and which now surfaced, destroying my cheerfulness.

Much remained obscure, and was only touched upon. Once I went to the toilet at night and disliked the sight of my large, aggressively coiling stool. "What does it remind you of?" Whence my uneasiness? It was the size of it, the dark, black color, the sense of its being separate from me. Were these my childhood fears of self-disintegration and loss emerging from my dreams and my weakened defense? Was I afraid of losing too much of myself? Penis—long stool—child? I couldn't think of anything further in the atmosphere of that session; it remained a matter of intellectual acrobatics. I knew how heavily laden with symbolism the feces are, but I could not really feel or remember anything in that connection, not emotionally. I could only be sure that my alarm was connected with something bad and sick in myself; if I could have defined it, I might have expected to find a great giant gob of something sick, dark and neurotic.

My awareness of being severely neurotic oppressed me. Sometimes I felt I had been pushed into my depression like a dachshund whose nose is pushed into his excrement. But there was still hope. I knew that analysands must "work their way through depression," which came at regular intervals, and was to be expected.

During a brief family gathering I felt tremendous anger toward nearly everyone present; I thought most of them impossible, cold and heartless, and could imagine myself splitting their skulls with an axe. Later, this frightened me; in analysis it appeared almost "normal." Certain remarks had reminded me of past situations, reviving latent rage and feelings of powerlessness which I could now perceive more consciously. So all things considered, I was making progress. This was a case of repressed feelings which had now been exposed and which I had to integrate. I found the usual ironic tone of family conversation clearly hurtful (with its expressions such as pettifogging quibbler—nervous virgin—social idiot, etc.).

*   *   *

Two months before the planned end of my analysis (after a year, because of my analyst's move) I registered for a group dynamics workshop. This was considered an important supplementary experience.

I was under a strain before it; I had taken on a great deal of work. One job I was doing gave me considerable trouble; we frequently discussed my difficulties with it. I had to deal with administrators and generally came off worst in any conflict with their smooth, prescribed routine; my failures revived my problems with father figures and authority; there was tension between myself and people important to me, for whom I would have liked to work more successfully. All this constituted a considerable tangle of feelings when discussed in analysis; tearful and discouraged I talked about the coolness, lack of understanding and rigidity I met with in administrators; I connected it with my lack of assertiveness and self-confidence, my inability to cope with life in general, my submissiveness and my inhibited aggression. My helplessness and powerless anger were similar to what I experienced as a child; as was my dependence on the judgment of superiors. Why was I not able to distance myself, to take things more lightly? I thought of simply giving up the job; resigning from it. But she said I would certainly experience this as defeat. The strain of the job told on me, however. Other people had had their difficulties in the same job, but probably didn't suffer from them so much.

At a private party, in quite a large company, an analyst I knew complained he was always getting into situations—during plane journeys, in remote places when he was on holiday—where he was called upon to help in childbirth; there were women in the last stages of pregnancy all over the place, and he was lucky if he wasn't recognized as a doctor. His story was only mildly funny; instead of coming to a point he kept describing more such situations, and finally I asked if he'd ever thought of going on holiday with a midwife. Judging from the subsequent laughter, I had made my point.

Since then, he had become my superior, and now he told me that even my first contact with him had been castrating. (And though he was obviously piqued, this was the diagnosis of a man who had been properly analyzed.)

I set off for the course feeling exhausted. I was afraid I would find the whole thing boring and I wouldn't be able to share in the general enthusiasm for group processes. Perhaps I would be unable to enjoy myself.

Driving there, and quite often afterwards, when I had just woken up, I found a tune was going round in my head: *qui a changé ma chanson?*

I saw this course as something positive for me; my analyst did not. Subsequently, I was put on psychopharmacological drugs, without really wanting to take them or even seeing why I should.

I learned a good deal at the workshop, anyway; I felt strong, capable of thinking clearly and independently without falling back on authority; I felt like a mature, attractive woman, able to put my convictions into words and stand by them; and I felt lovable. I had been sure enough of my own feelings of boredom, annoyance, tension, etc.; in this larger group I'd been able to see that a great many other people felt the same way, their feelings developing sometimes faster and sometimes more slowly. I had done my utmost and I felt good. The atmosphere was determined by people connected with the Church (pastor, priest, Father . . .), a world I did not know. By the end of the workshop I liked almost everyone there— everyone, anyway, whom I could understand. I had been told, "If you don't like someone, you haven't understood him," and that was true.

On the way back, I broke my journey and spent the night at a motel. I was excited; on principle I didn't want to take a sleeping pill, since such drugs cover things up, conceal them. I had short and intensive anxiety dreams which kept waking me. I wondered whether to leave the light on, or take a sleeping pill after all, or both: Then, however, I decided the dreams were important, and might help me get at things deep down inside me. And the fear with which I kept waking was bearable.

One dream kept recurring, with variations: the situation was a Last Supper type of scene, as in a painting, with many pious people present, men who suddenly and with one accord began to revile me, attack and overpower me, like wild animals, wolves. In my dream I fell to the ground on my back and they all fell upon me. The pack of wolves was going to eat me. At this point I woke in terror.

I thought of the men who had been in the workshop in connection with the wolfish wild animals; my father's name was Wolf, too;

there had probably been much erotic tension behind that ecclesiastical atmosphere. Some of the men present had liked me, but I'd also sensed a good deal of anger, contempt, condemnation, rejection. The dream basically was like an intense concentration and continuation of the real situation. The few women in the workshop had not had an easy time of it.

I kept coming back to one violent image, of something like a fenced area crawling with laboring, toiling beetles scrambling over and under each other, bloodstained, cramped for space, always on the move, legs becoming entangled and struggling, all the beetles trampling one another down, injuring, maiming, tormenting each other. It left a most unpleasant impression.

In another dream, I heard a shrill voice shouting, "You must remain small." Thoughts, remarks and ideas from the course came back to me too.

I wanted to delve into my own depths, follow my impulses: I had to urinate frequently, the warm gush in my urethra was soothing. My whole genital area seemed superfluous; if it were removed I'd have been at peace. My breasts were too diffuse, too soft and unclean. I washed my genitals and breasts; without those parts of me I'd be clean, vulva and breasts cut out. Masturbating had a soothing effect, and so did urinating. I could feel myself again in those two acts: I drank water, urinated, masturbated, tried to understand. My female body was something dirty, something to be punished, something to be fought.

The next morning I felt as if I'd been broken on the wheel, but I was pleased with my self-knowledge. I was sure now that I suffered from female castration fears and guilt feelings about attractiveness and potency. I thought I had gone through the experience described in my analyst's article about the penis/phallus separation, which I had just read. I wasn't sure what the beetles meant.

Exhausted and proud, I planned to unburden myself of all this in my session, but I never got that far. I began talking about the previous night, which I saw as the quintessence of my experiences. She did not seem at all receptive to my theories; she asked if I'd seen these things or dreamed them; had I been able to tell dreams from reality? This was unlike her: She generally listened to me carefully. After about ten minutes she broke off the session, saying I needed medication; my present reaction was too strong, and would be too much of a strain on me without drugs. I felt rejected, but agreed to her urgent persuasions, or at least I agreed to take something strong to help me sleep. I dreaded the thought of another such night as I had passed. She immediately phoned to make me an appointment with a physician. I was determined not to have my thoughts and feelings chemically altered; after all, I'd worked so hard to get at them. I would take sleeping tablets, but nothing else. The physician asked me more questions, and then prescribed psychotropic drugs. I couldn't see why: I had laid myself open to my dreams on purpose, and nobody had noticed anything wrong with me during the workshop. I accepted the prescription, meaning to pretend I was taking the drugs, as he realized; he told me so, in friendly tones, and gave me a sherry. I began to weep, gave in, and took psychotropic drugs three times a day until further notice. They blocked the connections between the brain cells, at least in part.

They calmed me down. Just before I was due to take them, I often became restless again, tormented, twitchy all over, without any definite reason. I thought I wouldn't be able to stand this condition for long; I shouldn't think anyone would.

At first I was upset because I hadn't been able to unburden myself of my discoveries regarding my emotions. Later I decided that was best. I thought my analyst didn't want to talk about them so as to spare me. The topic remained taboo as far as I was concerned. And the drugs had disposed of the substance of my easiness.

She suggested my going to a mutual acquaintance's psychiatric hospital for a while. I was surprised, and thought it unlikely they would have a job for me at such short notice. No, she meant as a patient! But she didn't insist on this solution. I then audited lectures at a medical clinic as often as I could.

She thought I was in a state of excessive depression; I was to ask the physician if anti-depressants were indicated. He thought my moods were understandable and said I needed no additional drugs.

I was finding dirty jokes and double meanings embarrassing, almost painful. They reminded me of something sad, now dead, almost beyond repair, and I thought other people would notice. I couldn't join in their laughter. Once I did try a light-hearted note—"That's all he ever thinks of!" The man I'd meant approached me later, saying, a query in his tone, that I'd sounded almost reproachful. I changed the subject. I couldn't tell him the whole awful, hopeless truth.

I found any kind of contact beyond the casual human closeness of people touching or leaning against one another unpleasant; my skin was either painfully sensitive or numb. I blamed myself, feeling worthless as a woman, a hopeless case. A man who had perhaps been through something similar himself, who at least understood, went to great pains to disprove my total denial of pleasure; he was very kind and took a long time, just getting very close without being too insistent, merely to convince me I could feel pleasure again, and I did, a little. "There, you see?" I clung to that for a while.

I'd had that song on my mind ever since the workshop. The tune soothed me; I would often play it for hours on end. I played it at night, too, when I woke, or if I felt restless for some reason. "Ils ont changé ma chanson—look what they done to my song," ran the words of the American original. This interested her; she encouraged me to sing it to her, but I didn't dare. Finally I hummed the tune for her. However, that didn't convey the important aspect of it, I lent her the recording of the song, and she listened to it, she said, "several times, very carefully." One line, in the German version, ran "ich wollte singen, was ich niemals sagen kann"—"I wanted to sing what I can never say," and she thought I meant that for her, but she didn't understand what I was really trying to express; presumably it was something emotional.

I was pleased; she had liked the song and been receptive to it. Her record player was already in the city to which she was moving; she really had gone to some trouble to listen to it, and was interested. We never thought of just taking the text literally, not as a kind of cryptogram. (See p. 64.)

Several sessions were truly paradise; there was total unity and a sense of relaxation between us. She did not seem to feel overstrained when they ended, either; she smiled, seeming gentle and relaxed. At such times I thought her, her whole room, the corridor and the staircase beautiful. However, there were only a few such sessions, and they were not repeated.

Another song encouraged me: "A time to love—a time to cry," ("Who knows, we both could find the way, we both could find the answer." It too was sung by Dahlia Lavi.)

We did not go back to those dreams and nocturnal fears of mine upon which I'd briefly touched, never even mentioned them. The nagging question remained: What had really so exhausted me, knocked me so badly off balance?

Once, towards the end of my time with her, I became insistent and asked almost desperately if my capacity for feeling would ever be all right, maybe after further analysis, she finally said, very cautiously, that I would probably "learn to cope with my feelings better." So this was her opinion after a year; the opinion of a recognized analyst. I felt the weight of it.

I could scarcely bear to see other people happy now. It made me feel desperate, envious, full of hatred, mean. Seeing a pregnant woman, I wished the child within her to die, wished it to wither slowly, have to be brought out of her in bits, I wished deformities on it, and so forth. I could only stand seeing happy couples in the street if I imagined them falling victim to serious illnesses, death, mutilation, accidents. Quite deliberately, I wished for disasters. I felt guilty about this, and isolated in my wickedness and hatred. I might be told that such feelings did occur, and at the moment I couldn't allow anyone happiness because I had none myself, etc., and it all sounded convincing enough, but it was upsetting too.

Our sessions were now concerned with current problems. It suddenly turned out that the analyst with whom I'd expected to continue my analysis was going away, and would not be undertaking any analysis for quite a long time; another man, to whom I then agreed to go, wouldn't be around after all because he was staying abroad. As I was in such a bad way, I needed to continue analysis directly, without much of a wait. So I couldn't stay in this town; moreover, a certain time spent working in organic medicine seemed a good idea, like a plaster cast around the mind, distancing me. I must find a new analyst and a new job.

My present analyst went to a lot of trouble for me, phoning around to find me a place in analysis. I spent many of my sessions with her in tears; some of these were additional sessions. Another song did me good:

> Tell me where can I go
> There is no place I can see (. . .)
> It's the same in every land
> There is nowhere to go

And it's me who should know
won't you please understand?
Now I know where to go
where my folks proudly stand
let me go o let me go (. . .)
for at least I am free
no more wonderings at me   (D. Lavi)

But I wasn't taking any notice of song lyrics at the time.

*   *   *

Parting from her was much worse than I'd expected, as if a vital part of me were being torn away. I dreamed she and I were wearing the same shirt, joined at the side of the chest like Siamese twins, one sleeve each. I wept my way through my sessions, couldn't imagine life without her. As if all the sap in my being would be drained away when she went, leaving me behind, just a depressive, inactive lump of flesh, unable to cope with life. I wondered whether to follow her abroad; asked friends if I could come and stay with them. However, it would have been very difficult to get a work permit, and she did not think it would be a good idea if I had no work and she were my only point of contact in a foreign city; it was too much of a burden to lay on analysis.

Then it turned out that I could continue my analysis with a man in another town.

I travelled three hundred and fifty kilometers for my initial interview; I had inwardly prepared myself, and was all tensed up. He was obviously short of time and under pressure; he listened to me in a friendly but rather superficial way, and then said, surprisingly quickly, that he was prepared to take on my analysis—this before I'd really been able to describe myself. He dismissed me after about quarter of an hour. Feeling rather flat and dissatisfied, I found myself out in the street, wondering how on earth he had been able to form an opinion of me in so short a time. Had he understood what I was saying? I had expected something more thorough and intensive.

I was very lonely at first in the new town and my new job. I felt an almost physical distaste for the tough, unforthcoming Swabian dialect. One Sunday, I drove through the Swabian Alps alone; all the restaurants as well as the outdoors, seemed full of well-fed, contented, and self-contained families of young people with small children, people who hadn't a care in the world, and no personal problems. The dish I had ordered made my mood even worse: A pile of noodles, resembling a cowpat, which I was expected to get down somehow. Well, I wasn't here by my own choice.

My new anlayst mattered all the more. He listened to me, was friendly, kindly, interested. We had acquaintances and interests in common; he did me good.

I knew men like him, men who were his type, and they liked me.

Soon I felt he was uncomplicated, casual, stable. His room looked comfortable, just the way it was; no kind of aesthetic constraint had gone into furnishing it. He did not dress pretentiously either, but casually, and the effect was pleasing.

He didn't seem to mind very much what he looked like, and he had obviously come to terms very well with a physical handicap. I liked his relative sturdiness, the way his trousers were not tight-fitting, but hung comfortably, his soft, supple suede shoes. He had a sense of humor, and particularly liked black humor, which he interpreted as a practical and skilful way of dealing with misfortune. I liked that interpretation. Soon I felt comfortably familiar with him as I might with an elder schoolmate.

The sessions were friendly and pleasant. I had a great deal to say, and he listened to it all readily. I looked forward to our time together. And now I was finding my feet relatively fast at my new hospital, too; I was getting to know people. My own field of medicine was in demand; suddenly I was a specialist. I recovered a little self confidence.

There were also sessions of analysis touching upon the taboo subject of what had happened after the workshop. It did me good to observe the calm, uninvolved objectivity with which he expressed surprise at the violent reactions I had aroused in those around me. It was comforting to hear that he thought there could be no question of any psychotic symptoms; if I would think it over, he said, I'd see this was something different. What had made me suspect psychotic symptoms so intensely? Well, I hadn't understood too well myself, and I couldn't work through the incidents of that time now; they had all been stifled ahd suppressed by the drugs I was taking. I had felt much as I suppose a fallen woman would have done in the old days upon bearing illegitimate, syphilitic black twins—deep embarrassment and degradation, anyway.

I was much better now. The mysterious stain on me was gone; I could even talk about that time again, and pick out those aspects I had thought pleasant and beneficial. Moreover, the reality of the work I had to do at the hospital brought me real experience of success. Here, in these particular emergency situations, I was really important. That fortified me. I felt I was blossoming.

By now I had come to think my analyst very attractive; his hair excited me. I bought myself a pair of beautiful lace-up suede shoes like his, and only realized what I was about when the salesgirl started directing me away from the men's department. Comfortable, easy, uncomplicated walking shoes. I was in love. I listened avidly to positive remarks made about him, and took no notice of negative ones, telling myself that people who had anything to say against him were stupid. They just didn't know him, or else they had problems of their own. One woman had met him at a party at carnival time, and thought he was impossible, described him as rigid, said she would never go into analysis with someone like that, he was really the limit—and to think such a man had been through analysis himself! At first I was indignant, but then I was quick to think what an idealized, mixed-up sort of image of men and father figures she must have, and wondered what was wrong with her if she had to defend herself so hard against such an attractive man. At least, I thought he was attractive: Rugged, casual, strong. I imagined he would be like that in bed too.

I tried to put my enamored state into perspective and to convey it to him by comparing him to a man on a desert island. And the analytic situation really was similar: Isolated, with the setting guaranteeing the absence of any other man by way of comparison or alternative choice; myself face to face with him and no one else over a long time and in a small space. However, it seemed this wasn't funny. Yet he usually enjoyed an ironic way of putting things, and sometimes even laughed at it. I was proud when I had made him laugh.

In my new job, I soon came to think one of my superiors was making obvious advances; my analyst immediately asked why I always, almost obsessively, had to interpret everything in sexual terms. I flinched, but soon came to see that I must just have been wishing for those advances. I felt embarrassed about my desire for my superior; I was less forthcoming in my manner to him, wanting to keep the situation under better control, and observed it more closely. I really couldn't see anything suggestive in his behavior now, and soon I felt quite indifferent about meeting him.

I fell into the depths of depression when I saw my analyst at a concert sitting between two women. The concert, played in a monastery, was very enjoyable in itself: Baroque music, of which I was fond. But it really was torture to see him on such familiar and easygoing terms with those two women. They both seemed to be very attractive, beautiful, confident, feminine, motherly, loving, intact, stable, lovable. Easy to see why he would be out with women like that and not someone like me. Would I ever be so desirable and desired myself? I felt smaller and smaller, and had to make a great effort not to burst into tears. My companion, who was fond of me, felt helpless in the face of my emotional distress, and then angry: Surely the point of analysis wasn't to torment oneself like this, he said; how on earth could I, I of all people, here with him, have such deep doubts of myself? But the evening was ruined. Such commonplace arguments, from a man who'd never been analyzed, carried no weight with me.

We discussed this in my next session, deciding it was Oedipal jealousy, which was good and valuable and had to be lived through. I was in the analytic process, I was a good analysand, experiencing things intensely. My analyst seemed gentle, tender; delightfully attractive.

I wanted to use the familiar form of address to him: "Du." I said so. I thought it was silly to communicate with someone so well at arm's length, by means of the formal "Sie." He knew all about my friends, my feelings and my fears; he knew about my breasts, my pelvis, my dreams, he knew what I liked. The formal "Sie" wasn't right for any of my real-life relationships. Communicating erotic desires and experiences in an impersonal, objective manner, using "Sie," seemed artificial and stupid. And for my part, I thought I knew him very well too by now. I knew what dreams he had, what he enjoyed. He liked soap, had once said he really enjoyed using it. He seemed to be aware of his skin, to be capable of sensitive feelings, although he had never really made the best of his particular attractions. He didn't choose his clothes with much care, had not quite found his own style yet. But he was obviously able to feel good naked, under the shower, in the bath; he could caress himself, let another person caress him, etc. He liked to be underneath in love-making, liked to be shown new ways. Liked it, or would like it, if a woman took the initiative and seduced him. (I had gathered this from his great enthusiasm for the film "Never On Sunday," in which a woman seduces an inexperienced man.) I was sure he was not forceful, was easily made to feel insecure, but was probably grateful to a confident, passionate woman. I'd turned the antennae of my perceptions on him, found out what he liked about me and other women, and I thought I had partly understood him. He seemed familiar to me, too, rather like a Hessian, like the boys who used to travel in from the country to my class at school: Sturdy, vital, shy, very nice at heart. I knew that men of his kind liked me. So why shouldn't I address him with the informal "Du?" I had heard that it was normal and indeed required in other methods of therapy.

However, there was to be no question of our using the informal means of address. He insisted on the more formal mode with some vehemence; it belonged to the analytic setting, it was prescribed usage, and he insisted on sticking to it. The parameters were laid down.

"But why I mean, what's the point? In Gestalt therapy courses . . . if it helps one get at the truth . . ." I knew I was behaving outrageously and that use of the familiar form of address was by no means usual. But why not? If something occurred to me, I had to put it into words, verbalize it. What values did the formal "Sie" protect and the informal "Du" threaten? Not the usefulness of transference, certainly; in our culture, the informal address would have facilitated transference. Did Freud insist, or would Freud have insisted, on "Sie?" Had he said anything at all on the subject? What values would suffer from the use of "Du?"

Arguments such as these did not go down well. He reacted sternly, insisting on preserving the formal analytic setting. Surely I must know, particularly as I was in training analysis myself, that "Sie" was generally used in analytic situations, and I was making unreasonable demands in wanting to get closer. But suppose it had occurred to me all the same? I felt rather cross; how was it that he couldn't produce intellectual arguments to convince me?

He didn't really have to go over the rules again. I felt embarrassed. Perhaps I really had gone too far. One analysand, to whom I cautiously mentioned the matter, smiled in a superior and knowing masculine fashion (she wants to sleep with him, she's acting out, a typical cause of transference). Didn't other people ever think the same way? Was it perfectly natural to them to impart intimate details while calling their analysts "Sie?" On the other hand, I ought not really to be revealing such intimacies of my analytic sessions to anyone outside—other people didn't do that either.

But perhaps their analyses were less personal? Did they say less about themselves and what mattered to them? I felt different. Or were they simply more discreet and unforthcoming, happy in their analyses? If they didn't have the urge to talk about any of it, discuss it outside analysis, well they must be finding analysis a wonderful, soothing, fine experience.

On the other hand, he did like me. I could sense that. So why was his present reaction so stern? Had I really been behaving impossibly, or was it that he felt insecure? "The use of the formal 'Sie' is part of the analytic setting." To be sure.

But then I thought yes, I really had gone too far. At any event, he didn't like me that way; I had better not make an issue of it.

During one session we broached the subject of masturbation. I said I thought, strictly speaking, I really ought to do it some time during a session, then he and I would know what was wrong with me and why. My playful notion met with decided rejection. I could feel it—and I hadn't really meant to carry out such a plan. "What do you fantasize about when you masturbate?" I thought about him; just him, at that time. I kept quiet. We didn't clear the matter up. I felt guilty, in that I had run on ahead of him.

Once home, I brooded about embarrassment and lack of frankness; I tried groping my way back to the theme at the next session; it had been too delicate a subject, I said, and that was why I'd kept quiet. "How do you mean, delicate?" Well, awkward. Embarrassing. He didn't understand. I was evasive. Wasn't it as clear as day, even to him, that I was talking about him? That I thought of him? How could outside acquaintances see how I felt so clearly, while he didn't? I began to feel annoyed. After all, this was the most important factor in analysis, something that absolutely had to be worked through and brought out: The transference love. Emotionally crip-

pled by fate as I was, this was my chance. Everything depended on
love, that was what gave the whole analytical effort its meaning.
Why was he being so slow to understand? How explicitly did I have
to express myself? I was quiet and subdued for several sessions.
Waiting for him to understand. I remembered a friend of mine
from Berlin, an experienced man; there had always been a strong
attraction between us, but I hadn't really trusted myself to sustain
a relationship with him at the time, and he had given up his attempts. He looked Jewish; my analyst's name was Jewish. They
were both dark. All of a sudden he seemed very close to me again.
"Why don't you get in touch with him?" asked my analyst, and I
phoned and arranged to spend the New Year holiday with him. We
had a crazy time: All the same, I kept thinking of my analyst—the
nape of his neck, his hairline, his hips. My friend's attributes
couldn't quite compete.

Back home again, my sudden surge of vitality could be explained
as repetition, father transference. My lover looked like a man my
mother knew, with the same thick lower lip and noticeably bow
legs, looking like the caricature of a Jew. This friend of my mother's had come into our lives after 1945 and had been very kind to
me. I had dreamed of a kind of primal scene with him. He came
down the stairs of our house, did something to my mother's nether
regions, I insisted on his doing the same to mine. He agreed, and I
was proud and happy. I could only hint at the fact that I'd kept
comparing my friend from Berlin with my analyst; it didn't go
down well.

Before I went away, we had an argument. He asked me to give
him the monthly fee in cash, not by bank transfer. That month it
came to 595 marks (seventeen hours at 35 marks each). I went to
the bank before my session, drew out six hundred-mark notes,
folded them and put them in my wallet. I remembered the money
when I was lying on the couch, sat up, took it out of my wallet,
folded up three of the notes, put the rest back and gave him those
three. That was the sum in my head at that moment. He immediately said it was five marks too much, and was going to give me the
change directly, but I said no, we could settle up when I paid my
next bill. However, he insisted on giving me the five marks at once,
took them out of his wallet, and the session went on without further
incident. On the stairs, I realized with horror that I'd paid him far

too little. I thought about it as I went back, and couldn't help laughing. After all, I had known the correct sum only half an hour earlier, at the bank. I knocked on his door, smiled, gave him the other three hundred-mark notes, and said it must be something to do with the number six. He looked at me blankly, surprised, and took the money.

I thought it all over again at home. Why had he initially acted as if the three hundred marks were enough, indeed too much? There's an obvious difference between three and six folded notes. He could hardly have made just the same slip at just the same time as I. Three notes also showed six corners, but it's not hard to tell six corners from twelve corners. Anyway, he had the sum of 595 marks in his head all right, and had seemed sure that the sum I gave him was five marks too much.

Had he shared the same slip after all, had he really, erroneously thought the three notes were six? I couldn't think so. Then he had probably been feeling his way into my own thoughts, my anxieties and inhibitions. "Sex" was too delicate and dangerous a subject for me, and my slip had occurred only in his presence, during the session. I had drawn the correct amount out of the bank. I had not made the mistake of thinking of the sum as three notes until I was lying on the couch, and then I had put the other three back in my wallet.

The most probable explanation, I now thought, was that he had gone along with my own sexual taboo, on purpose and with sensitivity, so as not to alarm and intimidate me with too quick an interpretation. I liked him for his mature, sensitive attitude.

This was my main topic the next day. However, the session turned out a very difficult one. He just did not understand my idea—at which I'd laughed, anyway, and which I had found amusing, and that in itself proved something. He insisted on his own interpretation: I hadn't wanted to give him more than half, I had wanted to keep something back from him. He would not admit there was anything in my theory throughout the whole session, he asked more questions and stuck to his interpretation: I was withholding something, castrating. I was indignant at his vehemence. Why wouldn't he even take my theory seriously? He was just being dense; an uncomfortable tension arose between us. He had always understood me very well before, and listened to me too. Why was he suddenly so unyielding and vehement? He also interrupted me in mid-sentence, giving his interpretation before I had been able to tell him mine properly, as I saw it from my own ideas and associations. I had been so sure of myself, I had laughed, too, and now I wanted him at least to understand my idea. A harsh tension developed for the first time. I left the session feeling dissatisfied and upset; I had not succeeded in explaining my theory.

In the next session, I did manage to do so: With effort and difficulty. However, he wouldn't see it. "No, really, it's too wild—very far-fetched." The tension came back. I didn't think he ought to discount my theory so firmly. It had given me some fun, and it was my associations we were talking about, after all. He stood firm on his interpretation of my having wished to keep something from him, to cut him down to size. The whole thing turned into a fierce struggle, an argument, a wrangle. I thought he was acting like a schoolmaster, poking his nose into my associations. He might at least have granted my theory the status of a possibility, instead of dismissing it entirely as "too wild."

Over the next few sessions a most unpleasant kind of atmosphere arose, a tension which was to persist, and which I thought of later as the "Westwall" atmosphere (indicating violent conflict, much shooting, both sides heavily armored and digging in, a hundred thousand dead, all adding up to not a millimeter's change in the front line itself).

We could not agree. The tension, however, relaxed slightly when he at least listened to my theory, allowed it into his mind. I still felt analytically and morally indignant at the way he dismissed my thoughts as crazy, foolish, of no value, setting himself so firmly against them. One friend of mine, to whom I told this story, saw the point at once, just as I did; he understood directly. I wanted my idea taken seriously, as a possibility. However, for all my careful explanation, it seemed to have entered his head only once, very briefly, only to be spat out again vigorously. Was I supposed to switch on some kind of inner censorship to eliminate, filter, and slow down at the source any ideas that were too "wild and far-fetched?" What then was normal, not over-hasty, not too obvious to which I must adapt? Why was he so keen to meddle with my ideas anyway? I didn't think much of such value judgments in analysis. Why had he suddenly become so dense? Previously, he had understood me, quickly and sympathetically. What was wrong all of a sudden?

Why had he excluded my possible interpretation like that? So severely, judgmentally. And why didn't he understand my infatuation? Couldn't he see I had really gone to Berlin for his sake, encouraged by him? Even if my interpretation had been very far-fetched indeed, totally idiotic and artificial, he still ought to have started by taking it seriously, he should have listened to it. And he should have thought that my own explanation was of importance to myself, my mind, my mental connections, however abstruse, tortuous and peculiar it might seem to him. It had felt right to me in the circumstances, it had amused me and brought me relief; why would I have wanted to castrate him and withhold half of something from him at this point? He had spent an entire session refusing to understand.

The tension had been horrible. I suddenly felt that he was different, inaccessible. When I was home again, I wondered why. Might he not just be a little bit in love himself, might he have warmed to me in the pleasant, gentle, comfortable atmosphere of the sessions so far, without actually noticing? And might that be why he was so painfully slow to understand now? Was it not merely a touch of erotic defense that made him act in so tense, negative, intractable and rigid a manner? But men of his kind liked me in ordinary life, and if I was so fond of him, well, he might be feeling a little bit the same way. I was taking pains to appeal to him, dressing well, grooming myself, behaving pleasantly.

I put this theory to him at the next session. Was his slowness to understand the result of a mini-infatuation which he had failed to notice? However, it seemed I had gone wrong here; I had been presumptuous. The tension returned. My idea was simply not for discussion. The whole session was a difficult one.

Some of that tension remained, and kept resurfacing later. For the first time, we had failed to agree. It upset me, and arguing was a strain, but after all, the incident wasn't as important as all that, and retreated into the background.

I went to sleep, briefly, in many of the sessions, and would doze off up to four or five times during the hour. At such times I had scraps of dreams. I was not surprised; I had always been able to take quick catnaps. But often we couldn't work over these brief dreams of mine during the session; time was too short and there was too much material in them. He did not seem to be entirely in his element with dreams. However, my dozing off didn't bother him. When I mentioned it to other analysands, they thought it a dreadful way to behave, so I kept quiet about it, and was glad he was so tolerant. He let me do as I liked, and the atmosphere was not a bad one. I became familiar with these quick dreams, and often remembered them after I had slept briefly and then woken. Early on, I had felt embarrassed for the rest of the session, but my going to sleep might indicate relaxation, confidence; not everything need be put down to anxiety and defense. We never actually fathomed the reason for my weariness; for both of us, obviously, it remained a neutral condition.

It was more difficult to accept the way he dealt with another incident. By now, I once more felt like taking my intermediate analytic examination, and discussed the matter with him. He approved, gave me some helpful hints as to the wording of my application, and encouraged me. (On my first analyst's advice, and after I attended the group dynamics workshop, I had applied for two terms' "suspension of training.") So I was now trying both to resume my training and to get permission to take the examination. I had wanted to take it in the city where I was living before, but at the time I had not spent enough hours in analysis, although I had enough under my belt in the way of seminars and therapy sessions.

Some weeks later, during my session, I remembered my application, and wondered out loud what had become of it. He seemed to be embarrassed: Hadn't I heard yet? My examination had been put off to a later date. After all, there was no doubt that I'd applied too soon. I was surprised. There could be no question of its being "too soon." Why was he acting so differently all of a sudden? I asked what he meant by "too soon." We had discussed that very point, most thoroughly, and he had been entirely in agreement with me.

I couldn't understand it all and pressed my questions to him. Finally, and coolly, he informed me that my application to take the examination had in fact been made too early. They had not yet admitted me for training, since they didn't know enough about me; it would be a good idea if I took part more in seminars and went to more lectures. I was being re-admitted to training at the date for which I'd originally applied, in three months' time.

My mind was in a whirl. How on earth could they not know enough about me to admit me now, but enough to know they would in three months' time? If there were any logic or honesty in that, then they wouldn't have been able to re-admit me at all, or at least not with a prophetic eye upon some later date.

Moreover, I actually had been to a great many seminars and lectures, out of sheer interest in meeting new people here. That remark was like an emotional slap in the face. In fact, I had thought I sometimes took rather too much part, spoke up too often in discussions. How could they turn around now and say they didn't know enough about me?

My analyst remained cool, objective and impersonal: Surely I could see that I had applied to take the exam *too soon*. This was the reality that I had to recognize; why was I making such a fuss about accepting it? I became less sure of myself; but I really had discussed the timing with him at this point, because that was what I wanted and I was feeling all right. And in fact, he had told me the wording I should use in my application. So, also in fact, he had shared my opinion. He repeated that I must see it really was too soon. By now I didn't know if I might have been mistaken in thinking he had agreed so positively. So I asked if he didn't remember approving of my plan, with never a word about the date suggested being too soon. He said nothing, and did not react, just as if I hadn't put the question at all. As if I'd been talking to a vacuum. After a painful pause, he said, "You're defending against reality."

But surely he had advised me to apply. Or was I wrong? I was almost quite sure, though. The atmosphere in the room became cold and unnatural; something suddenly seemed all wrong. Previously, we had been in agreement in principle, and he had been pleased to see me blossoming to some extent; now he wasn't approachable any more. The pleasant, soothing atmosphere was shattered. It sounded almost like a stock phrase when he repeated that I must recognize reality, I must see it really had been too soon. Why was I finding that so hard to accept?

Everything in me resisted. I didn't want to answer that second question; what I wanted to know was whether he had agreed with me a few sessions ago or whether he had not. How could he have swung around so completely to the opposite opinion now? And why wouldn't he explain it to me? Why was he persistently ignoring my question? Or had I perhaps been mistaken after all? Had I totally misunderstood him? Everything within me seemed blurred; he remained quiet and cool and did not answer. I also objected to receiving the news here and now, during analysis, as if by chance. Why hadn't I been told before, in writing, and with clear reasons given? He did agree that I had a right to have been officially informed earlier, and he did not think it a good idea for the matter of my training to come up during analysis. However, that still didn't explain his complete change of mind. I asked more and more persistently what was wrong. Didn't he remember the encouragement he gave me, quite clearly and unmistakably? We had discussed the quality of this analysis considered as training analysis, too, I said; so he did see it as a training analysis. Didn't he? He simply did not react, and just repeated that I must see it was too soon, and those were the facts. The session passed without bringing us any closer together.

Alone at home, I felt I was reeling. I could hardly say how I felt. His coldness was hurtful, too. Had the goodwill of our last few sessions existed only in my imagination? What other misjudgments might I have made? I had been so sure he was pleased that I was doing well. That was the very thing that had given me such a good sense of security. Had I been entirely wrong? Whence came his sudden stiffness, the change in him? Didn't he really like me at all? Had his apparent pleasure in my progress been part of his technique, something I ought to have seen through? But I'd been so certain that he liked me, and was pleased with the sense of vitality that made me want to take the examination now. And he'd said he had heard good opinions of me from other quarters. What kind of facts were they I was to accept now; what did "too soon" mean? Had he agreed with me or hadn't he? Had I just imagined his goodwill? Was I so eager for people to like me in this strange town that I had utterly misinterpreted things? Had I become so biased in my infatuation that I saw a distorted version of the truth? Had I, perhaps, been unable to accept his indifference because of my own problems, maybe because of my narcissistic deficiency, so that I had simply and systematically misinterpreted everything in my favor? The idea was a horrifying one; if it were so, then what on earth could I rely on? Was I in such a neurotic mess that I wrought wholesale transformations on my surroundings without even noticing? What was the matter with me? What were the facts I must accept?

This was my main topic at my next session. I wanted clarity, and pressed him for it. He did not seem to be at ease, and gave me a detailed account of the decision. But what mattered the most was the difference in the atmosphere between us, my uncertainty about my own perceptions. Finally he told me he had been at the meeting where the decision about me was made. Hence his change of mood. He had thought he wouldn't need to tell me, but now he thought it was better if I knew.

So I had been mistaken. My private self-questioning had been unnecessary; I had understood him correctly; he had agreed with me at the time. And had let them change his mind at the meeting. I hadn't known about that procedure, but it certainly explained things.

However, he still insisted that I had applied *too soon*. That made no sense to me, particularly not when combined with an assurance that I would be re-admitted later, which just didn't fit in with the argument of their not knowing enough about me. He couldn't see the illogicality of it. We were engaged in a dogged tug-of-war. I complained that he hadn't even tried to follow my train of thought. I was irritated, felt I had been systematically misunderstood, and thought he was being obstructive. I found this was no proper analysis. We interrupted each other. Why was he coming up with so many arguments at this stage? How was it that there was so much tension, so many affective factors in the situation now? My first analyst had never acted like this. I felt as if the session were a wrestling match. Arguments, wrangling, attempts to prove our points as if we were in a law court. Who had said what in what words. The revolting atmosphere returned. I still felt hurt, and we were getting nowhere. I wanted to reconstruct my thoughts about the lack of logic in this.

After several stressful "Westwall" sessions, I felt tired of it all. The whole set-up gave me a feeling that perhaps they really had something fundamental against me, perhaps they weren't going to re-admit me at all. At any rate, this was the strong and disturbing impression I had, a feeling in the air, made up of many little things and not really anything I could prove.

I brought this uncensored impression to the session, and it met with vigorous rejection. What on earth made me think of that? How was it I still wouldn't face the facts? I had simply put in my application too soon. Why did I have to resist that idea so stubbornly? My present feelings were "paranoid."

I was alarmed. He didn't know anything about it yet; I hadn't yet had a chance to explain what made me feel that way, what had caused it. A "paranoid" idea, delusions of persecution, meant severe disturbance, meant one's perceptions were definitely sick, with no kind of basis in reality. Once again, he was talking more than usual, and wouldn't let me finish what I was saying. I just wanted to tell him how I came to have that feeling, arising from the general atmosphere and many little details I had yet to tell him. But I could no longer tell him, so decisive was his explanation and his rejection of my idea as paranoid.

I felt I was under attack. After all, my powers of perception were part of me, something that had grown with me. So perhaps I had been wrong—but surely that didn't mean I could just allow my feelings to be erased, eradicated, destroyed? Even if it was a totally goofy feeling I'd had, surely he ought to take a look at it, understand and reconstruct it? It had probably constituted a considerable part of my problems as a whole. I was fighting for myself, since part of myself had been declared sick, paranoid, crazy. But no, he said, it just wasn't so, no one was planning anything against me, that was all my paranoid perception.

Then he asked if I'd ever had such a feeling in other circumstances; did I jump quickly and easily to the conclusion that people intended to harm me? Did I often feel discriminated against, rejected, even if not quite as intensely? Did this correspond to the nature of my problems?

With this question, he was moving discussion of my perceptions to my life story, and away from any question of whether my feeling corresponded to reality: Had I or hadn't I perceived something which was actually present? Was this a notion of which I must rid myself, as being pathological, an internal factor I must oppose, or had I after all somehow sensed the truth? I didn't want to go along with him at first. The facts were too important to me; if my impression was correct, then I must change my ideas about my career. I could carry on in organic medicine, with the dream of going in for psychoanalysis tucked away at the back of my mind. But I had to clear the matter up. I was not economically dependent on the outcome, but I must be able to make plans.

I came to my next session with this in mind. But his response was, once again, that of someone facing a paranoid, extremely sick reaction that must be countered. We were back with the "Westwall" mood. We fought doggedly on both sides, exchanging a rapid crossfire of arguments. I insisted that he should at least take a look at my reasons, understand them and judge the way in which I had come by my impression. However, before I could really make myself clear he warded me off again, brushing aside any chance of my explaining things as if that too were a factor to be obliterated and opposed. I felt I was under personal attack. Yet I still thought I had a right just to have a feeling, an impression, without necessarily being able to prove the truth of it. We had felt tension of this kind before, over the question of the six hundred marks, and it had passed over. However, on that occasion I hadn't, in the end, insisted on my own interpretation; I'd let it go. Here, on the other hand, we were dealing with something more essentially a part of me. A genuine, strong, intuitive perception within me: My innermost being. If there was something badly wrong, qualitatively speaking, with this reaction, then I must brace myself for more trouble. This was of major importance now. Our hours of discussion were a great strain, and left me feeling edgy. He could not see the lack of logic I had seen; he regarded my feeling as wrong and quite without substance. No compromise. Finally, I accepted his changing the subject to the biographical aspect of my impression. Yes, I could think of plenty of situations in which I had felt excluded, discriminated against, unappreciated: Unjustly, dishonestly treated, the subject of discrimination. And I also thought that given a cross-section of other people's feelings about me, I was selective in perceiving negative attitudes towards me more readily than positive ones; I was aware of that. If someone liked me, I frequently took little notice, but I noted anyone's dislike of me very carefully. I was familiar with that. People had always been able to surprise me by showing me sympathy; I had always noticed aversion. But had my present impression been plucked entirely out of the air, with no basis in fact at all?

The discussion took a new turn: Before a seminar, I had met an analyst who told me, in a very friendly and sympathetic way, that he was sorry. He was so kind and humane that I almost burst into tears. I took refuge in some empty, meaningless remark, more or less going along with what my analyst thought were the facts. I sounded so indifferent that he looked at me in surprise.

Here was a perfect example of the phenomenon which had led them to say they "didn't know enough about me." I had not shown how much I was affected, I hid my feelings behind a cool, indifferent demeanor. So we began concentrating on finding out why they "didn't yet know enough about me," and how far it was my own fault that I was so hard to understand. Why did they know so little about me, even though—or perhaps just because—I had made an active and forthcoming impression? What neurotic mechanism made my character so hard to fathom?

I did not care for this new subject of discussion at first; I hadn't yet managed to work through my rejection, nor the fact that my analyst would not take any of it seriously: My impression, or feeling, or fear that they never would re-admit me. The topic remained one of those that brought on the "Westwall" atmosphere. I felt I had been firmly rejected, swept aside, attacked, and significant parts of me had been found unacceptable.

So there seemed to be something incomprehensible about me. Though I was quite strongly committed to study courses, I obviously knew how to shroud myself in darkness, like an octopus, and make myself invisible. How had I managed to give several analysts, all of whom had seen me, all of whom had heard me speak some time or other, the unanimous impression that they didn't know enough about me? The same analysts had admitted a colleague of mine without ever seeing him at all. There was obviously something about me which in some way or other was confusing. Something that could not easily be grasped. Something that not even experienced analysts could see through directly. Something so unusual that even they, with all their experience, training and abilities couldn't classify it. I had a personality that confused other people and prevented them from understanding me. There could be no doubt that the problem arose from myself, was something I had triggered off in the analysts with my problematic nature, in fact a pure, dyed-in-the-wool counter-transference reaction.

I was particularly upset about one man in whose seminar I had felt very much at ease, and for whose clarity I had felt enthusiasm; I thought his method of interpretation excellent, an intellectual joy. The fact that he of all people said he "didn't know enough about me" was like a stab in the back. In my sessions, we worked out that in spite of what appeared to be my above average frankness and directness, I kept withdrawing behind my smokescreen again, perhaps to compensate for thus exposing myself, in some unconscious manner. However, the result was clear enough. Perhaps this was my way of distancing myself, showing my concealed fears of myself, which had also undermined my relationships with men to date, in that they hadn't led to marriage and children. It wasn't as if I were unattractive. I had always met men who liked me. It was possible that I had such deep, unacknowledged fears that I used this defense mechanism; perhaps that was part of my problems and had driven me to analysis, involuntarily, unconsciously, preconsciously, without my ever realizing it. At any event, the reasons for going into analysis that I had given at the time didn't seem sound ones to analysts. There was still some mystery concerning my motivation; by now I had come to connect it with the penis that was a drowned corpse, my father who had died at Stalingrad, the mediocrity of my sensual experience.

In this respect, the analysts' comment and elaboration made sense again; it showed me the logic inherent in good psychoanalysis. What carried conviction was the fact that I had had no inkling of my technique, and nobody had ever mentioned it to me before. In the long run, I could be glad I'd had so clear a verdict delivered, one which advanced me analytically. If it was so hard to see through me, I must be causing the difficulty as a defense against some particular painful disturbance. Something that bored away at me, going around and around, of which I knew just enough to know that I wanted to conceal it, and that this was why I must avoid all really close contacts.

I began to observe my relations with others more closely, comparing what they said about me with what I thought about myself. Their feelings with mine. The word "feeling" became almost sacred to me. Perhaps I didn't have feelings at all, or I had quite a different quality of feeling. Other people were easier to understand than I was, probably because they *showed* more feelings. I tried to do so too. It was difficult; I would suddenly remember, in mid-conversation, that I ought to be making myself clearer. Sometimes my confessions put other people off. One ward sister told me, with some amusement, that I didn't seem able to keep anything to myself. So now I'd shown too much. I felt helpless, and tried to convey and expose yet more of myself.

I observed, compared, became less confident, more doubtful, and in spite of it all I couldn't really perceive what was so odd about me, I didn't really understand that mysteriously different quality in the way other people behaved and I did not.

However, now I knew that I was the kind of person who appears hard to understand and enigmatic to other people, if she behaves in what seems to her a natural, uncomplicated way.

Most likely the poverty of my identification with my father was to blame for all this. If he had dissolved into nothing, a corpse, a vacuum in Stalingrad, becoming a figure reported missing, a man who could not be grasped, then presumably some of this unreal and nebulous aura had rubbed off on me. I had not known him as a living man: That could well be why I was so fascinated by corpses. There was a song I used to play often later, and liked very much, about praying to the power of Love, which I discovered to be a tune played by trombone choirs at gravesides. Another song by Degenhard, about a man leaving a newborn baby behind him in Paris, in the year '42, haunted me as well; my father had been missing for nine years, and I wouldn't acknowledge my stepfather. I had made him promise to get my father "back from the war" again, fetch him from Stalingrad and the snow somehow or other—bring him home again, anyway.

If this was it—well, how could I help waiting? Men had come home very late; you heard such tales everywhere. One man returned to a neighboring village in 1951, when no one expected to see him anymore. And his little girl—though he wasn't even her father—suddenly had a man there to love her and play with her. She was the illegitimate daughter of a soldier; her mother had persuaded the husband to accept her by asking whether he himself had always been faithful to her. Even people like that, men who weren't children's real fathers, came home. It all seemed unreal, and I was angry and desperate. What made me so hard to understand, emotionally and perhaps physically too? Was it that if I couldn't grasp and understand my father, I didn't want to be understood myself? My first analyst's interpretation, "you had no sensual experience of your father, so you can have none of this friend of yours either," had struck home, and had become generalized. I felt I had been ill

used. The Degenhard song recommended a father do his paternal
duty well or not at all. The only real thing I had from my father,
where he had concerned himself with me, was a letter-card sent on
what he worked out would be—and in fact was—the day of my
birth. All I could do was weep over it. He was sure I would be born
that day, he wrote, and would be nursed and suckled like the others. He could imagine it all very well from his experience with my
two brothers. That had been the only real thing from him about
me, to me. The rest was silence. Mortal, total, irreversible silence,
fully defined only nine years later.

"We don't know enough about her." Could I not say exactly the
same of my father? Was this my way of identifying? Was the difficulty of understanding me related to my sexual identification?

And how could such an unequivocal identification have arisen? I
did look like my father, no doubt about it; I had his nose, his East
Prussian calm. But I knew that only from hearsay, from what people said. Did I myself perhaps not really know who or what I was,
to what sex I belonged? If I hadn't taken my stepfather seriously,
perhaps I hadn't taken my mother seriously as a woman either?
Had my stepfather's brutality been so traumatizing for me that I
didn't want to turn into a woman, like my mother?

"We don't know you well enough" became a cardinal statement
about me. It ate its way into me. All I could be sure of was that my
own confusing ploy of concealment gave rise to that impression. All
else was mere supposition.

When my father failed to come home, I must have taken it to be
my fault, the result of my wickedness, of aggressive desires of some
kind. I probably concluded, from his absence, that I wasn't worth
coming home for, that I was a horrible person, that the sexuality
which had brought me into being was destructive, murderous, and
so on. Perhaps this was what I would not, could not understand,
and what, in turn, made it hard for others to understand me. Perhaps this was what others must by no means understand. Perhaps
it was what had kept me unmarried and childless, although I had
been told that my "pelvis was crying out for children."

Anyway, I now had to work through my feelings for my Berlin
friend. The mixture of pseudo-paternal, post-war, Jewish identification, and transference love was of analytic value. Perhaps it
would help to clear up certain points after all, normalize them,

bring them to the surface. My analyst did not understand my infatuation; I tried to communicate it by roundabout ways. He argued, interrupted me. I complained that my first analyst had never interrupted me; there had never been such tension between us, nor had she just imposed her own value judgments in such a manner. He thought his approach more direct; he saw it as a useful way of getting insight into reality; direct expression of emotions, he said, decreased the analysand's fear. That was his experience from his own analysis, and he had profited by it. This made only partial sense to me; he seemed so aggressive and committed, rather than detached and thoughtful. I had a little jingle haunting me, "I show love by holding my tongue, words destroy where they don't belong," but that didn't get through to him either. I felt cross.

My disagreements with him became important to me again. I wanted to clear them up. Our sessions became a bitter struggle as to who was right, who was going to put his or her ideas across, whose opinion and interpretation was accepted. As far as I was concerned, the tension between us had first arisen over those six hundred marks; then came the rejection of my application to take the examination, the illogical nature of the reasons given, and my feeling that he did not want to admit the facts in either case; in addition, he had ignored my infatuation. The "Westwall" atmosphere had been intense, and hard to endure, in all these situations.

There was part of me that he seemed to dislike, part of me he opposed and utterly rejected. A sensitive and important part of me. It concerned my seriousness, my search for the truth, my outlook on life, my ability to love, the truth itself; somehow or other, it concerned my deepest feelings, perceptions and judgments, my very identity. I often had the impression that my feelings were tender little plants against which he was waging war: Pulling them up, wiping them out, sawing them down, for some reason which wasn't clear to me. And he did not want to see, understand, or observe with goodwill what I actually thought and meant and felt. As if my ideas, my inner being set up an instant hostile reaction in him. I only wanted him to "ponder these things in his heart," like Odysseus in school translations, just to take them in. And then I would allow him to set me right.

That song I liked became important to me again; by now, I had it on disc in German, English and as an accordion tune. It

contained much of the essence of myself. I asked if he'd like to hear
it. My first analyst had been interested in the song, after all, and
we had left open the question of what I actually meant to express by
it. He was against the idea; he wanted me to "verbalize," since, he
said, "analysis means language." However, what it meant to me
couldn't be put into words, or so I felt; it had to do with the tune,
the mood, and my words seemed flat. I had the text of the song,
both written down and in my head. I had previously tried the
words alone on my first analyst. Anything I said now seemed neutral, did not get at the emotions in it, and the whole thing seemed
unsatisfactory. I urged him to listen to the song. He didn't think it a
good idea. Then I remembered how my first analyst had actually
asked me to hum the tune during my session with her, and had
then played the record "several times," listening to it, as she said,
"with attentiveness." I couldn't help crying again when I thought
of her. In the end I managed to persuade him. He said all right, he
would listen to the record at home. The American original (from
which some of the German wording differed slightly) ran:

> Look what they done to my song, Ma.
> Look what they done to my song.
> Well, it's the only thing that I could do half right,
> and it's turnin' out all wrong, Ma.
> Look what they done to my song.
>
> Look what they done to my brain. Ma,
> Look what they done to my brain.
> Well, they picked it like a chicken bone
> And I think I'm half insane, Ma.
> Look what they done to my song.
>
> I wish I could find a good book to live in,
> Wish I could find a good book.
> Well, if I could find a real good book
> I'd never have to come out and look
> At what they done to my song.
>
> But maybe it'll all be alright, Ma.
> Maybe it'll all be o.k.

Well, if the people are buying tears
I'll be rich some day, Ma.
Look what they done to my song.

Ils ont changé ma chanson, Ma,
Ils ont changé ma chanson.
C'est la seule chose que je peux faire
Et ce n'est pas bon, Ma.
Ils ont changé ma chanson.

Look what they done to my song, Ma.
Look what they done to my song.
Well, they tied it up in a plastic bag
And turned it upside down, Ma.
Look what they done to my song.

Look what they done to my song, Ma,
Look what they done to my song.
It's the only thing I could do alright
And they turned it upside down.
Look what they done to my song.

I very much wanted to know what he made of it; I waited, and kept quiet, and finally asked him. That song had become part of me; I had spent hours with it, and felt as if it were somehow connected with my whole life story. After considerable hesitation, he said dismissively and awkwardly that he thought the song was "trash" and the singer "a gold-digger." That hurt. I had wept so much over my song. I couldn't say another thing. If he didn't like it, then he didn't like me either. I was in it, or at least a large part of me was. "C'est la seule chose que je peux faire, et ce n'est pas bon, Ma." The song had been my companion so long. I had always taken it away with me on vacation; I didn't like to be without it. It had a very soothing, warm effect on me when life was not going well. "It will soon be time to understand," ran a line in the German version. I supposed he had got the "gold-digging" idea from "Well, if the people are buying tears, I'll be rich some day."

I could have wept; I longed for my first analyst. She had accepted my song, and I hadn't had to fight for it. She had tried to understand me; she realized there was something I wanted to say through it. All I got from him was a cold slap in the face. I couldn't get over it during that session; I went away disheartened. The song was part of me, and he thought it trash. He rejected it, and called the singer "a gold-digger." What could I say? He simply didn't like it. Had he really listened to it at all, set against it as he was? Had he let himself be receptive to the words and the tune? I thought not. He even seemed annoyed. This was obviously the last straw, as far as he was concerned. "Look what they done to my brain, Ma, look what they done to my brain. Well, they picked it like a chicken bone, and I think I'm half insane, Ma. Look what they done to my song." His rejection and condemnation just hurt. "Well, if I could find a real good book, I'd never have to come out and look, At what they done to my song," ran the words of the song. "Ils ont changé ma chanson." It had not been easy for me to surrender my song to him. I had felt naked. And now to be rejected like this. How could I get through to him, when he wouldn't accept me?

I knew another song performed by Dahlia Lavi which he'd probably have called trash too:

> "Words are all I had to take your heart away . . .
> You think that I don't even mean a single word I say
> It's only words—
> and words are all I had to take your heart away."

I had felt rather embarrassed, myself, about thinking so much of a pop song. All the same . . . by now I had several of Dahlia Lavi's LPs. This song meant the most to me, though I liked some of the others very much too: "If you could read my mind," and "Would you follow me if I searched for another life?" But that first one mattered most to me. I had seen the singer on a concert tour, and still thought this song was her best. What more could I do? My analyst didn't like me the way I was.

However, all the effort I'd made did seem important and necessary; this, after all, was an intensive analysis. The tension grew steadily worse. It made me edgy at work. Babies and small children are so sensitive to atmosphere. I accused my analyst of emotional vaginismus. Why couldn't he accept my ideas, crazy as they might seem, just look at them for once? If I didn't like a man but tried to

force myself to make love to him, I myself suffered from vaginismus. Could he be reacting the same way, emotionally speaking?

At this the atmosphere became icy. I felt compelled to place everything on this plane; obsessive sexualization. And yet, one evening during a lecture, I had caught him at the same game, flinging
sexual associations around. Why was it so wrong for me to put
things on the sexual plane? Why did I appear nasty, idiotic, mistaken and megalomanic when I touched upon such matters? They
used to say that "whatever can't be explained is put down to a vi-
rus," and now the fashionable diagnosis was one of "early disturbance," with a hint of something creepy and mysterious about it.
At my previous hospital they had regarded this modern diagnostic
fad with some irony, but here it was taken in deadly seriousness, as
scientific fact. I couldn't even really laugh at it any more.

Why didn't he understand that I was in love? We mentioned an
article on "Silence in Analysis;" according to it, the patient was
supposed to be fond of the analyst during this period. I felt the tension was just too much for me; his disavowal was a heavy burden.
At first I thought he was overlooking my feelings out of solicitude,
to spare me. But then I became aware that the "Westwall" mood
would arise when we approached anything suggesting the erotic.

I thought less highly of him now. This was not analysis, a previous source of enthusiasm. Why did he keep bringing his personal
opinions, assessments and judgments to bear on the situation in so
pervasive and dominating a way, without so much as noticing mine
or letting them develop? All this dogged argumentation, judgments
and tussles, and the way he contradicted me did not add up to good
analysis.

He thought I took it badly that he had destroyed our original harmony by forming his own opinion. A case of absolute
symbiosis. I had reacted as if to an allergy, he said, when he began
expressing himself as a separate person. Initially, he had shown
deep understanding for me, perhaps too much, and had supported
me strongly. I resented the fact that he was pulling away from me,
dissolving the symbiosis. And this, he thought, was my particular
problem: I could hardly stand having him express any opinion of
me diverging from my own. I said it all sprang from his lack of understanding (those six hundred marks), and the way he'd become
involved to a certain extent in a certain lie and dishonesty (when he

changed his mind completely after going to that meeting). I still felt that he was categorically rejecting significant parts of me. And if I stood up for myself and my feelings, I seemed repulsive.

When the tension between us was very bad, he often arrived as much as five to fifteen minutes late. He insisted, in mildly irritated tones, that this had nothing to do with me; once again, with my paranoid inclination to relate everything to myself, was reading too much into it. However, it was quite clear that his lateness occurred most frequently when we were going through one of those "Westwall" periods.

I drew the confidence to listen to myself and my own impulses from organic medicine. When I was going through a particularly tense, stressful time, a poisoned child had survived because I felt dubious about what the poison information center said; they had advised the wrong treatment, and the boy would have choked to death if I'd followed the official recommendations. That was encouraging, and gave me more heart for the fight. I was not so stupid and worthless after all.

Now and then, we still had pleasanter moments, reminiscent of our good start. At the beginning of one session to which I had come feeling very tense, while my analyst had been late, I just went limp, feeling exhausted and resigned, and lay there in gloomy silence. He liked me to be quiet and gentle, didn't he? Anyway, I lay on the couch for quite a while in that kind of mood.

"What are you thinking?" "I'm wondering how to launch an idea into your mind." My mild demeanor, the fact that I'd waited and taken things slowly instead of plunging straight in, the words I chose all pleased him. He laughed and relaxed, and we got along well again for a time.

I liked that sort of thing; it offered hope that, given patience and persistence and sensitivity, the whole calamity might, after all, be put right. Good analysis was very powerful after all, went right to the psychic limits, it turned one inside out and was exhausting, presumably to both. The "Westwall" mood was basically a good sign; something was going on, we were working through significant conflicts, at least tangentially. There was nothing lukewarm about it.

I developed diplomatic skills: Became evasive, shifted my ground, weakened when I saw the "Westwall" atmosphere com-

ing. If I put my mind to it, I could keep the atmosphere bearable.
Another song took on significance for me:

Ich hatt' einen Kameraden,
einen bessren findst Du nicht,
er ging an meiner Seite,
die Trommel schlug zum Streite
im gleichen Schritt und Tritt.
Eine Kugel kam geflogen,
gilt sie mir oder gilt sie Dir?
Ihn hat es weggerissen,
er liegt zu meinen Füssen,
als wär's ein Stück von mir.
Will Dir die Hand noch reichen,
derweil ich neben lag
bleib Du im ewgen Leben
mein guter Kamerad.

(I had a comrade, you will not find a better; he walked at my
side, in step with me. The drum beat for the fighting. A bullet
came flying—for me or for you? It tore him away; he lies at my feet
as if he,were part of me. I will give you my hand while I lie beside
you; be my good comrade still in eternal life.)

It moved me deeply, affecting my whole body, with a deep, warm
melancholy, but it was a fine, strong song, and fortified me even
though I wept. A grave song, with something important, romantic
and beautiful in the music—in the notes and the voices of the male
choir. I tried to discuss it, but the beautiful and the romantic did
not make their way into the session; they escaped my words. I obviously related the test itself to my father; however, there was something else in the music, something melancholy and lovely. It was
present, too, in "Hans Beimler, Kamerad," a Spanish Civil War
song sung by Busch, though not so strongly: This song didn't make
me cry:

Der Schuss war gut erwogen,
der Lauf war gut gezogen,
ein deutsches Schiessgewehr
starb Hans der Kommisar.

(The shot was well judged, the barrel well adjusted; Hans the Kommisar died, a German firearm.)

My uncle, who had fallen in the war, was called Hans. But language, words, seemed crude and unappealing compared with the beauty of the tune. That sort of thing made life seem worth living; there was real good in it. I didn't urge him to listen to my record this time. After his reaction to the first song, I wasn't risking it. This way, I could keep the romanticism of the song for myself and go on enjoying it. It would remain intact, though still unexplained.

Heine's "Loreley" had the same magic:

> . . . und singt ein Lied dabei,
> das hat eine wundersame, gewaltige Melodei.
> Den Schiffer in seinem Schiffe
> ergreift es mit wildem Weh,
> er sieht nicht der Felsen Riffe,
> er schaut nur hinauf in die Höh.
> Ich glaube, die Wellen verschlingen
> am Ende noch Schiffer und Kahn,
> und das hat mit ihrem Singen
> die Loreley getan.

(. . . and sings a song that has a strange, powerful melody. It strikes the boatman in his boat with wild grief; he does not see the rocky reefs, but only looks aloft. I believe that at the story's end, the waves swallow up the boatman and his boat, and that was the work of the Loreley and her song.)

But our disagreements did trouble me. For a while I thought of putting them to one side and communicating with him on a different wavelength. After all, mutual understanding on all points wasn't necessary. However, my confidence was undermined. I wanted to clarify it; I felt it was corrupt and dishonest to continue a relationship conventionally when it stood on shaky foundations. I resented the fact that he wouldn't admit the possible validity of my ideas: I felt he was fighting me as though I were poison, garbage, hopelessly feeble-minded. I wasn't, in the last resort, insisting that my ideas must be right. But why not let them grow and develop for once, as lunacy if he liked; why not just see them as a theme for discussion, the end product of a brainstorm? His hostility made me furious and aggressive. I wasn't going to try ignoring it any more. And surely these opinionated assessments and violent verbal attacks had no place in a proper analysis. I had not experienced anything like it with my first analyst. As I now remembered her, she was superb, intelligent: Wise, all-seeing, loving. I had never doubted her intelligence or her skills in technique. I was very sad when I thought of her, and all I had lost in her. I had never had such delightful sessions with him as some of those last ones with her. They had been paradise. I thought of her a great deal. Some things had certainly got under way sooner with him; well, he was a man. And he had been able to handle the episode after the group dynamics workshop with more detachment, more logically and fruitfully, than she could, when the situation was acute. Yes, he had understood all that better than she did, but then his own situation was different; he was farther removed from it, felt less responsibility for me than she had felt at the time. He had studied with her; was his work as good and his technique as expert as hers? He was not so very much older than I; ten years, but that didn't make any real difference any more. I knew men of his age, had had lovers his age, I could get along with such men. Was he really as proficient, mature and perfect as she was? She had been so sweet to me in the end, had taken a great deal of trouble, had actually phoned him to get me the place here. Perhaps he wouldn't have accepted me at all if she hadn't put in a good word for me.

I had certainly never had such pitched battles with her over meanings, associations, and observations. I kept telling him so. He interpreted this as the start of my work of mourning for the woman I had lost. That was why I couldn't recognize his authority any more; why I was looking for differences between them. And he could understand my sense of sadness and longing very well, he said.

I was indeed sad and full of longing. I wept easily, as if at the touch of a button. I felt lost, like a leaf in the wind. When she first moved away I had just dropped everything and entrusted myself head over heels to my new analyst. Now it was time for the extensive work of mourning. Only then would I really be able to accept him unreservedly. His arguments were convincing. I really did mourn her loss.

My doubts of him and my arguments with him, then, were all part of the analytic process. If I was still mourning a previous love, then naturally I had to find fault with him. My real criticisms thus lost substance.

A man I knew who was in analysis asked, apropros of my complaints, whether it was necessary for me to argue points so closely with my analyst. Didn't I want to keep some things to myself? I held him by the throat, on an intellectual level. If psychoanalysis was not the place for radical honesty and frankness, without diplomatic lies or conventional corruption—well, where was the place for it, then? After all, frankness and truthfulness were the essence of analysis. Free association was part of it too. I said something cutting about mendacious weakness of mind in reply.

Another acquaintance, also in analysis, once remarked in passing on the anger he himself sometimes felt with "the bullfrog," as he called his analyst. I wondered, with interest, how his analyst had reacted. Surprised, he told me he wouldn't and couldn't tell me a thing like that.

That struck home; both my acquaintances knew analytic theory. But obviously, there was a certain etiquette: Rules which they observed and I did not. Was it that I couldn't endure to be partially at odds with my analyst, in a kind of circumscribed discord? Could others do that sort of thing and still feel all right about it? Did they reconcile themselves to it, or was it that they just didn't mind if their analyst's view of important matters differed from their own? Did it depend on accepting the integration of good and bad in one object: A form of love that made all else unimportant.

Were other analysands adjusted and casual, or was I dogmatic, inclined to symbiotic feelings, intolerant and oversensitive? Why couldn't I accept the fact that in this particular case he just thought differently from me? Why couldn't I forget that and let the whole thing go? Interpretations rang in my ears: Why does this affect you so much? Why is it so important to you? Do you feel a need to spoil things for yourself at this point? Was it neurosis that made me stick so doggedly to my version of events?

I thought, consciously, that I was seeking the truth, and did not want to submit and accept someone else's view of it without being genuinely convinced. I had been right about that child with poisoning.

When the "Westwall" mood was upon us, or even at slight hints that it threatened to descend, he really did tend to arrive late for the session: Sometimes only a moment or so, generally ten to fifteen minutes late. In itself, this was nothing serious, since he could make up most of the lost time afterwards; his sessions began on the hour or ten minutes after it.

My first analyst had been very conscientious about time, and I myself had found her interpretations of matters concerning punctuality convincing. If I had something on my conscience, if I had anxieties or misgivings or was in a bad mood or anything of that kind, I used to arrive late, or sometimes early. After she had interpreted this behavior of mine a few times, it stopped, and subsequently I turned up on the dot, with almost hypnotic regularity. If I had happened to set off rather early, my journey usually turned out to take longer than usual. I might dawdle at intersections, or take my time over parking. In any case, I was often surprised to find how punctually, to the very minute, I arrived at her door. I was convinced I had an inner secret timetable. At least, I no longer thought it was chance when I arrived late. One could tell in advance, after all, that there would be a lot of traffic at mid-day, and there was no need for me to pick that time to drive through the town center; there were ways around it. Traffic lights had their own rhythm, too, and didn't all switch to red at the same moment, keeping time. If I did happen to arrive late, I had not allowed myself enough time from the start, and one extra red light had unbalanced the system. But I realized that I had secretly been planning it that way all along.

It upset me, now, not to have such analytically acquired insights admitted as valid by my present analyst. After all, he made the same journey daily. And the public works office didn't come up with time-consuming detours and closed roads every day, nor were these things selected specially for times of tension in my analysis. Come to think of it, family breakfasts could be foreseen, planned for and anticipated. It was unlikely that his children and his wife had purposely chosen just that moment to delay him. So many coincidences seemed improbable. And whether I came punctually on the dot, or unpunctually ten minutes late, made no difference in the last resort.

He did not care for this interpretation of mine. It really had been the traffic that made him late, he said, and the detours, the poorly organized layout of a small town now bursting at its seams, and his car, etc. Anything so long as it was not the relationship between him and me.

His way of looking at it confused me at first. By now, after all, I had experience of my own patients, and I knew what could lie behind someone's lateness. Only in exceptional cases did I believe in chance, or the workings of some outside power. I had adopted this way of thinking as my own, and now his objective, neutral arguments shamed me. In my egocentric efforts to relate everything to myself, arising from my megalomaniac fantasies, he said, I thought I knew everything. I had dreamed up these convoluted notions, relating an ordinary and unconnected event to myself personally, as if compelled to do so by some delusion of reference. Objectively, this was wrong, and it was no way for an analysand to act. His emotional rejection made it clear to me that this was not the way for me to think. Here I had no business to be wondering about slips; it was unsuitable behavior for me as an analysand, here we were discussing my problems, myself and my own difficulties. Perhaps we were dealing with the projection of my own wishes and ideas. Had *I* really wanted to come to this session? Hadn't the reluctance been in *myself?* If I was so quick in jumping to the conclusion that *he* had had difficulty in summoning up the will to come—didn't that indicate the state of my own feelings? And he had a point there.

(In relationships between two people, however, it often happens that you don't find just one of them feeling in a certain way; a simultaneous experience, differing only in intensity, occurs in both more often than is officially admitted, and this applies to psychoanalysts and analysands too. At all events, in my own medical work I could often get a very fair idea of another person's—the patient's—feelings and condition by taking notice of my own.)

However, he was not showing his feelings, and he was right about projection; I had not particularly wanted to come. Although I thought I had felt it, it was not *his* lack of enthusiasm I had perceived, but my own, which I had localized on him.

Projection is supposed to be an ubiquitous emotional mechanism, one we all employ in our mental processes. It was very strong in me. I could have sworn that he had not felt much like coming to the session. That was only to be expected, considering the way the last one had gone. I felt the same, and yet I was equally sure about him. However, back came my perceptions like a boomerang. If I had had only a vague suspicion, a playful notion, I could have laughed at his interpretation of projection and metaphorically filed it away. As it was, however, parts of my essential self were affected, feelings which had grown within me and which I valued.

However, before I could really come to terms with his objective argument and my own projection, another thought occurred to me: Why did I turn up so punctually anyway? Why was I so strict with myself? A minute here or there didn't really matter so much. Everything did not absolutely have to be done on the dot. That was probably the way my analyst felt. He just wasn't particularly orderly, punctual and compulsive. The idea had a relaxing effect on me, all the same, for I really had driven myself hard at times in my anxiety to be punctual. And when I hadn't made it, my failure had lain very heavily on my conscience. My superego was over-strict with me on this point. That was the truth—in isolation and aside from anything else— for other people really did take such things more casually. It would be better if I didn't take the whole thing so seriously, as a matter of such importance.

However, his questions had distracted me from my problem and the question I was asking myself.

I still had a feeling there was something the matter with this analysis. I had not been accustomed to such tension with my first analyst. So he and I agreed that I would discuss the point with her; she might have a better overall view, since she knew both of us, and it was to be supposed that the trouble lay in something personal between us: The "Westwall" atmosphere must have something to do with his being a man and my being a woman. I had found my way to a father transference very quickly with him, for instance, and I had soon fallen in love; the course of events wasn't the same as with her. He had also said that he had "never before had such difficulties in an analysis."

So I wrote a long, full letter to my first analyst, asking for an appointment. I expected much of her. I had a prompt reply: A short, unforthcoming letter, to the general effect that she really thought it would be best for me to talk the matter over with my present analyst, and she couldn't discuss anything with me except events in my analysis with her.

This was like a cold shower. It was just *because* I couldn't get anywhere with him, and my attempts to do so had failed, that I had turned to her. I had discussed that move with him, too. Couldn't she take it for granted that I would not irresponsibly introduce third persons into my analysis without agreement, and without good reason?

Her answer was the sort of thing to which any analyst in the world might react in his sleep.

And it left me on my own again.

My sense of irony was being worn down by the presence of that recurrent tension. My gallows humor was abandoning me. The tension was damaging to me, more so every time, opening old wounds, making old doubts proliferate; there was so much I didn't understand.

How was I to deal with my present analyst's partial rejection? I tried to avoid those themes and areas of conflict likely to lead to tension. I thought it must be possible to work through certain but not all areas of myself with one analyst, and take the remaining points up later with someone else. It must be feasible for me to integrate the frustrating characteristics of this analyst with my picture of him as a whole, and without rejecting him entirely. It seemed to be a classic case of mother transference: I was in the process of spitting him out, that is, my childhood image of my mother, of attacking, expelling him. Obviously the reason why I was reacting so violently and unforgivingly was that I hadn't taken the step of integrating good and bad in one object. That much could be deduced with fair probability from my life story. Other people had been able to fight their mothers, hadn't been entirely dependent upon them, had had a father there to make a third. In my situation, I had entirely suppressed my aggressive impulses; they would in effect have been suicidal. I was now making up for my lack of fighting and self defense. Very likely I was now insisting so firmly upon the validity of my opinions, my aggressions and my perceptions because I hadn't been able to let myself do so earlier, and/or because I had refused to entertain the idea that even a mother might have her weak and sore spots, might have a frustrating and disappointing side to her.

There were times when this made sense to me, but I couldn't really reconstruct it, feel it, believe it. However, perhaps the barrier I put up was just the result of my defense; the vehemence with which I balked, struggled was the proof.

We were still at odds, however. This analysis was losing emotional substance for me. How could I let myself in for potentially devastating and dangerous processes which put everything in question, if I didn't really have obsolete and total confidence in my analyst? If I didn't feel truly understood by him and safe? After all, really fundamental emotional upheavals were to be expected, as was a process of emotional restructuring during which one was very vulnerable.

At all events, I clearly perceived the nature of the tension that periodically arose between us, and he felt it too. My infatuation was over, and he had failed to understand it. Something important had been missed: Those feelings, indeed, that mattered most of all to me.

Our struggles were tiring, and made me irritable. I felt tense and overworked at the hospital; other people felt the same, but I carried an additional burden. I couldn't live at odds with him like this for any length of time; it was terrible. Should I forget it all, put it on ice, take no more notice? Let it be? Was that the mature, adult thing to do? Must I overlook his weaknesses, yet still like him and feel I was in good hands?

He did not impress me any more; he had shown himself so uncertain yet so dogmatic and stern. Did I have to think of him as a good father figure, a good analyst?

Why couldn't he manage to convince me, if not because of his weaknesses? Surely I was not expected to submit quickly without really seeing his point. And what, for heaven's sake, was it that I didn't understand? And why his stubborn balking at many of my attempts to develop my ideas? In the last resort, wasn't it his job to understand me? Wasn't it *his* problem if he failed? After all, I was not too stupid to understand; hitherto I had been considered rather bright. So it must be possible to convince me and not merely coerce me. I functioned well enough in ordinary life.

I sometimes felt ruffled during case seminars; it was so easy to be dogmatic and intervene with a remark of some kind (father, mother, child, penis, transference); at least, no one could dispute it. This couldn't be the right kind of analysis. It soothed me to find that others shared my sarcasm, and to think this was probably a phase analysands go through initially. Interpretations often were made automatically, by rote, as by grammatical rules of Latin declensions learned by heart: Femina, feminae, feminae, feminae, feminam, femina, and the dative endings are all the same and certain adjectives always govern the genitive, etc., etc.—now isn't that incredible? The mere tone of voice can express an understanding of such symbolism, of the fact that a thing meant this, that or the other—not always logically and conclusively, of course, but frequently all the same. As with learning Latin grammar, you need only turn to the classic meaning and you are right.

When I had some friends in to dinner, another woman and I both felt attracted to the same man; perhaps all she really wanted was a little game with the man, a "sadist endowed with charm," as my analyst had described him. I had learned that mature Oedipal feelings can be expressed in rivalry and competition, and tried myself in this. She was shocked by my insensitivity and coldness, my lack of hospitable consideration for her; I ought to have noticed her increasing isolation and misery. I thought that an old-fashioned view; and the men present agreed, later, that I was right. The competition and rivalry were mature responses correct in this situation. However, I had one woman friend the less.

At a congress, a woman I knew described an analysis she had conducted. I felt rather irritated even as I marvelled, but then I felt admiration and resignation. I would never be like her; I couldn't have thought of any interpretation so quickly, or taken so dispassionate a general view. The subsequent discussion was equally intellectual and sharp. I could scarcely keep up with it, and felt wretched. Finally, an older analyst sitting near me stood up, shook his head disapprovingly, remarked to the man next to him that this kind of interpretation was just like ping-pong, and left. The little scene cheered me.

As I couldn't get much across to my analyst, I let off steam to colleagues who were also in analysis. One man said I was resisting something beneficial, perhaps a great love. That was a good theory, but by now my infatuation with my analyst was behind me; I knew it for what it was and didn't think it could be repeated. Moreover, he seemed to regard me as a nuisance at the moment; he often arrived late for the sessions, and appeared to find me a positive trial. At the very least, I was getting on his nerves. I often thought I was being pleasant, accommodating and sensitive to his feelings—I couldn't make out why he didn't like me when I was in that mood. It met with a response in ordinary life. What made me so repellent, or else the occasion of ironic mimth?

For a while, I tried telling him funny and interesting anecdotes from my daily life—on this plane, we could both laugh, and then we were in accord with each other again, united in laughter. All the same, I felt drained after sessions like these. Something was being done at my expense. I did not like that casual, noncommittal merriment. It felt like joining in a stag joke against myself.

I was at the end of my tether. I really could not stand such discord for long. Amusement seemed to be the only plane upon which we could meet. Gradually, I came to realize that I must either fight back or surrender entirely. He did not seem to understand *how much* all this upset me.

Why wouldn't he at least see how much I had liked him? It was a matter of importance; surely I couldn't be that nasty and obstreperous?

Should I submit? If I had bowed to authority in the case of that child with poisoning, the boy would have died. My instincts and doubts had been right on that occasion. I had not been a particularly obstinate character before, indeed, I thought of myself as rather too well-behaved and conventional, too much the well-bred young lady: More orderly and well-behaved, anyway, than one might have expected of me with a mother like mine, who was more of a fighter and less conventional than I. I had thought, by way of excusing myself, that perhaps her circumstances had been less complicated.

The sessions left me feeling edgy, seeing myself as unpleasant, someone to be avoided; I was in bad shape.

Then it occurred to me that if need be, I might change my analyst. This struck me as a major, decisive step to take, but an idea that might be discussed. It even was recommended to have two analysts for instance, a man and then a woman! I thought of one analysand who had not been able to get it together the first time, and had changed his analyst. I cited him as an example that a change might make sense, that these could be appreciable reasons for it. My analyst said, dismissively, "Oh, well, *him* . . ." I kept quiet and then asked him to explain. "Your situation and his are not at all the same," I was told. This man and I, it seemed, were "quite different in the capacity for social achievement." At the time, apparently, his analyst, a woman, had just "not been up to him, in human terms." Wham!

I had ventured to compare my case with his, which seemed to be hubris. Obviously I had quite the wrong picture of myself. At any rate, I could gather from the atmosphere that I was not and never would be as socially significant a person; I was so different, so very inferior, that there could be no comparison.

That struck home. I was functioning all right at the hospital, dealing with emergency cases. I did not make any major blunders. What was so inferior about me, seen from the outside? Why was the man I had mentioned so decidedly, unquestionably superior? I had not thought of myself as quite such a social liability; hadn't I even a chance of developing the capacity for social achievement?

I had far overreached myself. A change had been a good idea for the man I'd mentioned, logical and sensible. However, such things took place on a higher plane to which I could not aspire. I was not that sort of person. All my analyst had to do was bring me back to reality. "Oh, well, *him* . . ."

I compared my analyst with men who were personally important to me; he suffered from the comparison. I thought almost all of them more sensitive, quicker of mind, more intelligent than he was. I hid my fury; I saw him as dense, intellectually a sack of flour I had to drag along behind me, a headmasterly figure who wouldn't allow me to live my life, who was always formally correcting me in his narrow-minded manner. This was not the kind of father I would have wished for; he always seemed to be under such strain, worn out, overtaxed in the paternal role. My own father had wanted a dozen children. I had not even been able to make my analyst understand my infatuation, something which had been perfectly clear to other observers, without any expert training.

Surely he might have been able to understand it, at the very latest, after I was so upset by seeing him in the company of other women at that concert!

There came a session when I didn't find confession so difficult any more. Hadn't he noticed, I asked, that I'd found him attractive, had dreamed of *him*, thought of nothing but him? It was over now, and something of importance had not been worked through.

His reaction was both instant and reproachful: It was up to *me* to make myself understood by other people, and my difficulty in doing so was one of my problems. Why hadn't I shown my feelings more clearly—and above all, sooner?

Yet I really had exerted myself to the utmost, and it hadn't been easy. I *had* shown my feelings, though, had indicated them that time I mentioned the delicacy of the situation. "It's *your* job to make yourself understood," he said. "You must be able to get somewhere with your analyst, you must be able to make him useful to you."

So it was my fault: I'd left him in the dark, withholding essential information so that he hadn't been able to understand me.

He reacted vehemently, talked a great deal, and interrupted.

I was not inclined to accept his reproaches; other people had seen through me at the same time and interpreted my joy correctly. And mine had been a beautiful, tender feeling; I just had not been able to verbalize it flatly. I was sick of the word "verbalize." I went along with the saying that words, when out of place, are destructive. So *I* was supposed to have made my feelings clear to my analyst! In a natural, open, honest way: "Listen, I think you're very attractive, I'd love to sleep with you, I keep wondering what it would be like, how you look and so on, when I'm with other men I'm always thinking of you." Rather abstruse, I felt.

His interpretation was disappointing, and not, I thought, one of much analytical integrity. If he had overlooked something, and that happens, that was his problem as an analyst, not my fault, or at least not exclusively my fault. That was why I was in analysis!

I began to feel angry. Angry to think of all those sessions spent explaining myself, all the energy I had expended (unnecessarily, now that I saw it in retrospect) trying to understand his sudden complete change of mind over my application to take the exam. Of the way I had doubted everything—my capacity for perception, my memory, my own reality—until he finally broke his silence. Whole sessions had been unnecessarily wasted by my confusion; and by his slowness to understand and his obduracy over the matter of the six hundred marks and my exam application. It was his duty as an analyst to be frank, to exercise goodwill and show as much understanding as he possibly could. That applied to erotic matters too. Our times of "Westwall" tension still hadn't been explained. If an essential part of his professional competence were being withheld from me, I thought our agreement had been broken. Many sessions, it struck me, had been unnecessary or of little professional value.

I decided to withhold four weeks' fees. Strictly speaking I ought to be the one getting paid, considering the trouble I'd had with him. I wasn't going to work on his behalf, providing tuition in understanding, and battling against his own resistance too; I didn't want to have to drag him along after me, put the brakes on and restrain the tempo of my thought.

I explained that I was not going to pay for the four weeks in question at all; so I would always be four weeks in arrears from now on.

I considered I was handling over large parts of myself to him: Formulations, impressions, suspicions, careful thought, feelings. Once I had talked about them during my sessions, they were dead. I could not have revived them to the same degree; many were spoiled, their content changed, and had acquired a different emphasis; one way or another they were diminished. And these were important parts of me! As it was, my relationships outside analysis were suffering from the way I now chewed everything over; all the original vitality was lost. By now I felt guilty if I wanted to discuss anything really significant with someone other than my analyst. My conversation became superficial. A lover told me, seriously, that our relationship really had no chance: What would I say, how would I feel when with him, if I were certain that he reported all our intimacy to a third person, daily and as a matter of course? I laughed, diagnosed this as the sexual partner's typical jealousy of the analyst, and did not take him seriously. However, part of my being, my genuineness, my fertile humanity, my warmth did go into the analytic relationship. And all this was worth something. I was making a great effort, straining every fiber. If the analyst did not stick to our fundamental agreement, was no longer a good teacher, kindly, understanding and benevolent, then I was not willing to pay.

I thought I was being brave.

However, I was going beyond what he could tolerate. He did not conceal his annoyance. I was employing blackmail, he said.

I stuck to my argument. The tension between us, I said, meant we couldn't communicate any more. Then I hesitated, and asked if he was counting on that money, financially. In that case it would be different; it was the principle of the thing that concerned me. However, it concerned him too, and he insisted on payment.

At first I felt slightly relieved that he had not reacted more strongly to the boldness of my reasoning, but was concentrating his attention on the sum of money, on the month I planned to stay in arrears. I felt I was in the right, and stood firm.

If he saw my withholding of payment as impudent, going beyond what was personally and analytically acceptable, he had better say so. Or convince me by argument, if my reasoning was pointless, or an obstacle to analysis. However, I refused to react to mere severity.

After all, I had needed courage for this confrontation. It would have been easier to yield, accept, hold back my feelings.

All this was very important to me; I was not playing around out of foolishness.

With so much tension between us, his late arrival for the sessions became a common occurrence again. No, he said, it definitely had nothing to do with me. He gave no explanation for saying so—such as that he saw no point in inquiring into it—he just made the assertion. I felt as if he were forbidding me to think of the connection between finer shades of meaning. I could fantasize about slips I made myself; in him, either they were not slips or they were of no significance.

We were still at daggers drawn in the sessions. They were a strain, and a torment.

For years, the wish of analysands to have some kind of check made on their training analysis had been a bone of contention. The idea had always seemed to me valid. After all, this kind of analysis was particularly important and would have widespread repercussions later. Supervision was the rule in the therapeutic analysis, but illogically enough, the exception in training analysis.

My own analysis now seemed pointless, and I thought we urgently needed supervision by a third party. Either this third party would succeed in clearing up our problems, in particular the dreadful "Westwall" mood, or we must terminate the analysis itself: The alternatives seemed to me perfectly clear.

I had in mind a third person who would regard me and my

analyst on an equal footing: Both of us could explain those points
on which we were in conflict, and try to resolve the problems with
the supervisor's help.

He saw this idea as immensely presumptuous. If he felt a need
for supervision he would get it, independently of me and my urging, and certainly not with me present. I had no right to bring pressure to bear, he said. He categorically refused to seek supervision
together with me, in a set-up involving three people.

I was surprised; I had not expected contradiction on this particular point, which was more formal than anything. In itself, there
surely could be no objection to a situation in which we had equal
rights, with me as one partner with a say of her own. Were we really in this together, as he used to tell me, correcting me, when I
made the mistake of saying his analysis was something done *to* me,
or were we not? However, my suggestion of a trio seemed to be beyond the bounds of possibility. Surely we might have talked more
about it, about the mere possibility of supervision? But I felt he
considered me impatient, I had gone too far, it was just too much.

It had required courage for me to mention the idea of supervision at all. If I was to be true to my feelings, my convictions, expecting a correct analysis, my reaction was appropriate. To go on
as we were would be pointless, and would have taxed me beyond
my strength in the long run.

In the course of our discussion, however, the idea of a trio became comparatively unimportant to me; what mattered was to resolve the tension and get the analysis going well.

And the idea of supervision didn't seem to trouble him particularly in itself—what did was the fact that I was presenting him with
an ultimatum in demanding that we either adopt that idea or end
the whole thing. Yet further analysis would have seemed to me a
daily lie if we couldn't clear up our problems.

But whether he thought supervision would be helpful, and
whether he told me about it if the event arose, would be *his* decision
and his alone, he indicated. And *he* would determine the time of it.

My presumption obviously lay in externals: In the fact that I had
demanded the introduction of a third party, and soon, as an ultimatum. *That* was the impertinence he couldn't stomach. The chill of
the atmosphere told on me.

He did not react to my saying that I really did feel I was under *great* pressure, I really was suffering *very* much from the strained atmosphere, and such a struggle was almost more than I could take. We returned to the mood of irony and humor, which did at least make the sessions more endurable than when the full "Westwall" mood was upon us: That felt plain horrible and destructive.

I thought my alternatives—either supervision, or termination of the analysis an honest approach. Either I took a method seriously or I didn't.

But it all had something of the character of a game too; we were having a vigorous debate, in the context of transference reactions and all the intra-analytic factors and complications. If I were really to end the analysis then it wouldn't be for another six months (so as to work through the detachment).

My analysis was, after all, a training analysis, done on a grant, bound up with examination marks and a research project at a university hospital. All perfectly respectable. And I had felt enthusiastic about psychoanalysis.

I had not been thinking entirely seriously of ending my analysis now, though I had certainly entertained the notion, and I had often felt quite clearly that such a move would be better for me. At heart, however, I couldn't think that our difficulties might not be cleared up by our own efforts. Surely it couldn't be so; we neither of us felt any malice; he was a training analyst, after all. The matter of social status impressed me too. I had my pride, too. Almost everyone I knew urged me to carry on, whatever I did, and said this was just a problem I was facing. My doubts and questionings rebounded on me like boomerangs. True, almost everyone I knew was in analysis, or had been analyzed. I could find no understanding of my doubts anywhere among them, though I could with other people, who wondered, with some lack of affective feeling, why I let myself in for this kind of thing. And my first analyst had referred me back to the second. So obviously I really had to clear the thing up, just between him and me.

I often felt I was at the end of my tether. It was a blow when, during one of our arguments, he remarked wearily, and with obvious irritation, "Then you just will have to end the analysis."

The worst thing about this remark was his tone of voice. I couldn't help seeing that he had had it with me, was utterly, totally fed up with me, and just now he could wish for nothing better than to be free of me at last: I disgusted him, he hadn't the slightest objection to ending the analysis, far from it. As if he were saying, contemptuously: Go on, then, go ahead and finally do it!

This was a decisive moment.

I had never known his attitude to be so definitely and fundamentally negative before. I went away, dealt with a few jobs, and then wept my heart out at home.

This time it had nothing to do with sensitivity, transference, exaggerated perception or anything else of that sort. I had felt that as far as he was concerned, he would like me to end the analysis at once, here and now. He really did not like me any more; I irritated him intensely, like a troublesome burr, like something to be vomited up. I couldn't count on his steadfastness any more; he would make use of the first legitimate reason he could to rid himself of my analysis. I was sure of that. He had been so irritated, disdainful in his rejection. He really did not want any more to do with me. After four months. He couldn't stand me any more. Our relationship really was at an end now.

I couldn't discount any of this as transference or a neurotic error of interpretation, either. His negative attitude was the real, sober truth, and nothing could shake that fact.

A few sessions later, he confirmed my perception for me. If I would keep talking about ending the analysis, he said, then I ought to envisage doing so as a real possibility. When I brought it up he actually had been in a state of considerable vexation and apathy. He had wanted to confront me with the reality of what ending the analysis would mean; I must, he said, get it clear in my mind.

I had spoiled the relationship. With my directness? My pervasiveness? My claims and demands? Or with my infatuation? My seriousness? All this was, in itself, part of a regular analysis. You found conflicts and transference love everywhere. And so you should; otherwise the analysis was not a good one. In my case, these things had sometimes occurred sooner and perhaps more intensely than usual, but after all, I had had earlier experience of analysis. And I was someone quick to react, quick to feel, quick to fall in love.

But what else was there about me that made me so trying and repulsive? I had tried to do my best, intellectually, during analysis, and by endeavoring to make him like me. I'd taken pains with my appearance, made myself up, dressed well, been very careful what I said. So it was rather brave of me to stand by my own opinions. It would have been simpler not to insist on my subjective view of the truth. However, I couldn't lie, not in a proper analysis. At school, they used to say I had a marked sense of justice, and it had not seemed anything out of the ordinary then. Nor had my way of thinking ever given offence before: On the contrary, here and now, when I had responsibility to bear at the university hospital, I had learned yet again the value of trusting my own feelings, misgivings and fears. If I didn't, a patient might be lost in one of those situations where the risks and responsibilities weren't subject to control.

So why was I now in danger of departing from all my internal points of reference? Was my analysis really to end? Just because I had delivered an ultimatum? Hadn't he understood how *very* seriously I took the whole matter of this analysis? Would someone who wasn't so serious about it, someone who merely wanted to get her analytic training behind her, have taken such risks?

Why was I now to be so firmly rejected? I had applied myself, energetically.

Would I have done better to follow the advice other people gave me, to be more quiet, and leave certain areas untouched? But was I supposed to lie in analysis? Had I kept silent about anything essential? I didn't think I had.

More likely I had been too frank. Was that what he disliked, me as a whole? Had other people in analysis reacted as I did? From what little they would say, they did seem to be more tranquil and less aggressive about it. Had I gone about something in a fundamentally wrong way? But then again, I didn't think this was the correct way to look at it. As an analysand, I had the right to basic goodwill, to good-natured assessment, to kindness and patience. My fatherly friend had written me, "I wonder what roundabout ways she will yet go." He understood my escapades.

What was so fundamentally unlikable about me? What was it, deep down inside me? Something that no one could ever possibly love? Something of which I knew nothing at all myself?

The way I fought back could not have repelled my analyst so much. That, after all, had been something honest, basic, and true to me. It couldn't be that which had so irritated him. It must be something in me.

I could no longer count on his reliability, emotional steadfastness and basic goodwill. "You had a difficult childhood; what you need is long and *reliable* analysis"—I could still hear those words, spoken at an interview, ringing in my ears. I believed them, too, after my experiences of the war, of air raids, of missing men.

Did my analyst realize what his coldness and edgy rejection must mean to me? He insisted that he had had an obligation to "convey reality," and I must not just threaten to end the analysis, I must be ready to do so in earnest.

"You think that I don't even mean a single word I say," ran the words in one of those songs I liked. Why was he repeating what I said to me? Because I didn't really know what I was saying, what I meant? Or I didn't mean what I said?

So what was it about me that could alter the situation and the mood so quickly? A few weeks ago, before the emergence of the "Westwall" atmosphere, we had been getting on well. I was in love, was working through the episode after the workshop, I was blossoming. He had been pleased with the way things were going; he had shown he was glad.

Was there something about me which was repellent, seeking conflict, revolting, secretly malevolent, extremely unlovable???

A steadfast analytic relationship seemed to be of the greatest importance to me. If there was one trauma, one neurotic failure to work things through which really weighed on me, it surely had to do with my father. The probable interpretations were: (1) Sexuality is deadly; conception is destructive. He had died after my conception. The day is done, it's time for Johnny Walker.[1] Each quickly lays an egg before it dies.[2] (2) I am deadly, annihilating, destructive: According to my mother's account of it, life had been delightful before my birth, and after it everything was over: My father gone, wartime, my uncle shot and bleeding to death, economic difficulties. Paradise was lost at my birth. (3) The evil within me had driven my father away, put him to flight: He didn't want to come back for someone like me. It wasn't worth staying or coming back for such a malevolent, competitive creature, jealous of brothers and

[1]Commercial in Germany.

[2]Translated from Maxund Moritz-Wilhelm Busch.

fathers, burdened with death wishes. It was my fault he didn't come back. There had been plenty of real and suspected cases where fathers preferred to stay with other women and other children in other lands. I had had plenty of time for such ideas, suspicions and anxieties during my first nine years, until news came through.

If I was not married now, or at least living in a stable relationship, it was repetition. I remained alone, waiting for Mr. Right, as I did when I was a little girl. I annoyed men to make sure they wouldn't stay with me.

In my present situation with my analyst I was reinforcing, repeating and confirming the traumatizing situation: Picking at old wounds. I was the kind of woman no man could like in the long run, who put everyone to flight, who needled men, upset them, and made them so angry that all they could do was withdraw.

The fact that he had been so annoyed with me was my fault: A counter-transference reaction. I had forced him to reject me; it wasn't *his* taste, *his* evaluation of my person, but my own evaluation, which he must then express and act out for me or for those close to me earlier in my life, because I had forced the role upon him. Maybe he ought to have seen through the counter-transference mechanism quickly, so that he could put the brakes on his negative feelings and modify them, but I was a difficult, complicated, sly person, leading him up the garden path, robbing him, as analyst, of power and potency. He was the recognized analyst; I was the hard case.

His dislike and rejection were wearing; I felt I was at the end of my tether. However, I could still find relief in my work. When this prop too proved shaky, and I saw that envy, rivalry and economic anxieties existed among my colleagues, I had reached my limits. I was to speak about the boy with aniline poisoning at a class one morning. It was a fairly horrible experience, although I had prepared well for it. "They really tore you to bits," said an acquaintance, afterwards. My superior was just back from vacation, and set the tone at the very start of my lecture interrupting me with a question. After that the interruptions came thick and fast; I could hardly get to the end of a sentence, so bombarded was I with questions, most of which were not within my terms of reference at all. I had my notes, of course, but as those brutal, destructive questions rained down on me I wasn't tough enough to give my lecture first and put off further questioning until later. What really hurt was the bitter rivalry behind it all; the emotional satisfaction felt by others in seeing me become weak and uncertain, the pleasure they took in striking at open wounds. I could not make it out. I had reason to be proud of the boy's treatment; I had used my brains to get my way, and I had been successful. Why the brutality, the pleasure in seeing me wounded and bleeding and suffering? A friend said, "Think nothing of it. Your rise has been a bit too meteoric—they had to put a stop to it sometime."

After this class, I did a few routine jobs, but I soon felt quite done in. I went off duty and walked about town for a while before my analytic session, weeping. The savage attack on me, together with the tension of my analysis, were just too much. I arrived for my session very upset, and met with a surprisingly pleasant, friendly reception. My analyst had seen me in tears in the town, he said; I "really was in a bad way."

I had convinced him at last. (His "really" confirmed my impression that hitherto he had not taken the extent of the strain on me as seriously as I had tried to convey he should. I had not misinterpreted him.)

He reacted to my tears, unhappiness and miserable despair in a considerate, friendly, supportive way. His ironic coldness, the "Westwall" atmosphere, his arguing and interrupting me, his severity were things of the past.

It was a long time before I recovered from that destructive episode; many people were surprised by my sensitivity. It had been a perfectly obvious mechanism among colleagues, they said, a total discharge of sibling rivalry, plus economic fears (for my job), plus simple envy. I had, indeed, been damaged: My notion of my happy family background destroyed, my confidence in myself undermined, my analyst's liking for me gone; and now, in addition, I'd lost my prop and stay in everyday life.

My colleagues' reaction was, to me, analytic proof of the fact that I was not lovable, was a cause of conflict. My analyst was quite right not to like me anymore; I was insufferable, with my neurosis and my monumental failure to work through my problems. Or at least, sizable and important parts of me were: Those parts that I actually rather liked about myself, which I thought showed me as strong, militant, attractive, intelligent. But this side of me seemed to be what men found annoying; what rendered them cold; it was probably castrating.

No doubt the fact that, when the "Westwall" atmosphere first set in, I had entertained the notion of my analyst's being blocked by his own feelings for me was simply a delusion of grandeur, a disavowal of reality, a defense mechanism to keep me from having to perceive my unconscious, but strong and effective, castrating tendencies and hostility to men.

Those men who still liked me in spite of it were not worth anything. One, who was very friendly to me, was extremely religious, which I took as the explanation of his goodwill; it was his basic attitude in general, and didn't actually refer to me. I attracted another man physically; so of course he would overlook my bad qualities. I thought a man whom it was very hard to affect was deceived by my outward appearance. It was my desperate mechanism derived from the counterphobia to conceal my inner ugliness. The fact that he let himself be deceived and wouldn't see through me, kept arguing against what I said in denigration of myself, just showed that his blind partisanship was not to be taken seriously. He had not been analyzed.

My active upswing of mood, together with a relative feeling of good health had lasted four months, and now it was over.

I felt trust and gratitude towards my analyst for taking so much and probably such unrewarding trouble with someone like me. For being caring, supportive, sympathetic, concerned. I wept a great deal, and felt helpless, ugly, horrible, at the end of my tether. He listened in a friendly manner; not a trace of irritation or the "Westwall" attitude to be felt. We were at one.

I might well be glad I still had him at all. I really and truly had been on the point of ending the analysis, even though not for another six months, merely out of defense and my failure to see eye to eye with him. Out of a repetition compulsion, I had first treated my analyst so that in spite of his original liking for me he couldn't stand me, and then, when that didn't work, and I still had him near me and hadn't put him to flight like the men in my real life (for I wasn't married), I had tried removing myself from his orbit.

Obviously I had overpowering, catastrophic fears of intimacy, of any kind of close tie. I couldn't even endure an analytic situation, made sexually safe by its setting and by guaranteeing the keeping of a certain distance, without frantic struggles and neurotic acting out.

It was proof, and discouraging proof, that I had almost no emotional access to this mechanism of mine. I could tell what my inner plans were by deducing them from their result, as a mathematical calculation is seen to be right if correctly worked out, even if it comes to a surprising conclusion. However, I didn't actually notice anything. Was I so swamped by my affects, anxieties, defense mechanisms that I couldn't even feel, for instance, a slight fear of infatuation, my sexual desires, my symbiotic longings, vis-a-vis the proximity and reliability of my analyst? Or after my chaotic wartime experiences, had those feelings been irreversibly repressed and extinguished in me? Or had they never developed at all? Were there holes and vacuums in me? As with my lack of proper sensual experience? I read an article about the way in which it had been possible to fill in the emotional gaps in the case of one woman analysand, through a particular analytic technique, so that those qualities of emotion she lacked could at last be formed and grow. That gave me hope.

I was still doing my work, but I didn't have to think of myself at work, I could just function. I was depressed for a long time. If I looked at myself really closely and was quite honest, I had to admit I didn't genuinely love anyone, and I was not secure in my few positive relationships. How could anyone like someone as unloving in herself as I was? My analyst was right. But still he behaved in a friendly and solicitous way. Psychologically, I was a social welfare case, yet he still, responsibly, concerned himself with me, although he knew me and all the evil within me. It was quite understandable that he couldn't think as well of me now as he did at first.

I had given evidence of massive failures of perception: There was my feeling that he had fallen a little in love with me, and my suspicion that I would never be allowed to take my examination. I agreed with him that those perceptions had been paranoid. It troubled me that I had been so sure of them. I could have sworn they were right, staked everything on them. But they had simply been crazy and mistaken. The whole "Westwall" atmosphere had arisen from paranoid perceptions. I needed analysis that would make a qualitative change in me if I were ever to lead a more bearable life.

Who was there I really liked? I felt outright hatred for my

mother and father and their egocentricity in getting me into this disabling situation. The one thing my mother could now see was that I really had felt great longings for my father. Otherwise, however, in her blind narcissism, she was unwilling to see any kind of deeper-seated flaw in me. I had always been sensitive, she said, I'd never been able to take quarrels and tension, that was why she once kept me away from school for three months, while she did battle with a sadistic teacher. I had been such a remarkably contented baby, almost never crying. She didn't believe a word of it.

My relationship with my brothers had been undermined; in the end I simply didn't know where my positive feelings were or where I might not be secretly hating, denying my death wishes and so on. My infatuation at the beginning of my analysis had turned out to be transferences and defenses from my first analyst. Inwardly, I had questioned my feelings for most of my acquaintances. Everything had been chewed over and over, was flavorless, not to be depended on. Lively convictions had been diluted into mathematically deduced, biographically intelligible, rational concepts, cleansed of their defensive aspects.

My analyst's solicitous concern confirmed my illness; my justified depressive weakness. I felt annoyed when acquaintances remarked on the change in me. They hadn't really ever known me, not my innermost being. They were naive and foolish, too undifferentiated, too different from me to be able to understand me at all. I could expect help and improvement only from my analysis. I was engaged in an intensive process. And the more difficulties and the more resolutions of earlier pathological structures I encountered, the more change I could expect. I agreed with my analyst there. Our agreement and the idea of the training function were just about the only concepts I had to support me, and I would defend them against the skeptics.

I had noticed how destructive the effects of my inner impulses were if I didn't entrust myself to my analyst's judgment, sensibility and empathy. I couldn't rely on my own perceptions. I could rely all the more on his. And they sometimes differed fundamentally from mine, but I had to come to terms with that. I just had to get through this difficult period; by doing so, I would be doing useful analytic work.

I did have one good relationship left, not undermined in any way, a pleasant one on both sides. A firm support to me. I could feel good when I was with this fatherly friend of mine, marvelous, ready for anything. And I had always been able to turn to him at any time when things went wrong.

I had kept him right out of my analysis until now; he had never been discussed. Now he made his way in through a back door. On account of my analyst's name, I had felt sure he was Jewish, and I was disappointed when he said he wasn't. In this connection, I suddenly found a whole area in myself where I had pleasant, good-natured and enthusiastic feelings for my friend and for everything Jewish. A kind of "philo-Semitism," as my analyst called it. In a brief aside he pointed out that it concealed "a defense against anti-Semitism." His tone of voice admitted of no doubt. I was taken aback. Was I really defending against anti-Semitism, did I secretly hate Jews, hate my friend? Was this yet another cleverly concealed, malevolent, disgusting and evil quality in me? I didn't want to believe it; I was so fond of my friend and felt so much at ease with him. He was an unusual person, and I always liked such people very much. Others were very fond of him too. Living means loving, he had once written to me. I just would not believe I harbored any evil thoughts in his regard. But my analyst assured me again, with sad and knowing overtones, "Yes, there's anti-Semitism in us all." All of our generation, he meant, himself and me, and all the rest of us. It was diffused through our being, through our surroundings; we were infected by the whole climate of our times.

With that, my last definitely positive relationship was shown up; the last little bit of love in me had turned out to be hatred.

It was a dreadful blow.

I consisted entirely of hatred, defense, reaction formation. My ability to feel was ruined so fundamentally that it was possible I could get nothing but purely rational access to my basic feelings. All I could actually sense was my act of defense, my philo-Semitism, my uncritical attachment, the fact that I simply cared for someone very much indeed. How could I have been so wrong? How could I have felt so much at ease with him and sustained a relationship that had no real foundation?

My analyst's certainty on this point infected me. My affection was an act of defense, was to be seen as such; I must live with my inner hatred. It had been prudent of me to keep my friend out of the analysis so far.

Somehow or other, that interpretation was a mortal wound. Pronounced with certainty, coolly, casually, it struck right home. Nothing much worse could happen now.

In my depression and wretchedness, I paid that month's arrears of fees without a word. If my fundamental character consisted of pure shit, I certainly didn't want to irritate my analyst any further. I was thankful that he would put up with me at all. After all, I was more of a burden, a strain and an imposition than most. I had nothing good to offer, only money.

There was not much sense in life, or much hope. I could see that there might come a point when only a very little more would suffice to make one sick of it all in general. I had always thought the comparison of analysis with a surgical operation strained and exaggerated, but now I saw the point of it.

And I had a sense of hopelessness, rising from outside causes, which I found hard to keep apart from my analysis: Berlin was now a source of depression to me. I had never met with such honesty and commitment as there, and I had clung to that. But I believed in analysis, and analysts knew that neurosis almost always provides the impetus for political activity, etc. They did seem to consider left-wing ideas valuable, but the basic tenet was usually that sickness lay beneath such things. Not wishing to give up my dreams, I explained it to myself by saying that every individual had changed because of his own personal problems—well, really they shouldn't have acted as they did.

Then, after Allende, I had a feeling of hopeless impotence. All that was good went under, and no one would help. Was it any use at all to fight? Those who were really honest, selfless and committed were defeated. Perhaps, however, it touched me so closely only because I was predestined to project all that was good, brave, fine, reliable, fatherly, serious and loving in the world on Allende (via my brother and my fatherly friend in South America). Perhaps I was grieving for something quite different, something that had happened earlier, and I had to work through that first.

Now and then, something in me protested. I couldn't believe that nothing but evil would come to light in me, time and again, evil without exception. Wasn't there something or other wrong here? It couldn't really be so. Other people did better in analysis, other people were able to like themselves, feel more friendly towards themselves, discover and develop their pleasing qualities. Why did I find nothing but bad and evil in me? In his solicitous way, my analyst pointed out that I was sicker than most. "You're more gifted, but also sicker" than the average analysand. These things had just been slumbering within me. Hitherto I had lived with all this garbage inside me. And my first analyst seemed to have formed a similar opinion of me.

I watched with resignation as a pleasant, attractive salesgirl lovingly handled her goods. It would never be like that; I was unable to love; my early deprivations, losses and dreams had flawed me. Women like that girl were the right sort of women, lovable, worthy of life, and able to cope with life. I had been an empty shell, held together hitherto with difficulty, and now artificially. I was embarrassed to think of my previous struggles, which I had thought courageous; they gave me guilt feelings. Not only had my perceptions been distorted; I had become aggressive and insufferable. That lecture I had given in the hospital, the episode which had wounded me so much, took up a good deal of time in analysis. It was a matter of understanding why so aggressive an atmosphere had arisen in the first place; how I had brought it about. We considered my deep disturbance, likely to make others react to me with extreme aggression; the repetition of my relationship with my brothers, and thus particularly traumatic. I remembered times when I had hit them, kicking helplessly, without managing to get my way. One of them once gave himself an electric charge with a stolen field telephone, offered me a friendly kiss, and I got an electric shock on my trusting lips. I remembered when they had worms which they said I'd brought home from elementary school. "Dörte, the rotten bitch, has given us worms again." And hadn't they been jealous of the way my charm won our stepfather over, as it now might win my superiors' liking? The way my colleagues now attacked me cast light on earlier circumstances: They were in no way as rosy as I remembered. Or perhaps my colleagues had simply been reacting in a perfectly ordinary way to my basically repulsive character.

Probably my brothers had been considerably cooler, colder and more aggressive towards me than I remembered. I found funny family stories particularly suspect. When nobody but me felt like celebrating Christmas with a tree, and carols, they had celebrated all the same, for my sake, but they substituted the words: "Dörte is a dope" for "joy to all," in a carol. I remembered it as a joke, a bit of fun, but now I recalled my anger at the time, and how oppressive it had been to be treated as small and stupid. I reproached my family now, with much ill will. I could no longer understand how I'd found such an atmosphere at home quite normal, and a kind of release. I remembered a teacher who had reacted in an injured way to a remark I thought funny and clever, and of which I had been proud. I could understand him better now.

I recovered, gradually, but I was still depressed. I had to work through my depression. It was burdensome, and other people who were in analysis or had been analyzed sympathized with me. But for all that, I was getting a good training, and upon the whole everything was going as it should. During my analyst's next summer vacation I felt lost and abandoned, and was particularly downcast at the usual time for our sessions. I felt ill at ease with people who were not in analysis, and could make myself understood more easily by those who had been analyzed. I envied them their confidence, though; what they had discovered about themselves was not confined to the negative.

As I had now been re-admitted to training, I again applied to take the examination. I had the backing of the regional group this time; they obviously knew enough about me now, and had not taken me up on my offer to be interviewed. My previous doubts had obviously been unfounded and paranoid. I felt confident; the decision had to be taken by the supra-regional group and was generally a routine matter once the regional group had given the go-ahead.

I was informed that my application had been postponed. It had been referred back to the regional committee, because one of the representatives from the regional group had been unable to answer a request for more information. This was unusual. I thought it odd that the regional representatives had not made more of an effort on my behalf; after all, the regional group meeting had decided in my favor. I then learned that it so happened neither of the two regional representatives had been at that meeting at all, though they were to present its decisions to the supra-regional group. Thus they had been unable to state circumstances of which they had not been adequately informed. That explained it. On the other hand, I felt vexed; if they were proposing something, I thought, they surely ought to inform themselves about it if they'd been unable to attend the original meeting. The whole thing seemed to me unusual and illogical. I also doubted whether I had been told the real reason. Was there not, perhaps, some general objection to me after all? Back came my "paranoid" feeling.

My analyst felt for me, and tried to soothe me. Here, as everywhere, one found differences of opinion within a group, he said, and that could be the explanation of what had happened.

I felt that the representatives had let me down. What was the idea of getting two people who had not been at the meeting of a body to represent that body, anyway? Why did such illogical disorder seem to proliferate around me?

But then I abandoned my old feeling that a firm decision had been taken never to re-admit me. Obviously I had just become mixed up in a group-dynamics muddle involving various rivalries. It was my bad luck. One of those responsible told me in private, by way of consolation, "But you won't have any trouble at all next time." So I felt confident about applying again on the next date, six months hence.

In my private life, I increasingly isolated myself. I couldn't offer myself to anyone with a clear conscience when I had the vague feeling that there was something bad about me, something that put men off, something enticing yet misleading, something hostile. I was handicapped by my life history. I directed the full force of my anger against my mother; with other people, it was more inclined to take the form of distancing myself, feeling different and at a unique disadvantage.

When I was feeling a little better, I sometimes felt attacks of the "Westwall" mood coming on, but now I wouldn't let them develop; they had been too terrible. I felt they were still there, they had only gone underground, and I must be careful.

Sometimes I felt that my analyst was annoyed, something was getting on his nerves, and that was why he coughed. He flatly denied this. But surely his cough wasn't just coincidence? After all, it occurred at the same time as his annoyance and his aggressive mood. He flatly denied this too. I stood by my perception. Finally he said he really was not annoyed at the moment, and as closely as he might examine himself he could find no aggression within him. It was my own aggression I was projecting on him.

My perception, then, had been false. But I thought there could still be some ambivalence, there being no such thing as chemically pure feeling. Couldn't it be that my sensibility in this instance was greater than his? After a debate of some length, he replied, in irritation, "Yes, the sensibility of a schizophrenic."

The explosive effect of his remark was heightened by his obvious affect; moreover, I wasn't going to accept such a diagnosis, for which there were well-defined criteria. He had been annoyed.

The "Westwall" atmosphere, which kept recurring, was discouraging. I could avert it, but it troubled me. One day, when I said, resignedly, that nothing basic had really changed: The "Westwall" phenomenon was less intense, but that was all, he told me that he had in fact sought some supervision in my case. We had been dealing with a "counter-transference trap": An emotional trap I had set for him, and into which he had fallen. My neurotic feelings had forced him into it; I had so contrived things that he couldn't defend himself in time. He had never before, he said, "had such difficulties in an analysis" as he did with me.

But the idea of a "counter-transference trap" did not explain everything to me. If that were all, then surely there should have been a fundamental qualitative change in something after the supervision, after he recognized the counter-transference? Basically, however, everything had gone on as before, only in a gentler, more muted, more cautious way. I had seen to that.

This was not how he saw it; the situation really was different now, he said, and had been for some time. He had never had a recurrence of those previous negative feelings of his. They hadn't come back. I didn't agree. He often refused to believe me when I felt that atmosphere coming on again, but I was sure of it; my sensibility was keen. I could feel there were important parts of me he didn't like; my combative moods, in which I felt well and vital, made him cold and aggressive. And along came the "Westwall" mood.

I couldn't force him to like these qualities in me, of course. That was an emotional process which couldn't be commanded. I could not draw his attention to it as if by legal right. And possibly the state of mind he so disliked in me did contain something very unpleasant, but he ought not keep reacting to it exactly the same, time and again. It made me feel quite unwell.

He did not say who the supervisor had been, but I remembered from our earlier discussion of the subject that if he did agree to a supervisor he would go ahead and find one. I guessed he meant his own former analyst, who was unorthodox, so that seemed a good thing. But when I thought how he still kept tackling the analysis in the same way, I felt it was hopeless. If I was repeatedly setting my counter-transference trap, why couldn't he at least manage to treat me neutrally? Without the same coldness and recourse to the same "Westwall" mood? If this was my repetition compulsion, why did he keep striking at the same flaws and wounds? How could I ever deal with it, undergo an experience that would change me, improve me, if he always reacted in an identical way, letting me irritate and annoy him and throw him off his balance? Such things happened even in our relatively harmonious periods of analysis, when I felt active, well and pretty, when my mind was clear and functioning in a manner that pleased me.

I was glad and proud of the *fact* of supervision. My analyst had reacted to me; he had taken me and this analysis and its problems more seriously after all, and my complaints had not bounced off him as easily as I had thought. That was reassuring.

But I also struck myself as powerful: How could I irritate a trained analyst so much? How could I land him in such difficulties? I didn't feel I was anything so very unusual. Even if I did display neurotic resistance and played it off with skill, wasn't I still a normal enough analysand, a neurotic one, with my own particular mechanisms arising from my history?

What was so unusual and impeding about me? What made me, a weak, depressive and inhibited creature, so powerful? I took a natural interest in my analysis, if on "too personal" a level, and not objectively and scientifically enough. Still, I felt committed; I had invested something in it myself. I did not consciously withhold information, I was trying to face my problems.

The lack of clarity about me, the sense of helplessness and the technical difficulties cropping up in my analysis bothered me; I felt dangerous and destructive. Why did I cause so much irrationality and illogicality? Not only in my analysis, but among other analysts concerned with my training. Why could no one ever give me any clear information?

There was obviously something confusing, obfuscating about me. Possibly connected with my death fantasies about my father (my inability to grasp him, lack of sensuous experience of him, his decomposing without a trace, dissolving in Stalingrad), and also, somehow or other, with my megalomania and my probably strong impact on others. One analyst—though privately and with annoyance—had said I displayed "a peculiar form of attraction."

I was helpless in the face of this; I didn't find myself particularly attractive—my mother, and other women, had more charm—nor particularly intelligent; my brothers were superior to me there. Nor particularly brave or militant—rather, I felt I was too conventional and easily led. At school, my brothers had taken far more risks, while I was inclined to trot along behind them. But even if I discounted possible remnants of a childhood feeling of being in the grown-ups' shadow, I seemed nothing out of the ordinary, not at home.

At a hospital conference, I had said something relevant to the discussion and backed it up by saying it was "known from the literature," without knowing exactly where this confirmation was to be found, though I was sure of the substance of what I said. At my session, I asked where I could read up on it. My analyst was annoyed. Where did I get the confidence simply to state such a thing without knowing my precise sources? I had been sure of what I said, though; it was just that I didn't now know where my knowledge came from. Hence I had used the expression "known from the literature," which had sounded convincing at the time. Maybe I had taken something of a liberty, but I was right. My confidence disturbed him. How could I have made such a claim without solid knowledge behind me, he wondered? Without a real foundation in fact? Yet people in the field of organic medicine lied shamelessly; it was common knowledge that medical examinations, and reports on congresses were falsified. I hadn't even been wrong in what I said, I had just implied a surer knowledge of the literature than I actually had. The discussion had been a lively one, and I had enjoyed it. However, I had obviously rubbed my analyst the wrong way.

Once, driving to a seminar, I took a man's right of way in a somewhat flirtatious manner; he had the right of way, but we had glanced into each other's eyes and come to an understanding. "Overweening ego" was the verdict of my analytic passengers, not entirely meant as a joke.

"You don't stick to the rules of the game," I had been told (by another analyst). Impulsive self-confidence was suspect; so, strictly speaking, was every spontaneous impulse. Analytic attention was given to my scruples, crippling inhibitions, guilt feelings. Naive confidence seemed to be a defense mechanism, manic overacting, and was no way to behave when viewed through mature and adult eyes. I thought some more about my moments of spontaneous, carefree verve, when I infected others with my good humor.

It was true, there was almost always some ambivalence, an opposing, hesitant impulse. Once I'd taken that into account, I found my impulsive verve gone, vanished; either that, or I felt embarrassment later over my lack of reflection. Indeed, the assurance of a sleepwalker, impulses put into action, were proof of defense.

Basically, I had no reason to be in any really good humor, not with my basic problems; I must get through my depression and then I'd be able to see ahead and start living again.

Some of my analyst's interpretations seemed familiar to me; they described or repeated notions I had expressed or at least entertained myself. But then, they did determine the nature of my own thoughts. And after all, his feelings about and evaluation of the situation and my experience were those of a normal human being, capable of reacting appropriately. "Don't you think that . . .?" Well, yes, I'd thought of it too; that was probably what I meant, if he saw it the same way.

Sometimes I felt rather confused when he made an interpretation of which I was well aware. "You will be asking yourself whether . . ." He would do this without moving to a different plane of meaning. At first I'd thought these interpretations were particularly clever and subtle, and believed there was some special significance behind them which I didn't understand, or he would hardly have repeated to me something which I knew perfectly well and had already taken into consideration. It was discouraging to be unable to find, in spite of my efforts and reflections, what the new plane, the unconscious content, was. Later, I decided that perhaps he was trying to create order out of my emotional chaos, the tangled mass of my ideas and possible reactions, and therefore simply gave me his opinion, his impression, his experience, and didn't really mean these remarks as interpretations in the strict sense of the term.

While we were slightly at odds, my analyst had to have an operation, so that there was a hiatus of some length in my analysis. I managed to fend off my anxiety about that by going on a trip to India, and in spite of various emotional upheavals it was a pleasant, enjoyable, satisfying experience, like taking a warm bath.

When I knew he was convalescent, though not yet back at work, I sent him a copy of a letter I had written to my fatherly friend about my trip, to keep him up to date. After putting it off for weeks, I had written this detailed letter in one night, when the spirit moved me, and had then gone to sleep feeling exhausted and content. I thought it was a good letter; it was a part of me. My fatherly friend reacted to it positively too; it showed an important dimension of my nature, he thought, something serious and adult which I ought to foster in myself. I had gone from one emotional upheaval to another while I was away, but I'd always been able to climb back out of the depths again, and it had been worth it; I had had some beautiful experiences and reached some firm convictions, won through experience, having left myself open to the prevailing atmosphere and gone along with it. What was very important was that I had not made any mistakes, had never felt anything "crazy" that had no real basis; indeed, I had felt "normal," reasonably sensitive, and sometimes rather dull compared to many of the Indians I met. My mellow mood and my perceptions had been beautiful, and had attracted people. There, anyway.

It was important to me to know what my analyst thought of my letter. At first I didn't dare ask, but he didn't mention it of his own accord. Finally, when I did inquire, he said, disapprovingly, that it was "like a school composition." In context, that meant boring and conventional; I might well have spared myself the trouble of writing such a thing, it would have been no loss, and I needn't have sent it to him.

That hurt; the letter contained something of myself. I just couldn't impress him, not with my most intimate thoughts and feelings. I had bared myself and met with cold, disinterested rejection; it would have been better not to reveal that side of me. The letter also dealt with sexual matters; it had not been easy for me to put those things into words. My analyst seemed annoyed that I had written to him at all. I explained (by way of excuse) that there had been such a long hiatus in my analysis, and a great deal had happened to me; I couldn't save it up for so long. In fact, I had written the letter only when I realized that I was beginning to repeat myself, using the same phrases over and over in answering questions from friends, and I always felt the urge to recount some things; I was dissipating my energies. I thought at first there was no one to whom I could tell it all, but then I wrote to my friend in Argentina, and sent my analyst a copy, not wishing to find several ways to phrase what I had to say. I thought he should have been able to understand my development; after all, he was the most important figure in my life in that respect. But I could tell that he was annoyed I had written at all. As an afterthought, he found fault with my "dealings with reality." I didn't know what he meant, "Why, the address." Then I remembered that I'd made a mistake in the street name when I first typed the address. I had been fairly sure of it and had put the street name I thought I remembered on the envelope, before going to the other end of the room to check in the telephone book, just to make sure. I had then corrected the street name. I'd started by typing the name I thought I knew because that seemed more expedient than getting up, going to check in the far corner of the room, and then writing the address. So I corrected the name in ink instead of using a new envelope.

This led to an argument, with a pronounced recurrence of the "Westwall" atmosphere, both of us interrupting each other and becoming cross. Why hadn't I gone to check first if I hadn't felt quite sure? But I had felt almost quite sure; moreover, the street name I'd typed lay parallel to the correct one, and I had friends living there with whom I felt at ease, so I wasn't as far out as all that. He insisted that this kind of thing was typical of me and my dealings with reality. Where did I get the confidence to feel sure the name was correct? I hadn't actually felt so very confident, or I wouldn't have gone to look it up at all; I just felt it was quicker, more expedient and sensible to get the letter ready at my desk, envelope written and stamped, before going over to the door at the other end of the room for a final check. It had saved me a journey, and was the easiest thing to do; it was just the luck of the draw that I had the wrong

address after all. However, that didn't mean I needed a new envelope on that account; I wasn't writing an official letter of application, after all, I was writing to my analyst.

He finally ended the discussion by stating that he personally
would have gone to check in the telephone book first, would have
looked up the address, and only then would he have written the
envelope.

It irked me that he concentrated so much on the outward form of
my letter. Why did it seem to be devalued by conforming to the criterion of the German school essay, with a beginning, a middle and
an end? And even if I had written a stilted composition of that
kind, why didn't he concentrate on its contents, on what I felt I absolutely had to tell him?

It was my unconscious motivation that ought to have concerned
him, after all. He wasn't there to teach me German composition! I
felt as if I had received a D minus mark, with many errors marked
in red ink. I was haunted by a pop song, Dahlia Lavi's "Words":

> "It's only words, and words are all I had
> to take your heart away.
> You think that I don't even mean a single word I say . . .
> This world has lost its glory
> let's start a brand new story now right now."

Another song ran:

> "My kind of life is love not to hate
> let's do it now before it's too late."

Why was he put off by the form of the letter? The business of the
envelope, and my style. That was not what had mattered to me.
And showing him the letter had been a kind of striptease act: It was
such a frank letter, originally written to someone of whom I was
very fond. Why should he reject it so utterly?

I was thinking in terms of song:

> "I don't know where we went wrong
> but the feeling is gone
> and I just can't get it back."

I did believe that my letter showed a good side of me: Clear-minded, capable of experience and endurance. On this trip, I had been capable of normal feelings, without excessive sensitivity, and my strong reactions had brought me to illuminating comprehension, to a state in which I understood, so that my perplexity and distress were relieved because I had seen through it all. Why did this put him off so much now? How was I supposed to be and behave, to satisfy him? Goodness knew I'd made efforts including the writing of the letter.

He might be friendly and solicitous when I was tearful and despairing, but that wasn't the whole of me, it was not my constant state of mind. How could I make the most of my happier side and still please him, so that there wasn't any tension between us?

I stood up for myself; I wouldn't accept criticism of my letter, or at any rate not of its form. I had lived, understood, changed, and I wanted him to understand and absorb *that* fact, so that my analysis could go on without too much in the way of initial problems, or a sense of unfamiliarity after the long hiatus he himself had caused. At heart, my letter was a love letter in disguise, and had been properly understood by its original recipient.

All the same, my analyst's rejection hurt me, and it added to those unexplained instances of difference of opinion between us.

My batteries felt recharged after my vacation; I still retained a little of my warmth. Babies would calm down for me; I tried to be as gentle as possible when giving them physical examinations, and it worked—they liked it, and would beam back at me.

And now, of all times, my analyst disliked me again. Either we had the "Westwall" atmosphere or jokes. Life remained a strain. However, I met a man who had been analyzed and found it easy to understand me. I was surprised to find how simply we could make contact, how little I often needed to talk or explain at all. Essentials he mostly absorbed through his skin. I could cry my heart out without having to explain; I met with good-natured, cheerful consideration. My edginess worried him; he asked some questions about it at first, and then said he wondered if my analyst wasn't too young for me. He thought ten years' difference wasn't enough, not in my case. There was something wrong; he could tell whether I'd had a session that day the moment he came in, because whenever I had I was irritable, changed, agitated. I didn't need to say a word, he could tell by looking at me; if any, I needed an older analyst.

I thought his objection funny; typical masculine jealousy. Naturally he would prefer me to have an ancient, sterile old man for an analyst! I came right back at him with my interpretation, and he said no more about it. Much later he told me I had been totally unapproachable.

He thought I was egocentric, concerned entirely and exclusively with myself, and complained that it seemed his only function so far as I was concerned was as the focus for my self-admiration; I was completely self-absorbed, related everything instantly and solely to myself, and would not adapt to him in any way. Had I any space in my life for him at all? Was there anything in me able to feel solicitude for someone else? I wept. Finally, and angrily, he said, "People just *have* to like you." So there we were!

All in all, I was taking everything very seriously again. I felt enthusiasm for psychoanalysis as a system of thought; professionally, it was enjoyable; some of my therapies were successful and satisfactory. Everything made sense; despite the strain I felt, and my depression, this analysis of mine was the right thing for me. I was in a training analysis within the framework of a recognized body, had a grant, at a university hospital.

There was a new development: I changed for the better during my analyst's vacation. I met people again, made easy, friendly, affectionate contacts (even if they were only eye contacts, at the baker's, or in a stand-up café). I recognized the feeling I again had a sense of a good life—little human contacts and reciprocal minideclarations of love could make the day seem worth living. All of a sudden there was something in me again that obviously made a friendly impression. I sat near a man in a café, and then he went with me to buy a lamp. We found each other's company pleasant, and that was the end of it. We had liked each other, a feeling absorbed through the skin, breathed in with the air, and we needed no more from the contact. But this pleasant side of me was gone again when I came out of my sessions. No doubt those minicontacts were fragile and depended on one's mood. I told my analyst about them. For instance, the proprietress of a baker's shop would kindly and carefully pick out for me the kind of salted sticks I particularly liked. She was glad I enjoyed her wares. Sometimes I met people in a stand-up café who communicated with me briefly, just with a word or so—"tastes good," or "hot!"—and then I felt at ease, part of the bustle of humanity. I liked these people too, and that in itself did me good; there was more to me than rejection and criticism. My analyst was surprised. I felt a bit peculiar.

A foreign analyst, who himself had trained my first analyst, came to give a lecture. I found him inspiring: A kindly, confident man who liked women. He resembled my grandfather, and analytically speaking, that is what he was. I felt we were on the same wavelength. He was pleased when I went up to him after the lecture, and invited me to attend his seminar; it would be like having a part of his family here, he said.

Moreover, he lived with the woman analyst who had written what I considered the most significant and best thought out work on female sexuality I knew. A beautiful, successful, luxuriant woman.

My analyst acknowledged my activities here, but seemed surprised. I didn't think there was anything odd about it: I had always liked that kind of man, mature, and appreciative of women. I had felt the lack of such men.

The French woman analyst's book had encouraged me; I had been able to reconstruct very little of value for myself from orthodox theories, which were also very depressing, and no doubt the women analysts were sad as well. This writer's theory, however, postulated an independent female identity of which I could be proud, with which I could identify, which could give me a satisfying sense of self-confidence. (There were in fact, less well-known theories put forward by other women analysts which were not at all that depressing; I read them only later, and learned that they had simply been passed over in silence. Helene Deutsch had won recognition.)

The Frenchwoman's theory was an extension of Freud into a field of which he himself had admitted that it was "terre inconnue." My own first analyst had mentioned the book, which made it additionally important to me. I was irritated to find that men analysts scarcely seemed to have registered its existence at all. And I found gaps in my own analyst's knowledge. I wondered whether in the last resort a man could ever be in a position to have genuine, deep understanding of a woman: According to the theory in the book, only if identification with the opposite sex had occurred from time to time. Each partner must identify some time with the symbolic aspect of the other's genitals in order to become an empathic partner, and be able symbolically to admit in him or herself the qualities ascribed to the opposite sex. In the course of this, one had to learn to separate the organic and the symbolic meaning.

Otherwise, a woman would automatically associate dominance, assertiveness, potency, etc., with the penis, and have guilt feelings concerning unfeminine behavior; a man, conversely, would feel guilt for those creative and passive capabilities which he had not separated from their organic aspect and with which he had not identified, and then they would cause him castration fears. I found this very illuminating; at congresses it had often annoyed me to see intelligent and active women almost automatically regarded as "castrating" and "phallic." Of the woman analyst of my very first interview, whom I greatly admired, one of her male colleagues had told me: Secretly she goes about with an enormous phallus under her arm, taking careful aim and then hitting out with it. I had felt much disconcerned on her behalf.

I had felt the force of this same theory myself, on the night after the workshop I attended; I had clearly perceived my guilt feelings concerning activity, thought, assertiveness, recognition—those qualities symbolically connected with the male genitals in our culture. More than likely, I had not accomplished the separation clearly and adequately.

(At the time, I was not aware of the real pressure put on me by the men in the class, who really had felt jealousy of such potential in me.)

So I had identified closely with this book; I wanted to translate it, and had been looking around for a publisher. When an English women analyst came to give a lecture on female development and female sexuality, I asked during the discussion period, what she thought of the Frenchwoman's theory. Her answer was only a vague one, so I then asked if she rejected the book, or if it was just that she didn't know it well enough? She said in a matter-of-fact way that she personally couldn't make much of it. Which told me where she stood.

At my next session, my analyst, who had been to the lecture, said he was taken aback my way of expressing aggression and yet appearing naively innocent. A query from anyone else as to whether the lecturer actually knew important literature would have seemed sheer impertinence. Obviously I had a childlike ability to say such things without giving offense. I had not been aware of it.

In addition, he said, my question had clearly risen from my personal problems; that was very noticeable. But why shouldn't I think sexuality an important and personal subject, I asked? What did it matter if every soul in the lecture hall had noticed? I insisted that all interesting subjects were emotionally charged and directly personal anyway. He wouldn't accept that. I had had a wholly personal interest in the matter, he said, just as I did in my analysis. I lacked objective, scientific interest. I reduced anything and everything to the personal level. I got angry, and expressed doubt that anyone ever felt abstract interest at all; you could find personal motivation everywhere, even among scientists researching into the peptide chain.

We had another fierce argument; it was different with me, he said, he had seen very clearly that my remarks during the discussion arose from my personal problems and not from objective interest. My opinions were less detached than other people's. I, on the other hand, said I could guarantee, I'd noticed it time and again at congresses, that every utterance, all interest ever expressed, could be traced back to a personal problem if you really put your mind to it. We wrangled. My interest was different, more insistent, he said. I was too unsure of myself to question and compare other people. He stuck to his opinion that I lacked an objective and scientific interest in psychoanalysis. I felt misunderstood. Ought I really to approach such subjects in a quieter, calmer, more objective way? What was it that upset him about my manner of showing interest? All I could clearly feel was that he had some objection to it, and that he did not like me. I had sounded "too personal," my interest was "more insistent" than that shown by others, it wasn't "detached" enough. Something about my manner was wrong and disturbing. Yet my curiosity, my questions, my reluctance to accept too readily and my doubts were an important part of me, and what was wrong with them? Doubts, as Brecht has said in a poem, are sometimes the only right base from which something new can develop. How was I supposed to think, how was I supposed to show interest? At school, we had been supposed to develop "logical" thought, with the aid of the ancient languages; later, one was encouraged to adopt habits of "surgical" or "internal medical" thought, according to one's specialization. I thought this idiotic. But perhaps I really had gone wrong somewhere. There were times when I felt like a savage who must have table manners drilled into her, with difficulty.

At times I did wonder whether my analyst would treat me so much as a child in need of correction if I were married. Suppose, for instance, I were now living with a doctor in charge of a clinic or a professor? Would he have taken me more seriously then? My unmarried status was my weak point; it was the reason for my analysis. Why could he never see me as someone who could be simply trusted and believed, someone with whom he could agree?

Once, at a lecture, he did come down firmly on my side. The lecturer was describing the optimum way for an analyst to feel towards his analysand: Benevolent, assured, offering primarily positive interpretations, and so forth. I couldn't help laughing, and asked if this wasn't just a discreetly roundabout way of saying the analyst should be a little in love? This offended the lecturer, but my analyst intervened and said he agreed with me. That did me good.

I complained that he had very little feeling for my irony. His friends thought him witty, he objected. I considered this a dishonest argument; we were concerned with the analytic situation here, weren't we? I was the person he had to convince in this context, and other people's opinions were irrelevant. I wasn't calling in my big brothers to support me.

One day, when I was really in full flight, a mood of irritability arose quite quickly. When I asked why, he said I'd begun talking "at the door." I couldn't see his point. Was the setting more important than my affect, which he was holding back, belittling? I found it something of a performance anyway to ring the doorbell, take off my coat, settle myself on the couch, wait to conclude, from the cessation of movement and sound behind my head, that he was not comfortably seated himself and ready to listen, and then letting loose my affect. Not too fast, not with too much intensity, keeping within the fifty minutes at my disposal.

But suppose I was so full of something that I felt I needed to start talking about it even in the vestibule? Freud had analyzed patients while walking. And surely my taking my agitation seriously, not stopping it in favor of some stereotype, was in itself a sign that I was making progress.

I was particularly hurt by the emotional rejection which entered into his reasoning. I noticed his irritability, his tendency to keep me at arm's length, restrained, within clearly defined bounds and generally subdued; I could also feel unmistakable signs of the onset of the "Westwall" atmosphere. If he had told me that it simply bothered him not to be able to sit down and start concentrating before I began talking, I expect I could have accepted that.

As it was, his criticism seemed just a formal and emotionally violent pretext.

In any event, the fifty minutes did not constitute an actual biological or analytical necessity; they seemed more of a handy device due to the allocation of time.

I had often found it hard to pack an account of intense experiences into that space of time. Sometimes it was torture to leave the session, still immersed in some deeply felt and desperate trouble I had begun to describe, and have to wait till the next day or longer before I could continue. And when I did, it was hard to take up the thread of my account again. I had experienced this several times when discussing fathers, and the war; I had left my session red-eyed and with a headache, and could not switch off quickly. My sorrow was still there, underground, draining my strength even hours later.

Once, when I put forward the proposition that women's buttocks were of importance to the right sort of men, he swiftly and casually interpreted this as indicating something homosexual. All I'd meant was that it was those men who really liked women who would take pleasure in the female behind (or ass). I much disliked the fashion for very tight-fitting trousers, and men who squeezed their exiguous bottoms into jeans, actually aiming for a masculine behind—*those* were the people I'd have thought more likely to be homosexual, attracted to the buttocks of boys. I had really only been looking for some way of reconciling myself to my own figure. Many of my friends had been comforting on that subject, but I couldn't really convey my state of mind; I kept it to myself. The idea of homosexuality as a defense against castration fears—thus leading to sex from behind, to avoid the sight of the castration wound—and so on and so forth, was regarded, if ironically, as a classic one. It was persuasive. If those friends of mine were really defending against homosexual desires and satisfying them by roundabout ways, then there was nothing truly personal in the pleasure they took in me. I had thought an interest in women's buttocks refreshingly archaic, suggestive of the animal kingdom. My analyst's wife was thin, so obviously he wasn't one of those who employed that defense. I still wasn't happy with the way we were handling my so-called "work disturbances." I was at that time having problems in dictating anything at all; I had gone around for almost a year suffering ever sharper pangs of conscience over an expert opinion; I was constantly behind with my correspondence; my head sometimes rang with all the things I had on my conscience. I also had to write a report on my project, the one for which I had received the grant for my analysis. I didn't have the self-assurance to describe something mediocre in glowing terms. The idea and its planned execution were good in themselves. I felt stupid, impotent and inept in my inability just to put those experiences I was actually having into words, give them form, set them against criteria. It all felt too delicate and diffuse; I didn't trust myself to express it. I could have done with encouragement. I also was to write about the case of the poisoned child. A doctor in charge had promised that he would then go through what I had written with me. But I couldn't summon up the energy to throw it together. Subsequently my guilty conscience caused me to keep out of the doctor's way. I was in a tangle of feelings, felt like a flop, because I couldn't even cope with a thing like that.

The things I'd left undone weighed upon me. I felt constantly under pressure, and my weekends were spoiled. I wouldn't allow myself anything pleasant before I'd dealt those priorities, yet I kept putting them off, and felt tired and exhausted the whole time.

My analyst sympathized, but I didn't think he could really have dealt with such situations any better himself. He was visibly unenthusiastic and late in making out his invoices, or else would then do them all in a rush. Obviously he didn't find it easy to get things done either, and it took him a long time to make out any certificate that fell outside routine work. The sessions we spent discussing this matter didn't stimulate me.

He didn't seem skilled with words and the use of language, either. His motoricity was complicated, and rather difficult. One of my brothers had the ability just to sit down and start working. If he had something unpleasant to do, and he had made up his mind to do it, then he simply did it. He literally radiated confidence; I liked that. I could be stimulated by such people. However, my analyst did not have this kind of brilliant competence. I missed the refreshing contact with my brothers, I missed their encouragement. My first analyst had thought I wanted my mother to do everything for me. The present interpretations and theories didn't change me. My paralysis remained.

I could no longer really appreciate my analyst. I couldn't at heart take him seriously or fully accept him. He didn't inspire me; his interpretations did not strike me with a shock of surprise, there was nothing fascinating in the way he phrased things. Was I now feeling about him as I had felt about my stepfather? I had known quite well, at the age of five, that the latter was not my real father. My brothers too had refused to call him "Father." We had agreed on "Ather," and that was all. And it had been perfectly clear to me that he would have to go away when my real father did come home. Perhaps I was repeating the pattern of this early relationship now. But in any case, the success of my future relationships with men would depend upon whether I learned to accept, admire and appreciate my analyst. If my relationships were suffering from the fact that I was secretly waiting for Mr. Right, and those real men I actually knew couldn't stand comparison with him, if I had been true to him so far, then I had now reached an important point.

But hard as I tried, I couldn't find my analyst inspiring. I saw no intellectual charm in him. I was very much inclined to be enthusiastic about good phrasing and clever remarks, even in people whom I didn't otherwise care for. My father had written witty, delightful, ironic and outrageous letters. Not so my stepfather. I had not liked his lisping, rather pompous Hessian manner of speech, and was often embarrassed by it when he spoke at graduation ceremonies as a representative of the parents' association. However, fellow-pupils of mine thought he was impressive, and were surprised by my embarrassment. And acquaintances described him and my mother as "a good-looking couple" when they went out walking. He was inclined to bring discussions to an end, in his own favor, by employing a loud voice and his step-paternal authority, less frequently by means of convincing argument, and now and then by reference to the big encyclopedia. That was the effect my analyst had on me too: Clumsy, unskillful, inclined to insist upon his standing, on the rules and the setting instead of explaining and convincing. Many people described him as witty, too. They said he could react in an unconventional, original way during case discussions. That wasn't my own experience of him, but fellow analysands spoke well of him too. Nobody else seemed to feel as critical as I did, or at least none of them said so.

I thought my father had been a handsome man in his way, with a fine, distinguished face. I liked his figure and the casual pants he wore, as I knew them from photographs. My brothers' appearance was similar. It pleased me. My stepfather, on the other hand, seemed more the puffy sort, always a little too fat, distinguished. But then again, many people thought him good-looking. To this day, however, I don't like people with a gap between their front teeth; now that I have thought more about it, but in no way changed my opinion, it still seems to suggest foolish indifference, aggressive and authoritarian stupidity that will suffer nothing in the way of competition.

And after our initial pleasant period, my analyst really did look to me like my stepfather: Sturdy, rather heavy in movement and around the hips, not handsome, nose too small, none of his features strong enough. My stepfather's small nose had often troubled me. (Never mind the possible analogy one might make—nose = penis.) Anyway, the transference relationship was clear, at least in so far as I was now selectively perceiving features in which my analyst and my stepfather resembled each other.

Then I condemned myself for these negative sensations, and felt angry with my neurosis, which spoiled everything. I was frigid on every count. I couldn't manage to accept his interpretations with any enthusiasm; they tended to leave me either indifferent or hurt. I often thought them superficial, naive, far-fetched or tortuously constructed.

They could hardly fall on fertile ground, considering my inward sterility, my emotional vaginismus. No wonder I wasn't married and had no children. If I balked at everything as I was balking at my analyst, then I was not about to admit anything at all to myself. Other analysands went into raptures about him, felt they were in good hands, were delighted with his clever interpretations. This discouraged me totally. Everybody else had a different impression of him. But then of course I had my biological vacuum, my flaw; it was with difficulty, and step by little step, that I must learn what others had been freely granted.

I couldn't think his face handsome any more either. I still somewhat liked the nape of his neck and his hair. A woman friend said he had fine eyes. But I'd never paid particular attention to people's eyes. I hated it when someone conceded, of an otherwise unattractive girl, "But she has fine eyes," as if one were praising "fine landscape photography" in a stupid film. His eyes were dark and rather large, yes, but I could feel no enthusiasm for them. All that was over and done with.

I would have to learn to like men who were not very dazzling, not brilliant, the average kind of man. I must feel enthusiasm and genuine appreciation for such men. If I couldn't succeed in that, I would be clinging to my father forever, and my capacity for loving would remain on ice: Buried in the ice of Stalingrad.

I remained predominantly indifferent. If I tried hard to find his interpretations and the way he put things interesting, I could succeed to a slight extent. But only in a brittle, theoretical, intellectual way. I was learning how one gave interpretations, what they had to be like, what points they ought to make. But I couldn't feel fully involved, not in myself, not with my whole identity and all my interest. Many of our sessions were just dull, lacking any conflict or tension, boring—except that my very boredom was evidence of my neurosis. I felt altogether cool, unconcerned and uninterested. Attempts at anything more vital led only to self-reproaches and despair at the mess I was in, at my inner emptiness, my inability to love and lack of interest, my inability to appropriately respond to so normal, attractive and appealing a man.

I could not deceive myself about my lack of interest; it just was not changing. Comparing myself with other people was as discouraging as ever. Yes, perhaps defense would have been better rather / than this total vacuum, than the deficiency in myself that I had to perceive and understand.

The level of his interpretation was brought up short against the realization of my indifference. "You must be able to get along with your analyst and make him useful to you." But frigid toad that I was, I had no feelings. It was my own fault. I must make an effort,

develop more within myself and give more out of myself, show
more feeling, verbalize clearly. The main emphasis was on my reluctance and the way I stood aloof. (If we had remained on that
plane of transference, we should have been obliged to conclude that
this indifference did not correspond in any way to my history, that I
had reacted strongly to my stepfather, and that my present indifference towards my analyst—supposing it could really be understood
as transference—was the result of defense against strong libidinous
impulses. That I was possibly "playing possum" with him so as not
to be involved with Oedipal conflicts. However, we did not get on
to that plane. We noted my poor emotionality, my coolness, my insensitivity, my lack of interest in men such as himself: Average, reliable men. The fact that I scarcely reacted at all to his
interpretation by any change in myself was the result of my defense, which was hard to get at.)

I had to concentrate on the sort of men who would be good for
me. So far I had successfully warded them off. In spite of my pelvis
being ready for childbearing, in spite of my outer presentability, I
was unmarried because I had not learned to like such men, because
I had not carried this over to all my men friends, and to my analyst. The fact that I felt enthusiasm for men who were out of the ordinary, and was able to appreciate them, showed how cleverly I was
avoiding any close tie. Such men only supplied my narcissistic deficiency, and in general they were not reliable. I must develop qualities that were brilliant and out of the ordinary in myself, and not go
to others for them by way of compensation.

A woman I knew who was in analysis said firmly and with resignation, when I expressed surprise that she was leaving a gap between children in having her family, "Well you know, when you're
in analysis, the child is practically the analyst's." I was slow to understand, and found it hard to do so; I could scarcely remember
any such wishes in myself, and now they seemed uninterestingly
theoretical. Other women built stronger relationships, in analysis
and no doubt in life too.

Many things agitated or infuriated me these days. However, my
analyst seldom went along with me; instead, he reacted with something between amusement, surprise, skepticism and rejection.

An analyst gave a lecture in which he spoke at length on a female
patient with "severe early disturbance." I thought he was cynically

and contemptuously hostile to women, and I felt angry—so did other women sitting near me. It seemed to me clear that he was unable to cope with his patient's erotic attraction and intellectual potency, and treated her disparagingly, showing aggression in his diagnosis. I did not like the kind of interpretation he was presenting; it seemed destructive, and I wouldn't have cared to be his patient myself. There was a growing sense of restlessness and irritation in the audience around me, and I put several questions to the speaker. He reacted to them with the same kind of cynicism. As I had to leave anyway, to go to a hospital party, I thought it a suitable moment to walk out of the lecture.

My analyst showed concern again at my next session; had I felt unable to stand the tension that arose after my remarks? I had seemed to take what the lecturer said as a personal insult. Why did I have to take it so personally? I had some trouble in convincing him that my main reason for leaving had been the party; I had certainly felt outraged, but not deeply shattered by the discussion. I had enjoyed the party too, and thought no more about the lecture. I was surprised by my analyst's solicitude. He might have been dealing with someone seriously sick. He still seemed to feel some doubt, however, because I had made myself so conspicuous. But even if I had not been able to stand the speaker's cynicism, I asked, didn't he himself think the lecturer was hostile to his woman patient? Exposed to such destructive interpretations, she was lost. Could he sit by and listen impassively to such things?

He had thought the lecture "original." No, he had not felt there was any hostility to the speaker's patient.

My vulnerability seemed to arouse his concern. But even if I really had been driven from the lecture hall by the speaker's cynicism, such a reaction might be natural and fitting. At least one other woman member of the audience had felt the same.

Our argument ran aground on the observation that I had just stood up and seemed to be at the end of my tether.

A seminar on perversions made me angry. I was disturbed by the extremely authoritarian and stifling style in which the seminar was conducted. The chairman spoke nearly the entire time, and then asked for various people's opinions and noted them down (for later publications). Moreover, the term "perversion" did not seem to be precisely defined; it even appeared to include fellatio.

My remarks bearing on the polymorphously perverse drew forth patronizing masculine grins. I was so angry I couldn't listen any more; I'd driven forty kilometers for this! My analyst took pains to try and make me understand. To some extent, he did seem to agree with my criticism and smiled at it, but he insisted that I must see others' point of view and not take it all so seriously. He soothed me, so that I felt I had been unjustly categorical.

I found myself almost constantly at odds with the representatives of pharmaceutical firms, and a state of severe tension often arose. I thought they were unwilling to answer questions and listen to my arguments; however, I still believed in their professional responsibility. Others got on all right with them.

My anger, my fury troubled my analyst. I knew I was reacting "too strongly," and I would do better to be more like other people in this respect: Less combative people, people who felt more at ease with themselves. He realized that there were problems now and then, but why did I get so worked up? I could sense his tendency to calm me down, like a subtle prohibition of my sense of outrage. He was being solicitous.

I tried not to let things affect me so much, I tried not to take them "so seriously," to stand at "more of a distance" from my own emotions, to deal with my experiences in a more thoughtful and controlled way. But there was much that simply hurt: The sudden death of patients after difficult heart surgery; their panic-stricken faces, wet with sweat, before lesser operations.

Previously, I had felt dissatisfied with my lack of decisiveness and my political inertia. Now I felt that there was a suggestion of acting out, a display of auto-aggression, masochism, opposition to the father, and so forth, about those who did have firm opinions and spoke up forcefully for them—even if it was not to their advantage. That was how I saw them at the time. I hardly listened any more to the actual remarks of a speaker at a conference or congress expressing opinions which went against those of the group 'currently acknowledged opinions, that is), and were not all wrapped up in fine foreign terms; I was too busy figuring out what personal problem might have been motivating and sensitizing him, making him rise to his feet at what particular point, before or after or against what other speaker. With increasing practice, I could almost always find something. All strong effect became suspect to me; intensity showed a basic and insufficiently resolved problem in the person I was observing.

There was one congress which made me feel very discouraged. It so happened, though aptly enough for the times, that almost all the patients whose cases were described had grown up during the war, in decimated families, traumatized by experiences of flight, etc. I was sad to find how little these people had changed during long and intensive analysis; it was quite hard to find any kind of development in their case histories, and any improvements seemed artificially constructed. I had the sense of a gentle melancholy which remained unchanged, and did not seem to be touched at all by the course of analysis.

I also felt horror on reading the book about Freud's wolf man. A macabre tale: What a life, what torment, what effort to survive at all, and that after intensive, first-class, long-term analysis! If analysis could have no greater effect—well, it was dreadful, enough to make you despair. I would not like to lead such a life. Imagine living on in such torment only for the sake of the analyst. I thought it a horror story pure and simple. And yet the wolf man struck me as so vital; I liked his instantly renting an apartment when he had only seen a woman, with a second key for her. He was quite steadfast in this, and would not have his idea of the woman spoiled by interpretations and therapeutic considerations (transference: She was a nurse at the hospital where he was being treated). Indeed, they did get together later. I thought he was much more decisive, active and steadfast than the majority of the men I knew, who reflected, hesitated, considered. The wolf man had felt such trust in his analyst, and of course he had had the best analyst of all. A man I knew who was in analysis himself said he couldn't finish the book; if that was all there was to it, you might as well go hang yourself right away.

When we were dealing with my relationships with men, the basic tenor of the discussion was about the emotional detours I had taken, the maneuvers I had adopted, in order to avoid commitment to one person or to marriage, the anxieties and defense mechanisms which had led me repeatedly to those men with whom there was no chance of family life. Fear of ties seemed to be the reason why I had chosen lovers who lived a long way off, narcissistic deficiency the reason why I reacted so positively to social status, a happy way with words, intellectual charm (but you can develop brilliance in yourself, I was told, you have it in yourself, why do you need such compensation? Do you feel you're not worth anything without it?). Conscious of my own intellectual and emotional emptiness, I sought out men of renown; in conformance with my feelings of inferiority, my minimal ability to stand on my own feet, my almost "as if" personality. "Why can't you appreciate a man who is not so dazzling?" My little history seemed to show that I avoided reliable men. How is it, I was asked, that someone like yourself, so reliant on warmth and dependability, makes for emotionally wary men? My relationships could be entered on the debit side of the account, when set against the criterion of marriage/family/children.

I actually was impressed to see how poorly I had managed with men, how little I had got from my relationships, how cold and grudging my lovers had been to me. (I had no standard of comparison with other women.) I felt rotten, miserable, deprived, and bewailed the fact.

After my vacation I attended a hospital meeting at which we discussed a girl with a severe generalized infection; everyone was worried about her, for her case was a matter of life and death, and her lungs, liver, heart and kidneys had all suffered damage. So far her fever had not responded at all to treatment with antibiotics, even rare and particularly effective ones. I thought of a fungus, which seemed quite a likely diagnosis, judging by laboratory tests and the progress of the sickness, but my idea was rejected impatiently: Pneumonia of this nature was never caused by a fungus. I still hesitated: You couldn't tell for absolutely certain from an x-ray. Later I asked how the case was going. It turned out that the presence of fungus in the patient's blood culture and urine had been detected several times, but was interpreted as the result of contamination. So then they decided to treat her for fungal infection. I was left, however, with a strong feeling of having said something unpleasant, inappropriate. Yet it was easy to understand how, amidst such widespread concern, fungal sepsis had been discounted, as the worst possibility of all. Drugs to combat it had only recently been developed, and they were risky, not having been fully tested. A diagnosis of fungal sepsis was practically a death sentence. Thus the general repression was understandable. I had not participated in it because I had been on vacation. However, I was upset by the reception of my remark. It was as if I had expressed some very troublesome, disgusting, unfortunate and reprehensible notion. When we discussed this point in analysis, we concentrated on the way I made my statement: Had it been with overtones of aggression, triumphantly, competitively, or what?

Intravenous antimycotics had just been developed by two rival firms. The basic substances were not precisely the same, so that one could conclude that their toxicity also differed. As it was a question of the girl's survival, with her heart, kidneys and liver only just functioning, though it was her heart, relatively speaking, which was in most danger, we tried to find out from both pharmaceutical firms what side effects were known to exist, particularly any affecting the heart. The regional representative of one firm said that no damage to the heart had ever been observed, so we used that drug, and the heart soon became enlarged. After some anxious and eventually furious and threatening telephone calls, a higher-ranking spokesman for the firm admitted that "in isolated cases" damage to the heart muscle had indeed been noted. We took the patient off the drug, gave her the rival firm's drug, which had a rather different spectrum of side effects, and she survived.

I was outraged that we had no access to the results of the firms' drug trials (probably because millions were at stake). I asked, at the hospital meeting, if such things ought not be published. Wasn't there any kind of authority, say the Ministry of Health, to which one could turn if need be? I met with solid rejection. Basically, it seemed, everything was all right. I remained alone in my outrage. It was the same in my analysis. My analyst acknowledged the reality of my feelings, but as if they were those of a pubescent girl. He was concerned about their extent and the form they took, the effect I had on others, the possibility of my acting out and repeating.

Once he heard, from other people, that they were pleased with me at the hospital, and told me so. It was a valid and admissable description if it came from *other people*.

Artificial respirators quite often broke down. They had to be taken apart to be disinfected, and now and then they were incorrectly reassembled. The reassembly process was complicated, involving possible sources of error; anyway, the fact was that they frequently failed to function properly, thus harming the patients using them, sometimes fatally. Appeals for better care and greater control helped, but there were still cases of harm to patients, which were then regarded as personal failures on the part of individual members of the staff.

I thought the firm manufacturing the respirators was responsible; they had the monopoly, and ought to have made the apparatus safer to use by means of color coding, or marking the separate parts in some way or other. In any case, the firm ought to know about it; it was possible that they hadn't even been informed of the frequent incidents. People involved in them felt bad about their carelessness, and kept their mouths shut. After several telephone calls, I managed to get in touch with a senior doctor, who said he would discuss the matter in a fortnight's time with the firm's representative. I was rather annoyed,; somebody ought to do something at once— change or test all the apparatus. If we had so many instances of failure here in this one hospital, what was the general picture like? However, the senior doctor was the person in contact with the firm, and he preferred to deal with the matter himself. In some irritation, he suggested I write it all down and let him have it. Couldn't I speak to the representative myself? This seemed undesirable. Later, I came up against a tangle of conflicting authorities, involving two professors, senior doctors, departments whose interests were or were not to be promoted, financial contributions, loans of equipment from the manufacturing firm; I was exhausted.

I had no support from anyone around me, neither from any group in the hospital nor from any analyst. My outrage seemed perilously close to querulousness, trouble-making, a failure to integrate and fit in happily.

Other analysands were also inclined to ascribe dissatisfaction and excessive irritation to themselves and their unresolved problems. But scarcely anyone else I knew fought back. In theory, I also thought it correct to free one's sense of outrage from its neurotic aspects, so that one reacted only in an appropriate way to any given situation.

But in my analysis, the real aspect hardly seemed to exist at all.

If my analyst had had any really telling objection to make, I might have been able to understand him, or at least incorporate it. His rejection, his skeptical and laborious reconstruction discouraged and crippled me. So much was left vague. Did he think I was

repeating my relationship with my brothers in that I tended to react aggressively to everything institutional (mothers and fathers)?
It wasn't really clear. "Don't you think that...?" he would say. The
uncertainty of his tone, the way he put the question was irritating.
Sometimes I felt sure what he meant, but then again the opposite
would seem to be the case. Sometimes he seemed to be forcing a
decided opinion into a detached, analytic form of questioning, but
later I would think he really meant it that way; sometimes he
seemed to have changed his mind entirely. However, I could never
actually prove it. All I knew for certain was that he regarded my activities with anxiety and suspicion. Not that I was particularly active at this time; I often dragged about for days or weeks in a state
of exhausted depression.

Basically, life wasn't worth living; I was rotten all through, full of
repulsive, hateful, evil, repressed-mendacious qualities, hardly
able to like anyone at all. My last positive feelings had turned out
to be defense. It was a poor prospect. This was the truth, the basis
underneath my conscious feelings; this was what I had found with
the help of analytic techniques. No one could easily shake that
certainty.

I agreed with those who judged me in similar terms; they seemed
to be in the right, but it kept me at a distance from them too. With
those who were well-disposed to me, I could at least dispute, argue,
prove my inner rottenness, or else I could put up a pretense until
they too saw through me. I had sometimes offered resistance as
more and more bad qualities and traits were uncovered, but that
was part of it too, proof of the defense mechanism which had previously spared me such insight.

A woman acquaintance who had been analyzed was unwilling to
believe my sad lack of relationships, considering the spontaneous
way I could make contact with children and so-called ordinary people. Hadn't I had some good relationships at some time in my
youth, she asked? That kind of ability didn't arise entirely of its
own accord. Or was it that I needed some kind of social distance
before I could feel at ease? Did I have to be sure I was definitely superior? She noticed the discrepancy between the way I got on with
my (analytic) colleagues and with other people.

I was surprised: I didn't think I was any good at making human
contacts now. My general irritability had done away with that abil-

ity. A friend's chubby little son had drawn back from me; I constantly had a bad conscience, fearing I wouldn't be able to communicate with my child patients and might treat them too
perfunctorily or too roughly. My analyzed colleague, however, was
an intelligent woman, and I took her seriously. I came to the conclusion that I was living in mortal terror of intimacy; I could keep
my fears at bay, to some extent, with people who were out of the
reckoning as close friends because of their social class or their age,
when the distance between us was made clear anyway by my white
coat, my position, and so on. I got on much better with hospital
porters and cleaning women than with my colleagues, too. At least,
there was greater familiarity between presumption. It was only my
social equals who seemed to feel that in me, and with whom I had
problems.

I didn't have to call up my anxieties, my secret need to stand at a
distance or my distancing ploys with those who were already distant from me; there was no need for me to fend such people off.
That was why I made easy contact with them; I needed to bring my
anxieties into play, along with those sharp remarks which served to
put a distance between me and other people, only when they were
on my own level. It was really quite a striking phenomenon. A
Greek cleaning woman, with perfect naturalness, pressed into my
hand plastic sacks for use in my move.

My easy contact with such people was now analytically clear to
me, but it gave me no reason to like myself. My generally better relationships with my Hessian godmother and with nonacademics
were suspect.

The official aims in my career would normally be to become a
medical director, head of a department, superintendent of a hospital, a lecturer; in any case, to have some authoritative function. El-
evated above other people, I would then have to lead, to correct—if
only medical reports—to give orders, if perhaps discreetly. Everyone, particularly the emotionally mature who had really resolved
their Oedipal conflicts instead of just surrendering, strove for leadership and responsibility. I intensely disliked the idea. I had felt uncomfortable, in my first post as an assistant physician, when a
nurse with her tray of syringes accompanied me around the ward;
from her disappointment when I went around on my own, I realized that I had deprived her of the privilege of accompanying the

doctor on ward rounds. This seemed understandable, as was my surprise at this. Even as a ward physician, I seldom cared for doing my rounds when I had to give directions, make pronouncements, and talk to patients in front of a number of people. I was never at ease; I felt unnatural. I preferred to discuss cases with the aid of patients' charts in the nurses' room, and then speak alone to the patients. And this was understandable, in itself. I could also rationalize the fact that I did not like making use of medical students or those assistant physicians assigned to me, as most people did, by saying that after all they were studying, and ought not be employed in routine work. However, there was emotional force in my aversion to such practices. Why did I never feel at ease when I had leadership and responsibility? I thought it was only teaching, giving orders and instructions without supplying sufficient reasons for them that I didn't like; I could work all right in my own way and feel happy in my job. I did not like giving orders when I encountered opposition and lack of understanding; I did a lot of explaining, and I felt unhappy if my explanation was accepted reluctantly or not at all. But anyway it seemed that you were better respected if you just made decisions in a flash without offering any comment; I could see that many people decidedly preferred and expected this approach. Yet I felt inhibited and out of my element when I adopted it. Still, it was obviously necessary, at least sometimes and with some people. Analytically, however, and in spite of my logical reasoning, some doubt remained; if a certain amount of the authoritarian style of leadership was called for, or at least was usual, why couldn't I just behave that way, casually and without feeling too many scruples? Why couldn't I make more use myself of the reality of the hospital situation as I found it, why couldn't I adapt to it? I had no basic objection, either, to working with a more experienced and older colleague if I liked him. What mattered to me was the atmosphere, the mood. My ability to work well partly depended on it; I found it hard to summon up much energy entirely of myself, alone, without some stimulating personality close by. I could do it, but it was an effort.

My dislike of, and marked lack of enthusiasm for, the idea of being in charge of anything (a medical team, a ward, a department, a hospital, etc.) was still noticeable. I couldn't even imagine feeling comfortable in a practice employing several persons whom I would have to control and supervise, or only as an emergency measure. I began to feel embarrassed the more I realized how little I felt ready to exert authority. My reasoning that I felt inadequate and inferior to experienced nurses who had been working in hospitals for years, because they had developed more feeling and instinct than I could possibly do in so short a time, whereas I must limit myself to knowledge acquired from my studies, was not entirely convincing. Why did I find it so hard to direct people, to give orders? After all, there were many unpleasant tasks that just had to be done, and it was not worth getting emotionally agitated about them.

My reluctance, however, showed how deeply rooted my old ties and inhibitions still were; I was too childlike and immature, I was determined not to be in authority, I couldn't (did not want to) get any pleasure from it, and didn't even want to take it on in a neutral way, I was still subordinating myself to big brothers, mothers, to higher authority, without realizing it emotionally at all. I felt only reluctance; I could feel much at ease in my child's role too. I had got on very well with many nurses, limiting myself to my own particular tasks and leaving their usual routine to them, without interfering. I had done well to take their finely-tuned perceptions seriously when they were worried about something, and yet I had left them to shoulder a good deal of responsibility—more than others did, anyway. I had let them exercise the authority of a good mother. There was one very energetic nurse, who had much wartime experience, with whom I had felt particularly at ease in emergency situations; she was pleased when I reacted quickly, and I learned a lot from her. That is what frequently happened. But another nurse quite plainly expected me to set the tone for the whole ward, be its driving impulse and determine the tempo. I didn't care for that. "You are competing for the role of the child," I was told, but I couldn't do anything about it. Discussing the problem was likely to make the atmosphere worse. I came to wonder if the nurse wouldn't simply have preferred a man as the doctor on the ward: An understandable feeling in itself, since she saw almost no one but women in the nurses' living quarters and at work. Even my analyst wondered if she might just be feeling envious and discontented. But his first interpretation had been that I was competing with her for the role of the child; I was the one who, despite criticism and all the difficulties it caused, simply did not want to grow up, out of spite, who rebelled against setting the tone for the ward, smiling, chasing people around, imparting verve to the place. And yet, I could do these things. My emotional underdevelopment troubled me, but I was not able to change it. I had remained an immature daughter who didn't want to give up her childish privileges.

Some old friends of mine used to go skiing every spring: one of them complained that I agreed to join them every time they went, and then for some reason or another I backed out. I realized that I was troubled by the idea of breaking a leg, with the accompanying blood and pain and splintering bone. At first I ascribed my fear to the fact that I'd broken a ski last time I went skiing, but had felt no such inhibitions at the time; I had gone on skiing, with borrowed equipment. The vividness with which I pictured the blood was disturbing, and was new to me. Perhaps I had carried courage and lightheartedness too far, and then my lack of interest came to the fore, as through a back door; or I rationalized that a skiing holiday was expensive—as the sun is in winter, anyway. Plausible, but unpleasant and impeding.

It was not just my love relationships that had become mediocre (a description which is scarcely adequate for my carefully thought-out, controlled feelings); my everyday relationships, my ordinary contacts were becoming tenuous; trivial, more restrained, formal and wary than before. I either had discussed, or would soon be discussing, what really moved me in my analytic sessions; I hardly needed anything more. Besides, relationships outside analysis were risky; I might expose my weaknesses. Now that I had discovered so many unpleasant facts about myself, it was to be expected that others would draw their own conclusions concerning the deeper meaning of my spontaneous impulses. I did that myself, with other people. If in doubt, they would stop to wonder what it meant when I laughed, or was excited or sad, or whatever other way I reacted. "How lovely to see you," says someone—ah, so he isn't really pleased or he wouldn't be so emphatic about it! Every effusive remark made by oneself or others can easily be explained as defense against an opposite impulse (which makes conversation with people who have been analyzed a particularly intricate affair, since they are taking this into account the whole time).

There was a story in the newspaper about a man who killed his brother with an axe, and then called the police in a law-abiding manner, explaining, "We were forever quarrelling—someone just had to put a stop to it." A man I knew (who hadn't been analyzed) roared with laughter; I dared not laugh myself, but was quick to diagnose death wishes directed against his brother; our mood was spoiled because of my inhibited neutrality.

Going all out to do something, feeling wholeheartedly pleased or enthusiastic about something, just letting fly—all this became suspect. There must be something else behind such a strong impulse. And among the analytically trained, who know about such things, it could be particularly embarrassing. Safest to hold back.

*   *   *

Shortly after this I found I had to revise or at least modify some previous interpretations: My superior at work really was very erotically orientated, and it was not just my imagination or the result of my own deficiency that I'd obsessively ascribed an interest in sex to him; he often did think of sex and nothing else, and in connection with a number of different women. No doubt I held fewer attractions for him now, with the reserve induced by my analysis.

I also discovered that an affair whose existence I had suspected earlier, but which I'd then put down to my own wishful thinking, writing the idea off as unreal, actually did not exist after all, or at least it did now. My instinct had been right both times. My first analyst was the one who had been wrong at the time, or else I had misunderstood her, or else maybe she had drawn my attention only to the role of my wishes, without actually ruling out the possible reality. But in any event, the effect of her intervention had been to make me totally exclude reality, convinced as I then was that my own hungry projection made me see chimeras.

And I found that there were people who no longer thought my first analyst quite as warmhearted, quite so perfect as they once thought. Some of them, too, felt she had partly misunderstood them and kept them at an emotional distance; they felt they'd been treated poorly. There was one woman in particular, whose attachment to her I had thought analytically ideal, and who now looked at me in surprise when I cautiously broached the subject. Very likely some of that sibling rivalry that exists between analysands said it was just that she was a very different type from me, and maybe she had had difficulty coping with the fact. To me, this sounded like slander—I hadn't thought that far myself. However, he was qualified. The friendly man who had told me I was in my "honeymoon period" with my first analyst admitted that he himself had been recovering from a previous bad experience of analysis when she analyzed him; it had cost him some pains to build up his self-confidence again. I could thus understand his attachment and gratitude to her very well. She might be different with men, anyway.

Possibly my poor "mother transference" wasn't so poor after all, or at least not in relation to my mother. Perhaps my feelings had been perfectly adequate.

The situation with regard to my training now brought me both insecurity and enlightenment. As the regional committee had given me the go-ahead, half a year earlier, I inquired after about six months, just to be on the safe side. I encountered reproachful surprise: Didn't I know the closing date for applications? I had overrun it by a week. Naturally I ought to have sent in a new application. But I had duly applied last term, I said; was there any confusion about that? No, but I ought to have kept to date. I had been relying on my former application, since the fact that it hadn't been accepted was due only to inadequate knowledge on the part of the two regional representatives. I could scarcely believe that my overrunning the date by a week was a serious objection. However, apparently everything was now fixed and I couldn't be fitted in. Back came my old suspicion: I felt I had been tricked.

My "paranoid" feelings again occupied many sessions of analysis. Had I actually any real chance of being allowed to take my examination? Weren't they just making excuses, hadn't they really and finally rejected me long ago? People aren't usually so persnickety over dates. Yet again, I was told, I simply must face facts; it was the facts I had difficulty in accepting. I felt upset because no one had reminded me of the application date: Neither my training supervisor nor my analyst. But evidently this was too much to ask; I should have dealt with the matter myself and not bothered other people with my own chaotic attitude towards paperwork. I ought to have made sure I sent in a new application form and checked the date personally. I had to go along with that; I was angry with myself for my carelessness. All the same, wasn't this sudden persnickety refusal to give way purposely directed at me—or were all

Swabians like that? My analyst sympathized to some extent, and
did not think much of the whole procedure. However, he said, I really should have seen to the matter myself; I'd neglected reality.
There was no justification for my paranoid feelings. A moderate
obsessional neurosis is not a bad thing in life, said my analyst, ironically, but I came up with such a quantity of illogical and atypical
coincidences; this feeling expressed my basic paranoid attitude.
Well, in the future I would remember what the Swabians were like!

I sent in my next application a term later, in good time and on a
fresh form. It was rejected by the regional committee on the
grounds that "they didn't know enough about me."

Once more, I could have cried. Six months earlier they had
known enough about me to recommend me for re-admission. And
now they didn't? What on earth was actually going on? If they
were really determined not to admit me, then I wished they'd say
so, and not keep me in a permanent state of doubt and uncertainty.
A considerable amount of my analysis, after all, was occupied with
the matter, which was weighing it down, making it seem implausi-
ble. Why did they treat me with such lack of logic? If I knew they
were rejecting me in principle, then I could make my own arrangements accordingly. I felt they had been lying to me.

My analyst came in for his share of this new shock. My so-called
paranoid feelings had turned out to be based on fact. How could he
have interpreted my perfectly correct reactions as paranoid over the
years? The entire thrust of my analysis, the frequent interpretation
of my feelings as paranoid, my supposedly distorted perception of
facts (a supposition mainly founded on that interpretation)—all this
just wasn't correct. I ought to have listened to *myself* all this time, to
my perceptions, I should have trusted *myself* and not those interpretations, nor the entire analysis. Now I was very unsure of myself, and
yet none of what he'd said was really fact. It had cost me a great deal
to submit to his interpretations and accept them as the truth, and in
exchange I had given up my own self, my own convictions. Now I
felt the internal truth of the analysis was wrecked. And what about
my deep, early disturbance, which was supposed to have distorted
reality? What of that was true? Why had I developed my capacity for
suffering? Where else had he been wrong? What was really so sick
about me? I had been very sensitive, that was all. What other analytic insights must I now revise?

My analyst was clearly concerned about this new rejection, and about the form it took. However, he responded to my furious reproaches by interpreting it as "a self-fulfilling prophecy." He still thought my perceptions paranoid; it was my own doing that they had now been confirmed and had taken on substance. I had acted in such a way that they had to reject me, so that I'd be right. I might well have caused the rejection with my anxious whining. I was too worn down to defend myself any further. I had probably been correct in sensing reservations about me right at the start; nobody had had the courage to tell me the truth, and then the authorities concerned had changed, and finally no one felt directly responsible any more—or I suppose.

Yes, there was such a thing as self-fulfilling prophecy. But I had long felt I was more sensitive than my analyst in many areas, and I had taken that into account from time to time.

All this time he had never considered the possibility that my perceptions might actually contain a grain of truth. And now that they had turned out to be justified, he thought of a tricky way around it. Couldn't he at least see that the inconsistency didn't lie in me alone, that there was, at the very least, a decided lack of logic in their suddenly saying they didn't know me well enough?

My basically paranoid attitude had been regarded as a large part of my disturbance. What was the right way to see it now? Why hadn't the "Westwall" atmosphere ever been clarified, or why hadn't it disappeared? What might be his part in causing it? Perhaps I was not a poisonous snake and cause of his countertransference? Had he, perhaps, stumbled over problems of his own? Perhaps the entire deviant analysis and his rejection of me were not *my* problem at all? Had he, perhaps, become hung up on his own personal problems, so that I had been given distorted and contrived interpretations?

At any event, I could make nothing of his interpretation now. The way questions having to do with my training had kept intruding into my analysis and had become so important had certainly made it unnecessarily difficult and complicated. But after all, they were part of my personal environment, and as such they belonged to it. It must be possible to deal with them.

I felt desperately angry and wanted clarity at last. I went to see my supervisor, who expressed surprise at the verdict of the meeting, and said he didn't understand the reasons for rejecting my application either. He referred me to another analyst. I thought, reading between the lines, he believed it was some personal matter between me and the other analyst. He was friendly, tried to offer something by way of explanation ("local tastes"—"You don't conform to the group") but this seemed to be his personal view and not an official opinion. His remark, "Why can't you let people love you?" struck home. So much of all this had to do with my neurosis. They didn't like me here. Indeed, why had I never felt really at ease in the group atmosphere with other analysands? Why had I always felt there was something severe, bleak, anxious and immature about it? Why could I not appreciate or like the look of any of my fellow-analysands as men? I had explained this to myself by saying that the men in our group had tacitly adopted a boyish, pre-genital, civil sort of tone, an atmosphere into which flirtation didn't fit, apart from such maliciously lecherous, depreciatory skirmishes as you might expect in an officers' mess, and so I was right not to feel at ease with them. Was my distancing myself, my inability to appreciate them, the reason why I wasn't liked here? An echo of my lovelessness? The remark now offered by way of interpretation gave some sense to the whole thing again, showed a connection with my neurosis. It was the problem, not anything fundamental. Perhaps I really had been working towards being thrown out. My fears that nobody took me seriously enough to tell me the whole truth, and nobody was really interested in the course of one analysis, were to some extent relieved.

Just to clear things up, I did make an appointment to see the man responsible for rejecting my application. It went badly. I left his room in a state of pain and confusion, feeling systematically rejected, a dangerous and disgusting creature to be held at an arm's length. I couldn't understand how anyone could so treat an adult person who was, after all, capable of insight. His point was, "We don't know enough about you," and however hard I questioned him I could get no farther. I just had to understand it, he said. I sat down in the nearest café and wrote until my muddled head was clear.

At least I was now sure that these people were not going to readmit me. They didn't want me here, and they wouldn't tell me why. I had to take that into account. I thought I had been treated dishonestly; analytically I thought it was criminal; it made me furious. After all, I had to make my own professional arrangements. It was about this time that my analyst moved to another town. I made up my mind that I would go over the whole thing again there in peace, in more relaxed circumstances. And there were a few people who were so friendly towards me, so easy and natural, that my general doubts were soothed.

But there was a crack in the basis of trust I ought to feel in my analysis. I thought "self-fulfilling prophecy" too smooth and glib an explanation. I began to trust my own impressions, perceptions and ideas again. At the hospital, I had learned a painful lesson: I myself was the only person I could rely on. If I wanted to remain to some extent clear of tangled interests, I must listen carefully to myself, my own brain, take note of my own responsibility; on no account must I blindly follow those in authority. They had their own interests, which didn't always run parallel to those of the patients.

Even if I had sometimes appeared extremely disturbed in analysis, there was nothing wrong with my perceptions in ordinary daily life.

Four times, my analyst had judged my feelings about my training to be paranoid: Always the same feelings. I felt something—he explained that I was mistaken; but I did feel it was so, I insisted—yes, he said, and that was just where my disturbance lay. And so I had generalized my false perceptions, relating them to all my sensations.

However, my feelings *had* been correct; my intellectual submission had been wrong and pointless. Was it based on his own inferior sensibility? Had I felt more than he did, more accurately and surely? Were my perceptions beyond the range of his—as with a bat, which hears higher frequencies than the human ear can catch?

The other analyst had partly confirmed my perceptions. "You don't conform to the group." "Why won't you let yourself be loved?" (With whatever reservations I took this remark, it did confirm my feeling that I was not popular here.)

In more real circumstances, I would never have accepted the humiliation of being rejected four times in a row. It was undignified.

In addition, my analyst had struck again and again at the trauma arising from my history, with the "Westwall" mood and his negative counter-transference, with his attitude of aloof weariness and his irritability. I had felt it; I didn't have to deduce it from the way he coughed or turned up late. I no longer believed I sensed things in a distorted manner only in analysis and not outside it, though that would certainly have been the ideal analytic situation— unadulterated neurosis concentrated within fifty-minute sessions.

Perhaps my first analyst's move had actually confirmed me in my trauma, and that was why I had been thrown so badly off balance?

All this time, he had not really managed to clear up the matter of the "Westwall" mood, or get rid of it. That horrible feeling re- curred again and again. Sometimes, when I discussed it with him, he reacted disbelievingly, and said he really felt no such thing now. Perhaps he was right, but I noticed it; possibly because of my "schizophrenic" sensibility, or as a burned child fears the fire. Per- haps he actually didn't notice the evasive maneuvers I employed to avert the tension.

I frequently felt pressure and constriction behind my breast- bone, and had to cough, bringing up thick mucus painfully and with difficulty. Sometimes the whole area behind my breastbone was burning, as it does in a classic case of bad flu. I imagined my trachea red, sore and inflamed, like the tracheas I had seen when studying pathology, distended by viral infections about which noth- ing could be done. I found it hard to get my breath, and coughing brought little relief. I felt as if something in myself, in my lungs, were destroyed, right behind my breastbone. I once had an x-ray done because the condition was so long in clearing up and made me uneasy, but there was nothing to be seen.

I also had this sore, painful feeling quite often without any real urge to cough, just by itself. As if something were rotating inside me, crushing everything in its path, and there was already a raw cavity of ruined flesh inside my chest. A poem by Gottfried Benn upset me: A poem about mice nesting in the rib cage of a woman's corpse. A destructive, rotating bullet, like the one that had killed my father? Or one set with iron spikes that made everything raw, leaving torn red fibers of flesh? Something like the head of a spiked mace? My vivid imaginings alarmed me. This was not like me; I didn't want to feel such things. But it hurt all the same, and trou- bled my breathing; something in me was injured and was gradually being destroyed, bloodily and painfully. My feelings were non- sense; I was exposed to many infections.

It frightened me that the idea could take root in me, when I knew very well it was nonsense. All the same, I felt the pain, and soreness, and urge to cough, just as if I did have a large bloody cavity inside me.

Sometimes everything seemed very hard. The moment I came into my analyst's room I would feel that dreadful mood of indifference. I could expect no sympathy then. "Analysis is language; do please verbalize." But what if I couldn't, and he didn't really want to listen either? What if he felt revulsion the moment I came into my room, saw me as someone to be rejected and kept at an arm's length? I was supposed to accept his evaluation of reality. It was a great effort to struggle. But obviously, even in this context, I gave an impression of being stable, robust and indefatigable, just as I did outside. I was well aware of this: I seldom aroused sympathy. People didn't readily notice when I was exhausted—that is, close friends did, but not people at work. My first analyst had told me, "You're not as stable as you seem."

But what could I do about it, when I kept on saying—verbalizing—expressing my conviction that I would soon come to the end of my tether, and he didn't believe me? If I said I really had almost exhausted my strength, and I aroused no sympathy at all, just irritated rejection of my demanding behavior? The worst of it was his cold rejection. There was no trace of friendliness left. What was I to do, what was I to change in myself? What was so bad about me? Was it normal for me to spend whole weekends in tears? Was this the way a proper analysis ought to go, leaving me feeling destroyed or at least damaged after a session? He might at least recognize my exhaustion, my pain; instead of showing such casual, sneering coolness, almost audibly sighing with relief when I left. If I asked probing questions or complained, the atmosphere became even worse. I knew quite well at such times that he would be glad to be rid of me, was only tolerating me, but would not, out of decency, end the analysis on his own initiative. But could he not at least see my desperation, my seriousness, my efforts? Was all that so very evil and vicious, such a denial and indeed distortion of reality? Why did he feel such disgust?

I obviously had to see it through. And when I was in a calmer mood, the atmosphere was easier to endure. It sometimes dispersed altogether. But it hurt me, it injured me, as if with many tiny little pinpricks.

Sometimes I felt like hating myself for my inertia, my painful, edgy, spineless resignation—or else like crawling away to hide.

And at times I could happily have murdered him. I said so, too. I could well imagine shooting him; after all, when someone felt as beaten down as I did, it would be a healthy, life-saving reaction, something I ought to do before I was entirely destroyed. I quoted that Sartre interview in which the analyst ended up shouting, "Help! Help!" out of the window, just because his patient had put a tape recording on. My analyst reacted very gravely. Could I really imagine doing such a thing? Yes, indeed I could. With a revolver. I said I thought I must have great ego strength to refrain from doing it. I had the urge all right; I could easily act on it if I had less self-restraint. I was rather surprised there weren't more murders in analytic situations. If someone kept slapping me down, subtly annihilating my identity, wasn't it healthy to fight back and save myself, by removing the basic, permanent threat to me from the face of the earth? My analyst was genuinely alarmed.

Just how aggressive, explosive and powerful did he think me, just how unpredictable and uncontrollable, if I really frightened him?

But I wasn't actually a raving lunatic, a real danger. I had been quite annoyed to find so much of the well brought up, good girl in myself: I was politically inactive, contenting myself with dreams. What was so alarming about me? Did he truly think it possible I might turn up for my session with a pistol, forcing a decision at gunpoint? Obviously he did. He had thought that Sartre interview funny too, once; we had already discussed it. But the fun had gone out of those intellectual pleasures.

Briefly, I thought: If I really scared him—if there was no humor or irony or playfulness involved—then surely my analysis with him had no real point. Didn't he understand my irony, my manner of ironic aggression? He really was genuinely alarmed. I was annoyed; good heavens, I wasn't some kind of highly explosive monster, I wasn't a bloodthirsty hyena. I would have done better to keep my anger to myself.

The atmosphere was scarcely endurable now. I thought he was not a man of intellectual integrity. But under pressures from outside, I put this episode out of my mind again.

After an intensive phase of the "Westwall" atmosphere, the

tension had slackened. I kept hearing tunes running through my head, several of them, in quite quick succession. I felt tired, couldn't concentrate well, spoke in a high little voice (he had once, in friendlier times, remarked that a rather deeper voice, something like Zarah Leander's, would suit me). I felt playful, not ill at ease, just rather foolish. Suddenly he blew up at the popular songs and folksongs I was humming, with scraps of their texts: I was acting like a bed wetter, he said, many small dribbles, and anyway my behavior was extremely aggressive. At first I felt hurt that he wouldn't take the words of the songs seriously, rejected them so firmly and reacted so angrily. But after a while I felt some relief to find him showing interest again all of a sudden. So he was still irritated; he wasn't as indifferent to me as he had seemed; I caused him agitation; it annoyed him when I did not express myself in a way that would be easier for him to understand. So there was something in me that still got through to him and didn't just pass him by, leaving him unaffected. He wasn't merely sitting through the sessions letting what I said bounce off him; he did feel with me.

(This taught me how viciously arrogant one can appear in showing consistent neutrality to someone, acting with "understanding" and "goodwill" which doesn't really exist. It can convey that one totally fails to take that person seriously, doesn't even think it worth losing one's temper with him. Which can imply more contempt and cause more hurt than fighting back.)

I had not hitherto noticed that my basic mood was one of aggression, but I believed it all right. I was much relieved to find his cold composure wasn't so perfect after all. I would really have liked to spend some time over those songs and their words, and the moods associated with them. I found songs haunting me a great deal just now. His remark about bed wetting was unkind, disparaging: At the wrong time, in many small dribbles, not letting go with force. I never had been a bedwetter, except once, when staying at a children's home where we were forbidden to visit the bathroom after eight at night, and I had held out as long as possible, but then lost control in my sleep. So that interpretation didn't hurt me.

All things considered, however, he had shown that he was approachable again; he was not entirely indifferent to me.

I was always in the wrong. There were some women who took an instant dislike to me when we met, uncompromisingly and without getting to know me any better. "So what did *you* do to her?" asked my analyst, when I had been exposed to a well-aimed act of aggression which found me unprotected. It was always supposed to be my fault; others were innocent. What had I done to her, what effect had my basic structure had on her? *My own* experience of the situation was secondary. He brought it up against me as if the remark had been slumbering within him all the time, just waiting to be called forth. In dubio contra reo.

Such an amount of aggression, such contempt and refusal to take me seriously had come to the surface in that woman's laughter that it really hurt me. Others present had felt its force too. It saddened me to have to keep citing other people to back up what I said. He took no notice of this perception of mine; he started from the presupposition that I had caused her reaction. Very unlikely, but surely not entirely on my own; it was her problem too. And I couldn't be held responsible for that.

But did everybody require protection from me? He had taken sides—and taken sides against me—without even hearing me out. *I* was the one who caused the traumas, I was the cause of conflict.

When I went skiing I had met a man who had then, to put it in bluntly organic terms, reacted with impotence. My analyst asked, "What did you do to him?" My dealings with him had not in fact been perfectly straightforward; he was sensitive; it had been, strictly speaking, a little power struggle. The question did make things clearer; previously I had felt I was the injured party, was half-hearted about it, and then attacked, as it were, by the atmosphere. In any event, I felt very powerful on the sexual plane. My analyst, on the other hand, instantly and without knowing the background placed the blame on me. Not even on the relationship between the two of us. For the man I met skiing had interacted with me in some manner, and my ambivalence had not come out of the blue. I thought my analyst's question very severe. Was I so very destructive? A woman who made men impotent? I did see the question as significant in itself, but the implication was awful. His opinion, a man's, bore weight; his judgment affected me.

I had had a long and beautiful dream, in which I was caressed for a long time, tenderly and pleasantly. I lay there doing nothing, just feeling good, and woke up feeling relaxed and comfortable. His comment: There was something of the teddy-bear in my passivity.

I was embarrassed. He didn't like me that way; I'd do better to be active and independent. I had made no progress in that respect; I still had passive dreams in which I was inactive and didn't move, instead of doing something wild for once in my dreams. I did not like to remember the dream any more; it was painfully revealing. I reproached myself. He himself would not have cared for a woman like me: I could tell that.

I might have seen such a dream as indicating longings, desires, a sense of something lacking; I could have taken it as wish fulfillment.

I had emerged from a brief and tentatively sexual contact with an acquaintance feeling thoroughly disenchanted; I now thought the man horrible, clumsy and inexperienced, a muddling dilettante, I thought he and his room were both aesthetically hideous; even the food he had cooked with care lay heavy on my stomach and I had left as soon as I could, unable to stand it there any longer.

What had bothered me so much, asked my analyst. Oh, the awful table in his room with its tapering legs, the feeling that we weren't on the same wavelength, he was out of sympathy with me, a dilettante. What bothered me about that? Well, I just didn't like it, it bothered me to find someone so totally inexperienced, and his whole apartment so ugly too. But couldn't I have taught him a few things? Well, I'd never been with someone like that before, and I really hadn't expected it, not at his age. It had all been so ugly and unesthetic. My analyst remembered the film "Ein Schiff wird kommen" ("A Ship Will Come In"), in which a woman had shown a man how to do it, in a friendly way; she'd helped an inexperienced man. I hadn't seen the film. She had been very kind to him, said my analyst. I could be like that too; it was one possibility, after all. But I had found everything ugly and repulsive; he suddenly turned me off. Of course I could have, for once, taken the active role. My analyst was right there.

It made me feel childish and unkind to think that I couldn't even act towards this man like the woman in the film, who had obviously been mature and maternal; she gave much to men, she helped them. My analyst had described her warmly. I was not that kind of woman.

I often used to think, in cold fury, that any ordinary person, any normal woman, any non-academic, any Indian had more sensitivity and sense of symbolism than my analyst. Folksongs contain much more of such things, and expressed much more naturally, than I could have put them in my analytic situation.

"Ein Schäfermädchen sass im Grünen
und pfluckte sich der Blumen viele.
Da dachte sie in ihrem Sinn,
ach wär ich eine Jägerin.
Kaum hatte sie es in Gedanken,
da schlich der Jäger durch die Ranken.
Er sprach zu ihr ganz liebevoll:
Mein Kind, kennst Du die Rose wohl."

(A shepherd girl sat out of doors, picking many flowers. Ah, she thought to herself, I wish I were a huntress. No sooner had she thought this than the hunter came prowling through the green shoots. Most lovingly, he said to her: My child, I'm sure you know the rose.)

The Upper Hessians, at any rate, would have known what was meant by the rose, without any interpretation or analytic training at all. A cheerful building worker once arrived, who told my mother, to "stop up the crack" between the street and the garden wall; this was self understood; and there was no need to presuppose any obsessive sexual allegation, any narcissistic deficiency in the building worker which induced him to show off sexually. He just liked the idea, and carrying it out would not have been beyond him. Or you'd hear it said, when something didn't quite fit, "A real gent ain't that fussy how he screws."

Dialogue between building workers: "Ah, what a real dumb fuck, and he stank!" "Why, he has to stink!" says the second, robustly—and surely, in his appreciation of the sense of smell, not stopping to think upon what pre-Oedipal mode of satisfaction he is pathologically fixated.

*   *   *

I was extraordinarily moved by a meeting with my first analyst, over a year after the end of my analysis with her. I had looked forward to seeing her again, but thought that my relationship with her was now a detached one. However, when I did not see her directly at the party where we were to meet, I felt quite miserable with longing, hopelessness, a sense of being alone and abandoned, separated from what mattered the most in the world. I killed time dancing formally in friendly arms, upset and in tears. When she did arrive I would have liked to sit or lie very close to her, intertwined; sitting diagonally opposite one another on chairs was not enough and only increased my yearnings. I wanted to know everything about her; her answers came slowly and were nowhere near full enough to satisfy my need. She had changed; she was wearing pants and no make-up, though her hair shone. Was she at all happy? Could I help her? Did she need anything? She seemed a little lonely, but independent. The intensity of my feeling found me unprepared; my alarm at its extent and vehemence was worse than the yearning itself. That night I hardly slept; I lay thinking, strangely moved, upset, longing, weeping. One question kept going round in my head: "How can I ever really love anyone if I'm so utterly wrapped up in her?" So mysteriously and incomprehensibly had she drawn all the love in me to herself, taken it over, as if by some ruse. Yet I had long had my doubts of her and her supposed warmth, of the way she kept her distance; by now I thought her more inclined to be cool and withdrawn. There really was no present reason for me to feel such liking and longing; it had been lurking in me unnoticed and unneeded, pointless, threatening.

In a conversation we had the next day, she said she didn't think my feelings at all surprising. After all, the break had come at a difficult time for me, and I had not yet had the leisure to work this through because of various changes (in my career, analytically, in my private life). I would have plenty of time to do so yet.

All the same, this great, monstrous and as it were subcutaneous longing and dependence that had insinuated itself into me at some point did alarm me. If it is true that early deficiencies are reactivated in analysis, thus to be worked through and assuaged, then this was all right. But could I really be sure? Suppose the mysterious bond I felt were to endure for a lifetime? Yet it was an entirely artificial relationship. If I were unlucky and did not succeed in resolving the transference, would I be true to her, without actually noticing it, all my life? And yet I did not have any reasonable grounds for such a yearning; I knew that quite well, from others as well as myself, people who thought her rather cool, detached and uninvolved, at any rate not a positive alternative to my mother, who had breastfed me for eleven months, and basically was a warmer, more loving person. I wasn't the only one to think so. The discrepancy existed; I had no reason to make attempts at transference and look for my first analyst to provide me with anything in this area. But could a transference ever be entirely resolved again? Looking at couples I knew (analyst and analysand after the analysis was completed) I felt rather skeptical. I saw so much reflex submissiveness and boyish or girlish behavior, along with so little that was bold ʼand vital, independent and daring on the one side—and on the other so much (questionable) detached mildness, such pseudo-paternal aloofness, such a natural assumption of authority and sexual neutrality. Many people who were aggressive with me lost this quality when their analysts were merely in the vicinity; they seemed to shrivel; "scared shitless," an outsider might say. However, many male analysts could be confident and aggressive entirely on their own, aside from the presence of any analysand. Sometimes I just didn't believe that it would be really possible to resolve such transference; these people seemed so strongly linked.

Mine could, of course, be described as a clear case of transference; probably my strong umbilical cord had been impeding me in life and love all this time, and I ought to be glad I could at least handle it thus. The development of a transference relationship did show that my ties with my mother had not been adequately loosened.

But I didn't want to be told how loving, intense, tender, or otherwise, my contacts ought at their best be. Such a bond as this was horrible, anyway, and I wanted none of it. I didn't want to be tied to someone not really very close to my heart, in whom I could find things to criticize. I wanted to seek out my close ties for myself, not to land in something inadvertently.

Sometimes, with my present analyst, I felt as if I were in an unhappy love affair, but without the frankness and honesty possible in such an affair (whereby one partner may say, "I don't like you, can't like you, there's someone else and it doesn't look as if that is going to change in the foreseeable future"). For in a real love affair I could have worked out where I had hurt my partner, what I had done wrong, what it was he didn't like in me, what bothered him. I could have looked at the other woman involved with him, and perhaps have understood that the two of them suited each other better and would get on better together. Such things could have been understood, however painfully.

But my partner in this affair was beyond such considerations; his reactions, likes and dislikes, impulses of rejection and anxiety, his attention, boredom or weariness were only a response to me and my behavior, the echo of my inward being. Not his own personal characteristics, for which he might have had good reasons. His counter-transference, I had discovered, comprised two elements: The feelings of people with whom I had previously been involved, whose roles and reactions I forced upon him, and his personal feelings towards me, arising from his own problems. However, it was clear that as a training analyst he had this second element under control.

Sometimes I was happy to return to my distorted sense of reality; then he was not irritated; I had not angered him with my transference and my neurosis.

The group dynamics workshop was still on my mind, an unresolved problem. I had found it useful, meaningful, illuminating, but a great many people had not. Later, my reaction to it had come up against general suspicion. But I retained some abilities I'd found within me then. I wanted to get to the bottom of the whole complex, find out about my supposed instability. I registered for another workshop, with the idea of dealing with this.

*   *   *

This course was conducted, without much zest, by three men, and I found it a strain. I encountered great hostility towards women, hardly recognized at all by our instructors; even in the exercises we did, which were good and instructive in themselves, the man-woman relationship was emphasized (i.e., female subservience). I did have several very intense experiences, which were of significance for my analysis. (They sound "crazy" out of context, but in the circumstances they were not unusual.)

1. The firm and solid rock of the Swiss mountains seemed to me unreal, incredible: I tried it with my foot, but it didn't wobble, did not give way, explode or collapse. I recalled falling, exploding air raid shelters; death caused by collapsing buildings, suffocation,

devastating explosions sending everything flying into the air, so that it was destroyed, lost, never to be found again. I thought of everything dying, dissolving, coming apart.

2. Brown cows—not black and white cows such as I was used to—were grazing peacefully and with infectious enjoyment in meadows full of flowers. This sight too struck me as unreal and false. Brown cows, to me, were burned, scorched cows who had only just escaped with their lives. Like those on my stepfather's farm after a fire in 1948. The cattle had been chained up; they lowed and reared, and were rescued in a partly scorched, charred state. After that I was afraid of going into dark rooms on my own for a while. Emotionally, I couldn't understand these cows now grazing so peacefully, without any fear, nothing hectic about the way they munched, or the peaceful impression they made on others, the Swiss. I lived in expectation of catastrophe: Of earthquakes, explosions, blind panic.

3. On top of a mountain, a Swiss companion pointed out the skyline, he was proud of every individual peak. Soon I couldn't bear to listen; almost all their names reminded me of ghastly accidents: The north wall of the Eiger—men falling and freezing to death; members of expeditions missing in the cold and never found again; classes of schoolchildren lost, starved, frozen; mountaineers falling to their death, bleeding, crushed; hikers falling into the crevasses of glaciers, perishing in pain, bleeding, frozen and starving. And so on. My Swiss companion was trying hard to make me like his country; I felt half sick with misery, thinking of those dreadful things, all the dead, all the disasters. And I realized how very different I was from him.

All things considered, anyway, it became clear to me that I was doing myself no good by stirring up memories of that whole insecure, chaotic period in this workshop. It weakened me and did me harm. Nor did I see any areas that I had previously not been conscious of and had avoided. Remembering more intensely did not endow me with any new qualities of feeling. It weakened me, opened old scars and paralyzed me, and I had better let it alone. I felt clearly convinced of that.

In this state of mind, I heard that my fatherly friend had been kidnapped some weeks before, and no sign of life had come from him for a long time. The parallels with Stalingrad were clear:

Uncertainty, lack of any news, a man missing and perhaps shot long since. Perhaps there would never be any more news, perhaps the end of the story would remain unknown.

It was the uncertainty I found hardest to bear. Maybe these were feelings from my first nine years of life coming back; my grief seemed too intense to be normal. None the less, it made me feel whole and strong; it was a vehement grief, having in it much confidence and assurance. I imagined my friend and how he would be spending his time: In control, planning things out. As I was used to conducting a dialogue with him, I went on writing letters and kept them to give him later.

I returned to my analysis in a state of emotional upheaval. I was a sensitive creature under strain, fighting for self-control. My analyst was kind, friendly and solicitous again. The "Westwall" mood seemed like a bad dream; my experiences interested him and he thought them significant. What I'd acquired was a distinct feeling that outside events—bombs, air raid shelters, fires, deaths, great economic uncertainty—had caused the disastrous insecurity of my early years, particularly as compared with the Swiss, who hadn't been in the war, and with people born after 1945, whom I had always considered rather different from me. I had gained the feeling that I'd do better to build a good, strong relationship that would give me security and stability. At any rate, I didn't want to go boring deeper any more. My sensibility was enough for me, and so were my insights. The early fears and disasters in my life had probably made me especially sensitive now to any fundamental threat; perhaps I found it easier to believe in the end of the world than, say, a Swiss person did; but it was all real enough; it was just that I had particularly strong feelings, and had had them early.

My analyst was already half-way through his move; analysis took place at his home on weekends. Once I arrived perspiring and thirsty, and he gave me a glass of water, which struck me as informed. Sometimes I met his wife and children; that seemed reassuring. I was grateful for his help and his analysis of me. His world seemed whole. He was a reliable father figure, one who at least was there. I felt different, and his wife again struck me as an impressive woman: Reserved and strong.

My whole body seemed somehow affected by my distraught state, and yet I could still feel basically good, intact. I had many worries, yet I felt competent. In addition, I had work which moved me a good deal. I was responsible for the delivery room and difficult births, I had to take the babies and care for them directly after they were born; I was the first person in the world to look after them. Moreover, I was responsible for all the newborn babies in the hospital, including the healthy ones.

Sometimes I thought I really couldn't be in such an emotionally shaky condition if I was coping with work of this kind. If there was ever anything likely to mobilize one's early anxieties, this kind of situation was it: Seeing helpless, unconscious women lying there bleeding, cut up by men; women in pain, pale, close to death, bleeding from their incisions, perhaps giving birth to stillborn babies. Blood, mucus, pain, fear, sometimes an orgasmic atmosphere during easier births. It suggested ideas of changelings—dwarves—bewitched children— malformations, fears of death. Moreover, being constantly on call was a burden; people had to be able to reach me at any time. I sometimes felt claustrophobic in my apartment in a new building; I would run down the corridor, do knee-bends to relieve the feeling. Was I really in such a hopeless state deep down if I could work like this? My sleep pattern altered. I might be called at any time, and found I could sleep at any time too. I got the date confused; if I had been deeply asleep and then woken several times at night, I thought days had gone by. It only needed someone to dial a wrong number and I was wide awake and ready to go. If I could do that, could I be in such a hopeless state?

My analyst thought I was identifying with my father, and that was why organic medicine was such a mainstay to me at the moment. Fashions were as they had been after 1945, too, with slightly puffed sleeves; I had a suit in which I looked like my mother. I never left home without wearing the perfume, Infini, my fatherly friend had given me. Driving the car, I would suddenly be unable to help weeping, weeping buckets; I felt ridiculous but I let the tears flow. I thought this was probably all right. Mine was not an abstract, artificial grief; my whole-body was in it, it was something warm. I wept my heart out with a friend, and it gave me confidence; something came up in me and out, and I let it come, and felt calmer.

The fact that I now felt my analyst's wife was a healthy, stable person was good, analytically speaking: My mother had almost died of starvation after 1945, and she was very ill; it was a long time before the cause of her illness was known, and the final diagnosis was a suspected brain tumor. She then deduced the probable correct diagnosis from a description of the effects of starvation and cured herself, by means of an illicitly reared and slaughtered pig. My reality was that the doctors had given up hope; we children were to be shared out among various acquaintances after her death. At the age of three, I had probably given her condition a neurotic interpretation: It was my fault, I'd sucked her dry, breast-feeding for eleven months, and I happily went on drinking even though I was then eating bread and didn't need to any more. My greedy drinking had endangered her life; her death and the dispersal of the family would be my fault. Quite possibly these guilt feelings had been added to guilt feelings over my father, and other people I knew who died around then, so that I had concluded I was altogether a bearer of death, not worth loving. It is well known that children connect early experiences of death with their own aggression and death wishes, and see them as consequences of their feelings.

If I no longer saw my analyst's wife as emaciated and on the point of death from starvation, it meant I had made inner progress and was reconstructing my mother in myself, my mother as she got better and became vital again. Perhaps I would be able to identify with her later, and to become such an adequate woman.

We were in agreement on this analytic plane. The workshop had covered all my problems, almost my entire life. And I had felt as if I were living through it all again, at breakneck speed. But the quality of my experience had been quite, quite different from what it was in analysis. What I remembered there with force, conviction and clarity had weight and cogency; more so than practically any situation in my analysis so far. In analysis, I had approached certain areas piecemeal, in small bits, I had addressed myself to them and digested them slowly, but in tiny portions, in a poor, meager sort of way, and never with such clarity. The workshop brought together my experiences in analysis. It was easy to understand why it had been a strain on me; in analysis, the whole thing was spread over hours, days, weeks, years.

Thus his relatively thin-blooded approach, his occasional coolness, were not first and foremost the result of our disturbed relationship; they were due to the method. Perhaps they were also, to some small extent, to be ascribed to my defense, which was intended to shield me from violent emotions, and quite rightly and logically too, I thought.

I buried my doubts of my analysis again.

*   *   *

The joint project we were now tackling concerned my youthful experiences, my wartime and post-war fatherless period.

There were songs relating to it: "What have they done to my song, Ma?," a song with words to the effect that, "I love the world and find it good, I don't want to see shadows everywhere," and "Get the tiger," which was particularly likely to run through my head in moments of tension and concentration, when it was hard to find a vein for a needle, when I was getting a tube into a patient, etc. I had become used to paying attention to the words, some of which were blunt and disconcerting: "Let's spend the night together," "If you see him, tell him I love him, I'd like to lie on his breast."

But I no longer dared come out with mention of those songs which really had mattered to me for a long time, songs like "Ich hatt' einen Kameraden" (I had a comrade); the Degenhardt song about the man who left a baby behind him in Paris in '42 and was shipped off to Stalingrad, "Mariechen sass weinend am Strande" (Little Marie sat weeping by the shore)—here my mind was on the baby's absent father who presumably deserts his child and yet loves it, perishing through the agency of outside forces. There was no doubt that these songs could be called trash. So could practically all the many banal hit songs which I had heard over the car radio.

"Analysis is language," he said; my world of songs, of music, notes and melodies had no place in analysis.

The street ballad type (almost always concerning abandoned young mothers-to-be) I could explain as childhood memories, and also because I knew them from village life and from my godmother. They tended to be sung when a certain mood arose on birthdays in the country, beautifully sung, with feeling, their words archaic and garbled.

My analyst was able to appreciate my gallows humor and

acknowledge it as an important ego function, a possible way of dealing with the atrocious. However, he was never quite on its wavelength; not the way my brothers were, and many of my friends, and now one of my supervisors. I could give my irony full rein with him; he laughed and didn't feel hurt. I found conversations with him a great relief. I never felt as much at ease with my analyst; his interpretations often seemed just too serious, boring down too deep, without any humor. We communicated best when I was very sad and in need of help. Perhaps I really was one of those depressive wartime children, full of unshed tears, and that was my real, genuine condition, while the potentially happy, secure, intact sides of me were just a thin veneer over castratory tendencies, aggression, hostility to men and mankind? At any rate, I was glad to have found something in myself again that my analyst liked too, an area in which I myself could take a professional and neutral interest in my analysis. These memories really did seem significant.

One friend of mine liked my songs, especially the street ballads. His paternal history was similar, and he understood me without the need for words. He did me good and supplied a deficiency in me. He sensed my lack of organization as far as paperwork was concerned, which so weighed on me, he plodded me, found a deplorable state of affairs, gave me a kick and forced me to deal with things that urgently needed doing. Hitherto I'd spoiled whole weekends thinking of all I'd left undone. The result was a troublesome, numbing weariness; the jumble of my backlog depressed me and absorbed any possible joie de vivre. I had given up trying to work this through analytically. My friend brought fresh air into the chaos; he simply forced me to tidy things up and get them done, and helped me when I couldn't manage on my own. He was cool towards all the interpretations I'd made after the workshop; they didn't convince him. With all this tension, I was eating a lot and had gained weight. "You're really chewing on something quite different, and that's why you're so fat," said my friend. His family background, he said, had made him quite familiar with the kind of tales I had to tell of my release of aggression at the hospital and the two workshops; he knew all about this sort of thing from his mother, who was successful in her own career. I could get nowhere with this, and I was surprised that he couldn't get anywhere with my interpretations, although he'd been analyzed, and that he saw things on such a curious level, one that was foreign to me. All right, he said, but why didn't I take a look at the Analytical Association; how many women were there in the top positions? An adequate proportion? Very likely none, he thought. Rather annoyed, I admitted that there was in fact just one. But I still thought this attitude odd; I hadn't come across anything like it in my analysis. It struck me as doggedly class-conscious—the class struggle on the man/woman plane. My analyst could make nothing of it either.

My friend saw nothing basically wrong with me, liked it when I was outgoing, and in my own ransacked mind I could discover parts of me that wished him well and felt concern for him. They could, of course, be explained, as father transference, which diminished and undermined them, but they satisfied me. I had at least the beginnings of a potential for love in me. Something in me did him good too, he said I made him feel refreshed and reinvigorated; so there must be some good in me.

I had many goodbyes to say: To the hospital, to my secret dreams, to people. I reproached myself for my inactivity; I'd been able to introduce far too little of a psychoanalytic approach into my work. The excessive demands of my work had totally absorbed me, and I had a continual guilty conscience over my lack of competence in organic medicine (which could have been overcome only by a great deal of reading), and over my lack of psychoanalytic competence as well. All things considered, I could have done with someone to prop me up, someone who wouldn't just be questioning everything over and over again, picking away at the neurotic element, belittling my convictions and tearing them to shreds. (Only later did I come across some of the basic literature on this subject, for instance B. Bowlby.)

And I saw no viable way of integrating a psychoanalytic point of view into my work. We were all stretched to the limit, almost constantly, and anything psychological demanded time and leisure. Moreover, I was in a permanent dilemma: If I let myself feel with and for patients, say a child having a spinal puncture—held immobile in a vise—or in a darkened room for an x-ray examination, or having a tube introduced into the stomach to pump it out after poisoning—I was left exhausted, worn out and upset. And that held things up. If I took time to explain to a child facing an operation the need for it, its reasons, the procedure itself, then I could

have used that time to dictate a backlog of letters, or read up on
something essential for me to know, or get my report written at
long last.

At any rate, I left the hospital with a bad conscience. I felt like a
failure. I had probably disappointed a number of expectations. My
positive efforts had fallen flat.

At this time of parting, my fatherly friend was released by his
kidnappers after six months. His survival, return and presence
gave me a pleasant sense of security, validating my world and my
dreams; I just felt well, as if my backbone were strengthened. I
didn't know if this was mere joy, or if I had now symbolically
worked through my early anxieties, wishes and hopes and given
them a happier ending. In any event, I had felt sad and also a little
bit crazy during this time, yet pleasurably so, and now my feelings
were validated.

*   *   *

A phenomenon concerning my relationships with men became
acute again, and occupied many sessions. It was something that
had troubled me deeply and for a long time; it occurred when I was
feeling good and enjoying life. Generally it went like this: I would
start by feeling I was liked, and then suddenly this was transformed
for me into alienation and distancing. Remarks I then made met
with no response, or only a reluctant one; I realized I was being
viewed like some strange animal. The next stage was that the man
in question would recoil if, for instance, I went up to him or made
any other such everyday contact; then came open to rejection. If I
tried to overcome the tension and alienation, and was more intense
in my approaches, I achieved the opposite of what I intended. I was
puzzled to find that this happened regularly only with some people,
while others liked me at those very times.

I had noticed it with my first lover; he always said he was frightened of me, though he didn't know why.

I caused the same reaction in the hospital. I seemed to intimidate
people and attract aggression to myself without having any idea
why. Gradually I registered that people were not treating me naturally, but with alarm, yet I did not entirely trust my impressions.
One man gave a start when I entered his office to give him the

night duty bleeper. As I had not been about to go for his throat, I was annoyed; in the end he admitted that he's felt somehow frightened of me.

It was puzzling that I never encountered this attitude in patients or in those who were clearly my superiors.

It sometimes happened at conferences that people wouldn't listen to what I said, or passed it over, or responded almost with distaste; this was always when I had thought I'd said something particularly good and clever. My ideas often went unappreciated, were hardly even listened to, but rejected as if they were repellent. Yet much of what I had just said met with general rejection, but might be put by someone else a little later, and then, after an interval, would be accepted without anyone's remembering my own remarks at all.

There had been a striking instance of this at the first workshop. We were a small and predominantly masculine group, and we were given the task of drawing up a paper; I had had some ideas, but when I expressed them they found very little favor. Some people didn't respond at all, just didn't listen. And after a while I realized what was happening: The actual content of what I had said was brought up again by someone else—a man—a little later, and immediately incorporated into the paper. I then put my mind to saying things in the expectation of hearing them taken over by a male speaker, so that I could be relatively confident that what I said would get into the paper that way. At the time I tried to explain it to myself by supposing that in the heat of the moment I just hadn't been diplomatic enough or found the right way of expressing myself, and had probably allowed an aggressive note to creep in, something stemming from earlier encounters with members of the group, or that was a family trait. Or else it was something castrating and over-confident in my manner. But now this kind of thing was happening to me in "normal" professional circumstances.

Once again, I tried my usual ways of explaining it: I was unobtrusively but efficiently repeating a family pattern set by my brothers, who had probably not taken my first attempts to talk seriously; they thought their own conversations, brother to brother, more important than listening to their little sister. And/or there was something conflicted in me, attracting aggression and contempt. After all, some women really were phallic and castrating, and masculine reactions were not unfounded. These possibilities confused me and shook my confidence. All I saw was the reaction, the end result, hard as I might try to express myself in a nicer, more diplomatic, adequate, suitable and sympathetic manner, one better adapted to the group process.

The fact that I couldn't remember any comparably painful situation with my brothers didn't prove there hadn't been one: A failure to remember, bland oblivion, could indicate repression of an especially traumatic situation.

Neither could I explain the marked way the phenomenon had occurred just now, in the first job where I'd started out with some professional qualifications. Or the way it didn't hold good with everyone. There were always a few who thought particularly well of things I said, when other participants in a discussion ignored them, and not just to comfort me either.

We couldn't understand the situation. It slightly resembled the tension of the "Westwall" mood. I noticed my analyst's efforts to spare me by keeping me away from conflicts, urging me not to be so stubborn. We would often agree that I had let some aggression creep in, that I'd been provoked or had failed to present myself with sufficient diplomacy or charm. And after all these suspicions, hints and suppositions, I was left suspecting something evil in me: My tendency to provoke conflict, my castration wishes, my hatred of men. "Much disturbance rises around you." So the norm stood outside me, in my environment.

I obviously didn't behave like other analysands. "No," he would say, in a tone of irritation, "you go talking about analysis a great deal outside." Which was true. But what was I to do with all that he didn't understand in me? With my rage, outrage, exhaustion, lack of clarity? And the remnants of my hope. Why shouldn't I try talking to other people? I might find illumination there. I might find the solution to my problems. Why was this prohibition supposed to be the rule? Why couldn't he take my intensity of feeling into account and see my unhappiness? I was more or less forced to make other contacts.

You don't need to be an analyst to see that a relationship in which one partner is constantly talking of intimate matters to third parties, discussing them and generally talking them over, is not in a very flourishing state. Obviously there's no need for further, out-

side discussion in a situation which is to any extent satisfactory. I
knew that kind of situation, too; moreover, there would be no inner
compulsion to talk any further about things which I felt were
cleared up and dealt with. My need to talk with others, therefore,
proceeded from an unanswered question.

But I felt the wagging finger of pedagogical authority always directing me back to my analyst.

How could I pack the whole of my inner life over one or several
days into fifty minutes? How could I give him so much information
that he didn't feel excluded from something, somewhere, somehow? So that I didn't incur the (at least implied) reproach of having
failed to impart something earlier, more thoroughly, or even at all?
My analyst prefaced his observations with such remarks as, "Why
are you mentioning this now for the first time? . . . You were able
to say this now because . . . What prevented you from . . . ?" and
other variations on that theme. Why such nagging and yet never
totally satisfactory curiosity about my life? Why didn't I have a
right to let something rest and come to maturity within me, or just
keep it entirely to myself? Mightn't that be exactly the thing for me
at this point?

The interpretation came pat: Mother transference . . . he
wasn't the one being so insistent, nagging, interrogating me, in-
quisitive, leaving me no private life and no secrets, it was my
mother. My mother as she had been, even if not now. My transference mechanisms caused my current misunderstanding of reality.
($[a + b]^2 = a^2 + 2ab + b^2$; therefore . . .)

But why did I keep on feeling this way? There'd been an echo of
it in his annoyance at my talking to outsiders, giving them access to
areas that belonged within analysis. I really did sense curiosity on
his part; I really had felt annoyance, too, in realizing that he liked
me to talk about congresses, describe what went on, give him background information that wouldn't otherwise have been accessible
to him. I really had sensed his pride in being well-informed when
he once mentioned that he had heard good things about me. Obviously he acted in this way with other analysands too.

It was a fact that my mother often knew rather too much about
me, and that I sometimes had to ward off her interest. Being very
sensitive, she noticed a lot; for instance, there was absolutely no
way I could conceal it from her when I was in love, she just knew,

and would laugh at any attempts of mine to deny it, dissemble or explain. She sniffed it out, relying on her feelings, which were to be trusted. However, I hadn't felt terrorized by the compulsion to tell all, at least not as I was now. Of course, she was good at creating the kind of climate in which I told all of my own accord. And I did that readily, anyway, not just with my mother. Nor was I then troubled by a feeling that I had to, that I was being subtly drained against my will.

She had never misunderstood me so totally; she had been basically on my side, her large eyes flashing defiance at the teachers or the school on my behalf. I could not remember her or my brothers misunderstanding me all the time.

So if my feeling actually *was* transference, transference from whom? The curiosity, perhaps, derived from my mother, but what about the way he got things wrong, his constant misunderstanding of me? Perhaps it was due to a query along the lines of "How is it other people feel they don't know enough about you?" Was I the one who so encoded and distorted the information I gave out, loading it with ambivalence, that I closed myself to others?

My teacher at elementary school, coming back to teach after a long period of psychiatric treatment, had told my mother I was slightly crazy. My mother laughed.

I'd been supposed to recite a poem to the class, and I refused to go up to the front; I would recite it from my seat. There were too many eyes looking at me up at the front of the class. In spite of her insistent urging, I didn't go to the front of the class. My mother wasn't surprised; after all, my ideas of school came from my brothers, and there had been no school at all for them for quite a while after 1945, and then with time off when there was no coal for heating; one way and another you could be absent as much as you liked. Why should I have to go to the front of the class if I didn't want to? This had seemed a rather funny story at the time—but then, I had backing at home.

However, suppose I actually was shielding myself in some subtle way from my analyst, making myself hard to understand, and thus undermining his analytic potency? An ability to understand, after all, was his professional qualification.

Still, I couldn't really believe in this theory. I had often and quite clearly felt myself misunderstood. Or anyway, understood with more difficulty, more laboriously, than I was used to. Moreover, these calculations had a mathematically cool and abstract effect; I had already assumed that much was due to myself and my neurosis, and now that didn't hold good.

Sometimes I did succeed in making such mathematical deductions. Then I thought the observant distance I kept and my stolid coolness an improvement on my earlier tormented bawling. Perhaps *this* was the objective and theoretical interest in psychoanalysis which I had lacked? It reminded me of translation exercises at school: A verb form might have several meanings in particular contexts, and other, less usual meanings according to special grammatical rules. The problem was to find what made most sense in the context of the sentence; that was the right answer. However, the teachers would *also* let pass meanings which were at least grammatically correct, if not quite right for the meaning—they weren't actually marked wrong, or if so, only with the comment "Meaning?" Grammatical rules always held good. If something was theoretically possible and correct, and just didn't quite fit the meaning, it didn't count as a mistake. The "Westwall" mood never came up in such sessions; I noticed, as I had already discovered, how I could deal with concepts. I was probably participating in a more suitable way at such times; I didn't feel so much affected.

*   *   *

I regained a certain amount of self-confidence at the new hospital; I took careful note of the way I went about my work, in comparison with others, and of what I was avoiding on account of my analysis; I didn't want to offend people. I paid a great deal of attention to tensions.

However, I noticed some changes in myself, which I didn't like, considering how I had been before. After all, there had been a pause of three years in my analytic practice.

These days I was more anxious, I kept to the rules more, making sure that what I did was technically correct; I was less daring, allowing the patients just that amount of freedom that my analysts had allowed me. When a patient asked for a glass of water, that was no problem; I had been given a glass of water on one occasion myself. But when the request was for orange juice (which was standing on a shelf nearby, no more trouble to fetch than water from the tap), I had professional scruples. When a male patient came along with a tray and suggested a cup of coffee together, if I was "allowed to," I really did feel unsure, and had to stop myself from reacting defensively. I didn't venture to go for a walk with another patient— because we could get to know each other better that way, and the countryside was pretty too—until I'd obtained permission from higher authority. Yet I could really have gone to Freud for my justification. A man with whom I discussed my self-restraint said I had "an unusually stern analytic superego;" though I hadn't been born with one.

I was now driving 75 kilometers, which took me fifty minutes, to get to my sessions. I had time to adjust, reflect, look at things from a distance; each hour was self-contained. I wasn't eating so much afterwards, I did more shopping, in a direct, confident way. At first I thought that city itself a fine, luxurious place, but I soon found that pressure of time, the distance I had to travel, problems with my car and the gas I was using were a nuisance.

After one analytic session I bought a coney jacket within the space of ten minutes: A pretty thing, greyish beige. When the jacket came apart in several places—the fault was in the fur—I went out after work and bought a wolfskin jacket, without consciously looking for one. It fitted, it was just right. A purchase strengthening my identity; I could protect myself with that jacket, it literally did give me a thick skin, it was a source of strength. I'd never paid so much for any garment before; my father's name was Wolf. I didn't think there was anything wrong about that. Why shouldn't I get myself that kind of symbolic support, instead of a rabbit?

I listened eagerly when I heard anything good or appreciative said in praise of my analyst. He thought this was "positively touching;" I went out of my way to find such comments; they gave me pleasure and validated me.

He did not always seem happy with his formally stern attitude. When I complained of it again, he said, "But this is a *training* analysis," and then I understood a little better. However, what concerned me wasn't to be given an exemplary analysis which I could then reproduce later; it was the intellectual and emotional result, it was what problems of mine I'd be able to recognize and work through. And supposing, with my particular history, I didn't fit too well into the usual setting, and might have found access to what was significant more easily if we hadn't stuck so scrupulously to the rules, still, he'd given me an inadequate reason. However, it came rather late; I had often been brought up short by his stern attitude. Was he really sure now that the classic setting was right, or did he just insist on it with me because I was an analysand in training? Was he in fact, afraid of his superiors and dependent on them? Those who among other things, would give him full recognition after the completion of my analysis? At this time he was in his early days as a training analyst, and this might be something that hampered him.

Sometimes I felt angered by his way of expressing his interpretations: "Don't you think that . . . ? Couldn't your emotion have reference to . . . ? Does this perhaps recall the fact that . . . ? Could it be that . . . ? Can you imagine that . . . would it be possible that . . . I might suppose that . . . could you think that . . . how would it be if . . . ?"

If I was already feeling edgy, this uncertainty, subservience or forced neutrality could make me furious. The way he put things was tentative, but I could feel what he meant, which alternative he preferred or at least thought the more probable. The way he put the question seemed a lie in itself. He had formed his opinion, so why didn't he give it, why didn't he stand by it instead of shifting the decision on to me, although he had already made his own? And he would not easily change his mind; I would have to fight for the solution that appeared most likely to me. His neutrality seemed a pretense; the fact that he made his interpretation as a proposition was more confusing than anything. Generally he was sure what he thought one way or another; I could hear and feel that. So why this shaky uncertainty, the tentative, cautious framing of his opinion as a question? Was he so uncertain and cautious in general, or was this his learned neutrality?

The final interpretation ought, in fact, to be mine; after all, these were *my* memories, my concepts, it was *my* life. I ought not be manipulated. But I could sense his attitude, and all the more clearly the longer I was in analysis.

This approach could make him sound very stilted, like someone giving spiritual guidance, when he might be thinking: But this is so clear she must surely see—it couldn't be more obvious—and then, making no judgments, he would disguise his firm conviction as a possible interpretation in the form of a question.

Even if I thought that I needn't accept a certain interpretation, that it didn't apply to me and I wasn't convinced by it, and even if he didn't insist on it, a doubt might yet remain. If that was what he'd suspected, perhaps it was right after all—it was just that I couldn't reconstruct the matter now. I kept a keen ear open for anything he suggested.

A powerful analyst whom I admired at a distance for his strength and certainty, but whom I had quietly disliked for his harshness in group work, shook me up because his son looked so bony, constrained, so much the good little boy, inhibited, puny, crushed; he hadn't even dared to grow as tall as his father. It was awful to see the two of them side by side. The son had had his strong father to identify with; you could end up as slight a creature as that without any father at all. It struck me that the pair of them discredited the theory. It couldn't be true—such a poor little mouse as the son was! I tried discussing my shock with other people, but a friend of mine said he thought the son was very nice. Well, yes, I believed him, but that wasn't what worried me. What upset me was the bony, pre-genital, inappropriately boyish look of the son. The steps that might have made him a bold, sassy man able to think of bottom-pinching and so on just hadn't been taken, even if his psychological processes were functioning in the normal way. But that wasn't real life. Such a good, friendly, mild sort of nature might be of moral and human worth, but that's not all, not what makes for fun. My friend couldn't go along with me; anyway, this wasn't his kind of problem, he had no weak spot in that area. Perhaps I'd have done better to discuss it with a woman. Then I felt I'd failed to be objective, I'd been unjust, had judged too quickly. After all, I really knew nothing about the two, and one shouldn't blithely make such judgments. I was probably mixing in my own problems.

I seemed to be a nuisance to my analyst again, an imposition which he bore only with difficulty. I often couldn't decide if he was under general strain, or if the feeling was confined to me and the stresses caused by my difficult character, my forever unlovable nature, all that was wrong with me.

This disdainful irritability, his efforts to distance himself, re-

vealed a distinct condemnation of me. I could have defended myself against words, I might have been able to clear up some misunderstanding. Language, after all, was the instrument of analysis.
However, the emotional rejection he had shown was a fact, and as
such carried conviction. At best, I could only go along with it and
aim to be in harmony with him on some point or other. I didn't understand why it was so, but the message was clear.

At supper, a colleague told us with infectious enthusiasm that he'd
started running, going round and round the track in the stadium,
and had been feeling much better ever since; he wasn't regularly
tired in the afternoons now, as he used to be, he felt far better altogether. He looked it, too: Healthy and relaxed, not under stress and
puffy-eyed as he'd often been about this time of day. A woman colleague (in analysis at the time) came over to our table, listened for a
few minutes, and then chimed in, with amusement, "So what are
you running from?" I knew that tone of voice: I'd never be equal to
such a voice, malicious, disguising aggression as humor. She might
as well have waved about a knife. Yet she was an analysand too, a
serious one, discreet, expressing positive feelings about her analyst.
(From the purely theoretical standpoint, if one kicks around interpretations in a simplistic way, one could find more pleasant associations: Ideas of getting going, picking up momentum, running after
something. But I knew her way of reacting and speaking; and surely
neither she nor my first analyst had been born with it, presumably
they had learned it and were now passing it on.)

A Polish doctor, a Jew, was making inquiries as to whether my
father or any of his family were still alive. My mother went to see
him; my father had found him a job as a nurse, and given him
warning of danger in good time. I wept, and retreated into my
shell; but my world seemed all right.

A depressive young woman who had attached herself to my
mother in India told me that my mother was the first contented
person she had met for a long time, and that was why she had followed her.

*   *   *

The patients wrought changes in me.
There was one, a young man, probably on the borderline of

psychosis by the usual criteria, whom I wasn't sure that I could treat, not in the setting of a hospital, and being the person I was, I had misgivings: I felt I might have problems with his aggressive impulses. He trained with body-building apparatus and did karate. I wasn't sure whether he was not too much at the mercy of his powerful affects, and I didn't know whether I, a young woman, was the right therapist for him. His seriousness, intelligence and commitment appealed to me.

I discussed this with an experienced colleague, with the result that he told me if I was alarmed, that was *my* problem: In practicing psychiatry he had seen physically slight male nurses who had no difficulty in dealing with highly aggressive patients. He indicated I should show more courage.

I still didn't feel wholly happy, put my problem to an even more experienced man, and was told concisely that my anxiety was typical of my inexperience.

However, I still had misgivings, and asked my analyst. After all, I'd once been put on psychopharmacological drugs, and I was supposed to be "more disturbed" than other people. Not that I had ever had a precise diagnosis—but I didn't want to undertake something for which I wasn't suited. "In fact you've already made your decision," he told me, acknowledging my commitment. I wanted to do it, and he didn't think my misgivings anything serious.

Subsequently, other people did take them seriously, and saw my perception as a real one, a statement about the patient. They were a help when complications developed. The patient had not been able to handle what he perceived as my turning away from him when I fell in love. Few of my dreams were hidden from his sensitive perception; he felt lost, abandoned and betrayed and reacted aggressively; after having quickly become involved in a love affair, he gave me an ultimatum—either I put him in a closed psychiatric ward at once, or I wouldn't survive our next session. His threat sounded credible; and he had to be protected from his own aggressive impulses too.

Later, I discovered that similarly dangerous situations, liable to have serious consequences, had occurred in his case earlier. His family hadn't mentioned that to me.

His deep seriousness, inward responsibility and clear gaze made a great impression on me. He had not simply attacked me; he had threatened, urgently indicating the dangers lurking in him with what means he had at his disposal, thus causing me to get him the care he needed just then for his own and my protection, to give him inward restraint through an outward structure (the closed ward), because he had pointed out the risk of his being unable to control his impulses by himself any more. He had forced me into a parental role which I ought perhaps to have assumed rather earlier.

However, I had been correct in my feelings about his problems and the risk of this particular therapy. I felt I had been treated too casually by my analyst, to whom, after all, I had told my misgivings. Supposing I had been throttled, or the patient had done himself some injury? Why had my analyst just applauded my courage, when he shaped none of my responsibility in taking the risks? That, after all, was why I'd asked his advice, since he was my analyst and knew me and my limitations, including those professional limitations I might be supposed to have.

As the patient's case history confirmed, I should have taken my feelings seriously. But no discussion with professionally experienced colleagues had been any use, and least of all had I had help from my analyst. Now he reacted with "concern." There was so much uneasiness around me, as he had said before. Was this incident my fault, then? But the patient had shown notably greater aggression on previous occasions, when he didn't even know me. A doubt remained, even though I consciously fought it off.

It became clear that I must be totally, entirely honest in my therapies, that those tensions which arose very often did so from genuine differences between me and the patient, seldom from transference pure and simple. At any rate, I had to clarify the actual relationship before I could venture to assume transference; there was no basis for it otherwise. And very often, in fact, the tension disappeared once we'd resolved our differences. I noticed that there is much more sensitivity around than I had been taught, or at least had learned to take into account. More than was credited to me, in my analysis, as a quasi-patient. It was no use my assuming the usual impersonal or at the most benevolent expression, anyway, because people had always been able to tell a good deal of how I felt by looking at me, and even with more self-control my sensations wouldn't have remained hidden from the sensitive antennae of many patients. All around me, I saw an inclination, in therapy, to interpret the neurotic and repetitive part of any conflict and take little notice of the actual part.

A woman patient said, in passing, she thought I had been annoyed with her. I wasn't at all aware of it, and said so, but I didn't reject the possibility in general, and then the atmosphere was more relaxed. When she left, I asked again if she really thought I'd been annoyed. Smiling, superior: "Well, yes, a little bit." I had to laugh too, and couldn't hide it. She was right, and she'd perceived more than I had.

I noticed that many patients did react faster and more intelligently than myself, and that I had to take this into account. Some had thought a whole situation through when I was just coming to grips with it; with a number of them, I felt I was plodding and laborious in my thinking. Many of them had lived through certain situations in life long before, or more intensely than I had. They knew more about human nature than I: All I had was my training, and by conventional standards a better ability to cope with life.

There was one man who liked me at once, and I liked him; I felt at ease with him. He had dreadful memories of the war, had been buried in rubble, and now suffered from diffuse anxiety states, work disturbances and depressive disorders. His condition was close to the psychotic; other therapists had described him as aggressive, and were happy enough when he wanted to change me. I did not think he was suffering from any delusions of psychotic symptoms, but was just very, very sensitive; he seemed pleasant and intelligent as well, lost his temper easily and vehemently over insincerity and the use of clichés; he was also quick to take offense if I didn't understand him correctly, qualitatively speaking. He didn't mind my lagging behind his own tempo, but I was not to misinterpret him. There had been some difficulties with one of the cleaning women; he had displayed his upper half naked, and asked her if she didn't think he was good-looking, to which she had replied no, just conceited. She was lying, he said, she was insincere and talking nonsense; he really was strikingly attractive, and she might have had some difficulty in pretending not to notice.

I thought him interesting, saucy and very witty. In his first session he spoke of nothing but how attractive he thought me, how he'd like to sleep with me, and so forth. He soon latched on to my own ironic wavelength, talked a great deal, flirted a great deal, and a considerable erotic attraction was established, which discomfited me; it had no place in a therapy session. He realized this, made some very plain propositions, sensed my insecurity, and felt— correctly, in this situation—that he had the upper hand. I forced myself to be neutral, feeling in duty bound to keep my distance and take an overall view, but I didn't know how I could create a "normal" atmosphere; I sought for some interpretation involving transference (myself perhaps as his mother, sister, etc.), felt stupid and was annoyed. I stiffened, tried to indicate the rules of therapy; he was to sit quietly in his chair, respecting the setting. An uncomfortable and indeed nasty tension arose; the end of the session came to my aid.

I was embarrassed, and felt awkward over my sudden tendency to be stiff and formal, just as artificial as my own analyst. I knew that kind of tension myself, or at least something very, very like it.

After some inner struggle I decided on the maximum of frankness with this patient.

He began the next session with further sexual propositions; the attraction and tension surfaced again; I said yes, I did think him attractive, I could well imagine making such contact with him, but that wouldn't be appropriate, and I called upon my learned knowledge to back me up. "But you would like to?"—that was what mattered to him. I admitted it, and he said, triumphantly, "And you thought you wouldn't be experienced enough for someone like me!" "I didn't say that." "But you thought it." I couldn't help laughing, and the tension was relieved. He needed acknowledgment, confirmation that he had aroused something in me and I did like him. Once he had that he was relieved of his obligation to assume a superconfident role. The atmosphere was pleasant.

Later, he was able to weep and show great anxiety, aggression and weakness; the sessions usually began with flirtation, until he felt sure I still liked him, and then he could venture to approach his dreadful misery. He had suffered a great deal during the war and the immediate post-war period, had had much bad luck in his life. He reacted to true brutality with extreme sensitivity and was much less thick-skinned and secure than others. He thought contemporary politicians were liars, and life was a cold struggle for power in which the stronger ground down the weaker and affection was rare.

He noticed that I thought life more pleasant than he did, but dismissed that, so to speak, because I didn't yet have a true perspective on it.

One session of therapy left me edgy, dissatisfied with myself; it struck me later that I had spoken much too briskly about masturbation, pretending to a false assurance and an easy acquaintance with the subject which I didn't really have at all, and which in any case was uncalled-for in this situation. My reactions had been insecure, insincere, and beside the point; I was not pleased with myself. The next session began in tense silence. I felt the atmosphere was very uncomfortable. Finally I plucked up my courage and had a shot at dealing with it. I told him I hadn't felt very happy after our last session; I had not been honest, pretending more assurance than I felt, as I imagined he might have noticed. He gave me a brief, mollified glance from beneath lowered lids; the matter was cleared up, and the atmosphere improved again. There was a trace of affection in the air.

He became taciturn and angry if his sensitive antennae told him I had not been totally honest, if I had been operating somewhere on the borders of my inner integrity. I might not always notice, until he suddenly turned uncommunicative, that I had not been really sincere, that I might, for instance, have said something merely conventional and not entirely my own. He had higher standards of veracity. He didn't mind if one was slow or unable to understand or couldn't reconstruct something, he could tolerate that; it was insincerity and lies that annoyed and upset him.

At such times I couldn't evaluate his mood directly as transference; I had, after all, given him plain cause for it. At most I could deduce that he was sensitive, and had probably had some unfortunate experiences of such things in the past.

I clearly observed the temptation I felt to interpret it as sheer transference when I found him too much of a strain (when he regarded me with suspicion, or when, caught in some insincerity, I felt angry). I would sometimes have been happy to dismiss his easy fits of temper as "mother transference," and to a considerable extent I would have been right. But I'd also given him direct cause. And if I didn't admit that, then how could he understand those elements in his past history which made him so sensitive?

My reaction was a successful experience as far as I was concerned; I brought it up eagerly during my own analysis, as an example of the way we—my analyst and I—ought to behave to each other analytically. I thought there was a good deal that was not sincere and open enough between us, things that we handled too formally. Couldn't my analyst behave to me in the same way as I'd described? He was impressed, and paid me the compliment of saying that he didn't know he would have had the courage to say what I did in the same situation. My sessions became very pleasant again; I felt I'd gone back to the early days of my analysis with him, with all their dreams. He was surprised, thought I had done well and said so. I began to believe, once more, that something good could come of my analysis after all; it looked as if our running battle was at an end.

One male patient ended his session with me with intense sexual fantasies and propositions. The next day something rather unpleasant had happened to me, and I was depressed, but I didn't want to cancel the session. He came to my room, and after a while became tense, agitated and anxious, almost desperate. Suddenly I thought that he might suppose my restraint and pallor were connected with him; the result of his importunity. I tried to make it quite clear that I was sad, but that it had nothing to do with him, it was an outside matter.

This obviously relieved him; he thought he had seen everything go up in smoke, and felt anxiety and guilt. The tension dissolved; he was quick to pick up my state of mind. "Are they being horrible to you, then?" he asked in a very friendly tone, kind and concerned.

I was so worn down that that made me cry; I shed tears and couldn't conceal them. My professional conscience as a therapist made this a difficult situation for me; I tried to recover my self-control, apologized, and wanted to end the session. He remained in his chair, very much on the alert, and looked at me gravely. "But if you don't trust yourself to weep in front of me, how can I weep in front of you?" This sounded so kind and made so much sense that I wept again, burying my face in my hands, and with a slightly easier conscience. He gave me time, and didn't seem to mind; he waited without taking any advantage of the situation, without despising me, without false solicitude, until I had shed all my tears and calmed down. I had not lost face with him by weeping; it made me human. He didn't expect me never to feel down and out. There was an additional bond of trust between us now.

One young man who had just had a telephone call from his father arrived for his session in a very aggressive state, threatening me by saying he couldn't control his feelings any more: Maybe he wouldn't be able to distinguish me from his on-the-phone-father. I was perspiring with fear, but finally decided I must interrupt him firmly, and talked to him until he would listen: I admitted that I actually was afraid, he was stronger than I was. He had regarded the telephone call as a plot concocted against him, interpreting it in line with his earlier experiences. And then his anger got out of control. Once I had convinced him that I'd been "really frightened," and had not known anything about the telephone call beforehand, he calmed down. He would have noted any lie I told, however small, and wouldn't have tolerated it.

Several sessions of concentrative movement therapy were important to me: The sensitivity, tension, warmth and eroticism that arose just from a simple exercise such as touching other people's hands or laying on of hands surprised me, and convinced me. If I had such intense feelings in me, feelings which could be so easily aroused, then I couldn't be so fundamentally sick after all; I might not even have those flaws which had caused me so much worry. My hot hands reminded me of some physical sensation I had once had before, and had forgotten. Compared to the others, I reacted with at least average intensity. There was one exercise where we were to lie down, close our eyes and feel our own faces, noting our feelings as we did so. One woman was alarmed; she had felt a pointed cat's face; another was sad because she found herself ugly; I discovered that my forehead had the same configuration as my grandmother's and felt more satisfied with my appearance than I thought I was. Surely I couldn't really be so shockingly sick and neurotic compared with other people.

I was much struck by certain ideas expressed at a seminar conducted by Kohut.

1. There are experiences and situations which have been so traumatic to someone that he has, so to speak, emotionally eliminated them, as a unicellular organism eliminates its waste. There is then no more emotional contact with these areas, and their elimination is a biologically healthy function, like the bursting of a blister. One

must let such things rest; emotional connection with them cannot be reactivated. To touch on them would be to weaken and harm the individual when he has helped and healed himself, with difficulty but effectively. He warned against trying to revive such areas of experience.

2. He distinguished between acting out in a positive sense, one which furthers analysis, and the kind which serves defense. In no circumstances, he said, should one obstruct the active sort, wherein the analysand thinks and acts for himself, in accordance with the intent of the analysis. This was a new idea to me; I had not encountered it in my own analysis.

Both ideas made a great deal of sense to me; I related them to my own wartime situation: Bombs, air raid shelters, fears for survival and everything else, explosions, fires, being blown up, etc.—to those fears I had re-experienced at the workshop, and from which I'd drawn the conclusion that I would do better to let them lie, and not weaken myself by picking away at them and reactivating such dreadful events. I had come to my decision to let them lie by myself; it did me good to find such an attitude was recognized as a correct one, and I could be theoretically fitted into the context of the norm.

3. The most important thing of all, we were told, was to take the patient seriously, whatever he might say: To take him seriously first and foremost, and particularly before giving any interpretation. It was precisely of a lack of such an attitude that I had persistently complained.

4. In this connection, he told us about an analysand who had insisted initially on not paying for the analysis. Granting this to be a valid position had probably been the most important factor, more curative than many later interpretations. It had made the patient feel secure, in that he could keep something to himself; he wouldn't have to give it up if he didn't want to; he was valuable as a person, worth analyzing; he wouldn't be viewed as worthless, obliterated and dropped entirely if he didn't pay. At the least, there were obviously other ways of dealing with a refusal to pay than those my own analyst had employed. The tone of this approach seemed so kind, benevolent and patient. Obviously I had been inwardly on the right track if such a well-known, famous and highly-regarded man thought the same way. Anyway, I found the seminar inspiring and salutary.

At a congress I saw an analyst whom I liked for his frankness and intelligence, figuratively speaking hacked to bits in discussion, because he had expressed some troublesome ideas which had been repressed. His statements were forgotten, and then, in retrospect, discounted as neurotic acting out, relating to his present personal problems, etc. I was struck by the vehemence and brutality with which he was attacked, in a totally unobjective way. It reminded me of my battles at the hospital. Obviously the attack on him and the intensity of emotional resistance to him also indicated that he had been right, pointed to the resistance and repressions which he had shaken up. He gave me courage; he hadn't given up, hadn't let himself be rattled. He had made the clearest and most inspiring statements of the whole congress; the attacks had worn him out. The others hadn't yet reached that point themselves, had not thought in such far-reaching discomforting terms. He had been a "cause of conflict" in that group. It wasn't his own neurosis, but the defense of the others, which had stamped him an outsider, one to be opposed in those circumstances. He hadn't given up his opinion; he may have moved some people along; I wasn't going to give up either, I hoped to draw strength such as his from conflict.

At last I met a man who aroused tender, maternal, caring and kind feelings in me again. A man I liked very much, simply and unambiguously liked. My feelings for him surprised and reassured me. No interpretation could have shaken them in a hurry; I proved that to my own satisfaction. I was grateful to him for enabling me to do more than hate, criticize, complain, entertain reservations. I suddenly felt I was a rich and opulent human being. That did me good, and so did his comment, "Well, I don't think you're as crazy as all that!" when I had told him the shaming story of my analysis.

I was surprised at the lack of ambiguity in my feelings both for him and for my patients; I couldn't discover any malice lurking in disguise there, or anatomize any chilly, defensive structure. I was amazed that a person like me could feel such sensations—and to find myself wholesome, too.

All of a sudden people were asking me "where my husband worked," whereas previously they would ask, at the most, *whether* I was married. At least it seemed possible that I could marry; it wasn't entirely outside my emotional potential.

I had fits of rage directed at my first analyst: Why had she supposed I was so sensuously handicapped? What had brought her to that interpretation at all? She had not met the man with whom I was then involved, didn't know anything about his neutrality and lack of pep. But she was quite clear that the fault lay in *me*. And a thing like that had made me suffer. What about her interpretation of the drowned corpse, was there anything at all in that? It could all be different: Had all once been different—I hadn't just been cleverly covering up. If I didn't really get on with a man physically, I was right to listen to myself; otherwise there would be something wrong. I must be something wrong. I must either do that or clear up little differences between us, creating a pleasant climate again. How could she have made so generalized a statement, so firmly—a statement, at least, which was capable of being generalized? I had certainly once been inclined to force myself too hard, hadn't felt confident enough to fight back; some men had just made a pass at me too soon; I had sometimes yearned for the kind of young men who attend dance lessons, for their hesitant gentleness at any rate. But really, I was not done in to that extent. How could I have forgotten all that, drawn a veil over it? Why should I suffer from *such* interpretations? And what was really true in all she had told me? Why had I felt I was in such a pathological state, so sick, so different from everyone else? I had also brooded a great deal over the incident of the psychopharmacological drugs; it was still a sore spot if anyone asked me about it. She had *not* accepted me then, she had stopped me in my tracks. She had firmed up in me the fear that I might be actually crazy in some way, on the verge of psychosis—anyway, quite different from other people.

I was snarling, boiling; old cow, I thought, sourpuss—more likely to sour things than any leading brand of vinegar, that's you—and so on. I wanted to write her a long letter, clear up everything, call her names, show my anger, point out her mistakes, demand a reckoning. Then I thought of the cool standoffishness which she'd employ to ward me off and shake my confidence; or of her sadness she'd feel in discovering I didn't think kindly of her. So much time had passed since then, and so much life too, particularly for her. I came to feel it would be irresponsible of me to write to her in such terms; she was lonelier and more isolated than I had imagined earlier. I knew that now. Her denial wouldn't even do me any good. It was in *me* that her interpretations had taken root, and now I had to pull them out; I had probably accepted them and made them come partly true, as well. She might not even remember; or if she did, it could be in another context. She hadn't expressed herself like that, she might say, hadn't meant that, how could I have understood her in such a fashion, given her remarks such an interpretation? And that would be *even* worse, for then it would *still* be my fault. I had heard her adopt such tactics.

I spent nine days in the city where she now lived, ruining my stay with anger, indecision and resignation—should I go and see her or not? Finally I took the advice of someone who knew her and asked me, in surprise, what I expected to achieve by meeting her. No, this was my own business now.

When I told my analyst of a lover I had met there was a pause, he gulped, and then asked a surprised question. I was feeling fine, I laughed and asked why he'd gulped, did he fancy me himself? Could he imagine sex being good with me? But I was overstepping the line. Back came the "Westwall" mood. My association was all wrong; he had not gulped. But I had heard him; I had taken particular note of his pause, his surprise, his incredulity and the difficulty he had in grasping my new relationship. I insisted that he had indeed gulped; I'd heard him. Why wouldn't he admit my description had excited him? I thought I was able to describe such things well enough to affect a hearer. Other people thought me attractive, didn't they? Why shouldn't he? If he didn't, then he oughtn't gulp. I persisted, playfully at first. Then I remembered all the tension that had arisen in analysis over those six hundred marks; I felt angry, and hammered away at the point. He became stiffer, colder, more distant.

Why, I wondered, was such a fuss made about sexual matters in analysis, anyway? There were accounts of its happening, there were couples (comprising male analyst/female analysand) who later married, and had slept together. They didn't die of father transference. And after all, you could do what you liked in analysis, so long as you thought about it. (This was a kind of generally accepted doctrine.) Did he really, at heart, believe there was a prohibition against it (sleeping together)? He said nothing.

At the next session he said, of his own accord, that yes, he *did* believe in such prohibition, for obvious reasons. I was disappointed; it was a conventional sort of answer and delivered after some delay.

The atmosphere became chilly again. I was irritated, and felt rejected once more. We managed to communicate better, if not more warmly, on a neutral subject, that of the tension to which I was subjected at the hospital.

Here I had found myself involved in heated arguments; outside factors had caused the formation of a power vacuum in which bureaucratic—and apparently anti-therapeutic—structures threatened to proliferate. This was bad for the most sensitive and sickest patients, those on the verge of psychosis; they could sense the conflict. I stood up for the patients' point of view at several large group functions; they were complaining that the doctors didn't listen to them enough, there was a lack of communication between patients and doctors, and such an atmosphere induced a feeling of resignation. I thought it was important to take these complaints seriously; some patients who were initially very inhibited found courage to express themselves in discussion; I took care that they weren't unnecessarily intimidated by the bureaucracy, and had a chance to say what they thought. At any event, in spite of a crippling administrative apparatus liable to cause insecurity, they looked after their own present needs to the extent of planning a party themselves; it was held and was a success. Afterward I got into difficulties over the giving of serious consideration to other complaints from patients; however, a number of people supported me at first. When the arguments with the bureaucracy increased—and with them fears for the security of their jobs—not many of them were still on my side. (I imagined it must have been something like this in the Third Reich.) However, I had warmth and expressions of solidarity from the patients and from people on the lower rungs of the hierarchy. I was happy as a fish in water; a glance from them was often enough to give me strength. But some of my colleagues purposely shook my confidence, with emotionally loaded remarks and vague threats of my being fired. I had been surprised by a petition against my dismissal which the patients had started drawing up quite early on, when I didn't think I was in any danger of that, and felt no petition was necessary. Later, I realized that they had perceived the general feeling about me with sensitivity, and quite correctly. "People like you don't stay long—it's the same everywhere, they get fired," a trade unionist told me. In any event, I had tension in my real life to worry me.

A mature woman colleague, who had not been analyzed, told me that the atmosphere which made me so uneasy was exactly the same as she had encountered as the first woman on the town council; she had really been stunned; later, she heard that the male councillors had been drinking to give themselves courage the evening before the council met. What was the matter with me anyway, she wondered—a woman like myself without a man behind me? I pointed out my status as an analysand; however, she couldn't conceive the analytic situation as meaningful; how could it be that two grown people, one lying on a bed in front of the other, wouldn't get into a state of sexual tension? Could one discuss anything at all in any sort of natural way? I couldn't convince her that it was possible, and I didn't feel happy with her criticism; I kept my distance from her.

My analyst was alarmed. I was conflict-ridden, he said, tension arose around me; I was regarded as the one responsible, the person who sets it off. At that point I could hardly endure the atmosphere between us nor my problems at work. The work in itself and many of the patients were a strain on me as well. I needed my strength for my real task, not to expend on outside friction. I was left feeling angry and edgy after my sessions; my cough came back, and so, at times, did that frightening feeling behind my sternum.

What with the stress I was under, all my bitter feelings of despair returned; during a manifestation of the cold "Westwall" mood, I asked forcefully how an analysis that was running such a bad course could leave him cold? Why didn't it even bother him to see me getting worse and worse as his analysis went on? I really couldn't bear this kind of thing any more. Didn't he even mind? I particularly disliked his cool indifference. I was furious and desperate, and I pressed him for an answer.

Finally it came, as if dragged out of him. "You know, if I were to tell you just how much I've suffered from this analysis, how it's worn me down, well, I just can't tell you; you'd never recover from your guilt feelings." His remarks sounded heartfelt, spontaneous, carried weight. I said nothing, and the session came to its end. Reaction came when I got home.

At the next session, I questioned him. What exactly had I done to him? *What* would inevitably give me such guilt feelings? He must tell me, I said, now. He didn't want to put it into words, and seemed rather ill at ease and embarrassed. I persisted; after all, I was certainly going to get tremendous guilt feelings, wasn't I, if I could only fantasize about the reason? He remained monosyllabic. Just what sort of guilt feelings did he think I was bound to develop now, if he merely dropped hints and then said no more? Anxiety was always stronger than reality. I thought of the worst things I could imagine: An accident or a suicide attempt. Finally, in response to my guesses, he told me that yes, he had had a car accident. I managed to extract the further information that it was a slight one. But that was no reason for me to entertain guilt feelings, or at least not such powerful and traumatizing guilt feelings as those at which he had hinted. I pressed him to say more. He seemed to be very uncomfortable. Yes, I had caused changes in the structure of his family life; his wife had been angry about the strain I put on him. In what way? Well, she would have liked to see the analysis come to a speedy end; I was doing him in. I was slow to understand this point; I didn't need to entertain guilt feelings over the jealousy of analysts' wives. That wasn't my problem. When I questioned him further, he finally and definitely said: doubt had arisen in regard to his general ability to live.

I was quiet. I had already heard trained analysts say, "She castrates laughingly." So it was all connected with my castrating tendencies, my destructive basic structure which damaged his ability to love and made him doubt himself. My hating, loveless, unloving inner being, bringing turmoil to everything. My character, I myself as a whole, had made him suffer like this and worn him down, until he was so badly affected and so near the end of his tether that even his wife worried about him. As a person, a human being, a woman, an analysand and an intellectual partner I was destructive, unwholesome, unendurable, exacting.

My inner essence had had that effect upon him.

At first I was still able to react with fury. Why hadn't he said all this before? Why had he gone on suffering because of me? Why hadn't he done something to change matters, why hadn't he at least expressed and verbalized his feelings? As it was, I had absorbed the atmosphere through my pores. My recurrent feeling that he was rejecting me, didn't like me and indeed couldn't stand me had been right all along. I had sensed something real, and the "Westwall" mood symbolized nothing but a pronounced state of

the suffering I caused him, his reaction to me. Wasn't all this dishonest in the extreme? How was I supposed to be frank and verbalize if he kept such a fundamental state of mind under control and
didn't admit to it? Didn't make it available to be worked through,
or at least be perceived??? The probability was that I had sensed
his suffering and antipathy all these years anyway, and had absorbed it after all. Didn't he see it that way too? What kind of picture of myself might I be expected to develop, in order not to
identify with his image of me? And how was I ever to improve
emotionally, to like, accept and love myself, if he could stand me
only with great difficulty, and by doing himself injury??? Wasn't
this an extremely dishonest, harmful and traumatizing way to behave? Could he seriously believe that I hadn't somehow felt his
attitude toward me — not, perhaps, in a way I could have put into
words, but felt it deep down?

I was really outraged about his lack of frankness. I thought there
could be no disputing it. And I found him ready to listen to me
here. I insisted on more honesty on his part too; I mentioned once
again all the examples of patients whose honesty had impressed
me. Suppose, for instance, and purely hypothetically, he had really
felt like sleeping with me when I told my story of sleeping with my
new acquaintance: Then what? Why his holding back, his minimal
frankness? We finally agreed to behave differently to each other in
the future, and practice a more candid form of analysis. Before he
went on vacation he said this was the first time he'd been sorry to
interrupt the analysis, and he was looking forward to resuming it.

During the ensuing break in my analysis, I began by submerg-
ing myself once more in the swamp of my hating, destructive, unloving evil-mindedness, as demonstrated to me once again. I could
scarcely endure what I felt any longer. Not only was I like that myself, I did harm to other people as well; probably there was no
treating this condition. But little moments of kindness around me
helped me to survive such moods. This was a critical period. Next,
I came back to thinking the whole story monstrous. What kind of
analysis was it in which I must actually witness, must actually be
shown, how unbearable, unlovable, destructive a creature I was?
In which I was barely tolerated, endured with the utmost difficulty,
like an ecclesiastical penance? And in which I was also explicitly
told just *how much* someone had suffered from me, from merely

being in my presence? If I were to take all this seriously, how could life go on?

I was all at sea: What kind of powerful, destructive, omnipotent person was I if I could do such a thing? Make a training analyst suffer to the point where it wasn't even possible for him to tell me the extent of his suffering and of my own destructive rage?

What kind of person was I, then? I no longer understood anything. Why wasn't it possible for him to treat me as he did other people? Why not an interpretation at the right moment, or simply a remark, and then I might not have been so destructive toward him subsequently? Or was I really so basically evil and unanalyzable, so malign? Why these reproaches, so late in the day? Why not end the whole thing earlier? Was there something I could do to make it up to him? Did I have to? Was it possible, anyway? What had I done, in my basic malignity, what had I destroyed, what had I ruined? And with what part of me? Without my really noticing, without even having any perception of it? What was going on around me if I didn't perceive or even suspect what radical, powerful and destructive effects I had on others? If even my analyst didn't venture to show me my rottenness, reveal it to me? Was I so fragile that he didn't dare—or so destructive that it would have been too hard a thing to tell me and make me aware of? What else about me had been kept from me? If I hadn't even had any real frankness in my analysis, if even my analyst hadn't trusted me to cope with such frankness—what was it like in normal life? Did a great many people, perhaps think me horrible, awful, and they just didn't dare to show me? Were they all lying to me? Was the liking and warmth to which I clung at this time not real either, was it all pretense? What on earth was still true? Was I altogether so mentally endangered, so insecure and so incapable of tolerance in the face of realities, in particular my own psychological realities?

*   *   *

Without analysis, I had more free time: Three hours a day. And I had the emotional space for other contacts. A mature young woman gave me a sense of security, and so did older people who simply didn't believe I was such a terrible mess and treated me as normal. These were pleasant, adult contacts; just eye contact, quite often, with many of my patients. A great many people understood my melancholy, run down state, and didn't mind. Mini love affairs strengthened me. The strain of work at the hospital didn't seem pointless; I felt strong all the same. I carried around photographs of friends and my brothers; they gave me strength too. I had ordered a fast car: A car such as I'd dreamed of, a car reminiscent of my father and my fatherly friend, in a color that would accentuate my feelings for them. I could withdraw into it, plunge into my own pleasant world.

While cleaning up, I found old things that brought back memories: There was a sense of well being, enjoyment of life and security that I had forgotten in connection with objects like my dancing class dress, my first bikini, a pair of beige poplin pants from my last year at secondary school, a carnival hat, a big red pullover from my first college term. I was sorry to think how I had changed, and to realize I couldn't spontaneously remember such pleasant states of mind. They came back to me slowly as I tried the things on. I'd seemed to myself grown-up and seductive in that Victorian hat with the ribbons, worn to a party before I reached puberty; I had liked myself, tanned and wearing the bikini; and I'd thought pretty well of myself in the shiny poplin pants and a loose sweater in that first semester.

I had suffered since then.

The fact that I wasn't married had been regarded as the indubitable result of my inadequate and unstable object relationships. I had envied people, felt inferior, inexperienced, retarded. Now, for the first time, I realized when I went to women's groups that those who were married did not necessarily have memories more loving than mine, that my experiences didn't really seem so meager by comparison; I could feel quite happy about a number of them. Perhaps not when set against my yearnings, but compared with the experiences of others. And my friendships were in no way fewer or less reliable than other people's; perhaps I even had more of them. Over the years, several friends had proved very faithful. There were many married women who had less in the way of pleasant memories than I did, and who had fewer friends of both sexes. If I started out from the assumption that what other people put into their marriages had, in my own case, flowed in various different directions, I didn't seem by any means so unhappily unusual. I almost felt guilty about my discontent. I might have had less happiness in love than I'd planned, but wishing for more seemed a personal indulgence, not something to which I had any kind of legal right, particularly not compared to other women of similar background.

I was often able to follow up my spontaneous ideas now. A patient diagnosed as psychotic dared not get into the car which was to take him home. I had met him briefly once before; his present panic was a sad sight. I happened to have a painted stone in my pants pocket and gave it to him. He got into the car with it, and the journey went off all right; he arrived home in a relatively calm state, as his mother told me later. I was glad; his confidence in me had done me good. All psychotics together, you might say; I had been given the stone by a courageous friend of mine, and had treasured it for a time. However, I had done the right thing for that patient in those circumstances. I would have been no use to anyone if I'd thought over my impulse and restrained myself from following it.

In a book about the primal scream, I read of the "toxic influence" of some people, and how it is then no use thinking the matter over, one simply has to admit that they are like that, and no one can stand more than a certain amount of it. The idea of not having to put up with everyone, not having to think one's way through every uncomfortable relationship, of having some justification for keeping myself away from influences I didn't like was liberating. I laughed at the idea, but I could make practical and considerate use of it.

I made my way back to a certain independence. Suddenly it struck me as idiotic to go on with something which was an ordeal for both parties to it. I thought it would be better to put an end to it as quickly as possible. Seen in retrospect, my analysis looked to me like a marriage gone wrong. There, too, I found it hard to understand people who stayed together when they merely seemed to make each other suffer. "If you only knew . . . " my analyst had said. The message was clear.

Why should we torment ourselves any further? Why should I torment him any further? Even if he had said he was ready to treat me differently, more frankly. Was there any point left in it at all? The supervision to which he had agreed had not noticeably altered anything. In real life, the healthy—or at least normal—reaction would be to terminate such a painful relationship, now that I really saw it for what it was and wasn't just dealing with my fantasies. A friend who had been analyzed said my analyst's reaction was as if a patient with psychosomatic vomiting had come to him, and the first thing he said was, "The sight of you makes me sick."

It seemed to be a good thing that at least he had now expressed himself so clearly. All in all, there was no point or substance in this analysis. I understood too much now. I would not expect any patient to continue with such a thing. Nor would I wish such a penitential analysis on any analyst. I felt increasingly sure of myself. However, I wanted to end my analysis in a formally correct, meaningful way, and so I made an appointment with a well-known analyst, discussed the course events had taken, and got his approval. Altogether, he thought, it had turned out well for me; my analysis had taught me to fight. He also thought I had come to show a certain seriousness, something that one could only have guessed at before.

*   *   *

When my analyst came back from his vacation, I surprised him with this new development. After our last argument before his vacation, he had, after all, been all in favor of a different form of analysis.

He agreed to let me sit.

I had thought out exactly what I wanted to say: During this break in my analysis things had changed a good deal for me. I had plenty of vitality, I was enjoying work at the hospital, I could realize myself more. I had started working with large groups, and found this a very significant experience. I wanted to do some writing, and felt the urge; it came pouring out of me. I told him about the well-known analyst who had described the course of my analysis as good for me. I'd also met many friends over Christmas who all agreed that I was my old self again.

Besides this, I had taken another good look at my mother and my brothers, and had come to the conclusion that my mother actually was an impressive woman, a reliable person, one who had always stood up for her children. She was now living with her third husband and was not as sick as we had supposed. I thought I could and should identify perfectly well with her after all. I also thought I could get on well with her now. My brothers were agreeable people too, and my position in relation to them was stronger now. I didn't think I would allow myself to be stifled as before, and I was not going to be a little grey mouse again. Altogether, I did not think my entire family such a pathological case after all.

All things considered, I also thought I wasn't so sick myself, not by the classic criteria; I had always functioned well professionally, had speedily passed my exams, and thought I could now overcome my minor block in writing medical reports. I didn't think myself so sexually disturbed either. (Here he smiled. "You like it with X?" I answered meekly, "Yes;" my inhibitions weren't too bad, they were really more like blemishes which could be cosmetically removed.) What seemd to convince him most was my argument concerning my mother. I had not been able to get on with her before, and if I could now, well, that was fine. He had listened to me attentively; the atmosphere was good. I then came to what mattered the most to me: I wanted to write, and whenever I'd been discussing this with him, the verve was gone, I didn't feel the urge to write it down any more. It had just vanished, and wouldn't come back. "You can always record what we say on tape; I've no objection." (This might have undermined my main argument.) In addition, however, I felt I was at the end of my rope: with all the driving, and even my minimum hours of duty at the hospital, I was on the go for eleven to twelve hours a day without a break, and I really couldn't go on that way. Also, my grant had run out, and I was obliged to take private patients for therapy; all this together surpassed my strength. He understood that. The driving was a burden under which my work as well as my analysis might suffer. I then told him that, for all these reasons, I would like to end the analysis; I had really made up my mind, and I was feeling well now. The atmosphere continued good: He asked some more questions, wondering why I had come to this decision so suddenly. I explained it by the break in my analysis, and my own nature, in which feelings of some intensity sometimes occurred. He did say he thought it was odd I needed to defend myself against him and seemed to feel something had gone wrong here. However, he agreed to what I suggested, and asked when I'd like to end the analysis: Today, tomorrow, next week or when? I became unsure of myself, asked what he thought was appropriate; I was surprised to find him so ready to consent.

We then agreed that he would consider the analysis duly completed, and would describe it in those terms if asked, provided that when I was doing analysis of my own I would also undertake to have some further analysis myself. Either with him or with someone else. He would be perfectly happy to do it, but wouldn't hold it against me if I looked for another analyst. He himself, he said, had had three analysts, ending up with one whom he wouldn't have missed for anything. I said I was in favor of completing that week's sessions as usual, then having a final double session the following week, and a talk after an interval of three weeks. In the context of the present session, this seemed to me a good plan.

I was surprised and pleased to find him so willing to go along with all this. Of course, I had prepared my speech well in advance; I thought it was a diplomatic one, and the best possible way to terminate an analysis (except that I wasn't married, or pregnant).

By the next session he had changed his mind. He said I was "unanalyzable." "With you, it's necessary to build up defenses rather than break them down." "We never had a working relationship." "Nobody else would have stuck it out with you so long. I've borne my burden, and it has weighed on me a great deal." "You often can't distinguish between *your own* feelings and those of others." I was, he said, given to "malign projections." He was annoyed. In the future, he said, he would take initial interviews more seriously, see that they were longer and more thorough; at the time of mine, several questions had remained open which he would have done better to clear up at once. He thought my reasons for ending the analysis sounded like pretexts; he would like me to tell him precisely why I *really* wanted to terminate it.

His tone reminded me of the early days of the analysis. He diverted me from my intention of ending my analysis formally and mendaciously. Suddenly I hoped we might yet clear the whole thing up, now it was coming to an end. "I'm tired of trying to win you over," I said, and this was really the essence of what I felt, that was why I wouldn't, couldn't go on. He was very quiet, almost as if there were tears in his eyes. After a pause of some length, however, the tension rose again; our moment of contact was over. Back came the hurtful "Westwall" mood.

Then he gave me his interpretation of my purpose in terminating the analysis: It was becoming genital, and at this point I took fright. That was all part of my problems and my anxieties. He had come to enjoy my analysis, looked forward to it eagerly, and that had obviously alarmed me; I was afraid of genitality. The way I saw it, I had experienced that plane with him already, and the feeling had worn itself out and then died. I couldn't retain warm feelings indefinitely for someone who made it so difficult. I didn't even feel jealousy when I really had cause for it; an affair of his had been more inclined to set my doubts about him entirely at rest. It didn't strike me as easy to revive things on that level, or certainly not now, anyway. In any case, I preferred men who were a bit crazier, more eccentric, cleverer with words, more ironic and humorous. At the moment I felt safe in a network of friends and lovers, brothers, patients, women friends. People who liked and understood me, didn't misinterpret me on principle. I felt loved. His interpretation struck me as routine.

However, he stuck to it. I could endure the tension better now, but none the less I felt injured, sharply wounded: A harsh, sore wound behind my breastbone, making me cough, impeding my breathing. It was something I knew well.

*   *   *

My present training supervisor had noticed the lack of clarity in my papers, and suggested we discuss the situation. I had been glad of his interest and the proposal to clear things up, and I resolved to set everything out in detail. When I wasn't able to tell him everything within an hour, we agreed that I would pay for further sessions, so that he could take his time and I wouldn't be under pressure; I liked this idea, since I had a great deal of complicated information to impart. What concerned him most of all was the matter of my inability to take stress; i.e., the question of my instability.

The first session was in his office in town, the second, just before Christmas, in his study at home.

The evening before the third session, after the New Year, I realized that we hadn't made an appointment for a definite place, or if we had I couldn't remember it. As I didn't want to disturb him during the weekend just for that, I thought the easiest thing was to telephone at a normal time for calls, when I was on my way to him on Monday; the first forty minutes of my drive were the same whether I was going to his office in town or his private address.

I supposed he would probably be working in his office, but he might be at home if the holiday break wasn't over yet; some analysts didn't like seeing patients at their homes, but then I wasn't a genuine patient of his. When I phoned, his wife gave me his private address, and as far as I was concerned that was the end of the matter.

He gave me a strange look as soon as I came in; I'd called up, he said. Yes, I said, we hadn't fixed a place for today's session. "But this is very odd!" I asked why; we really hadn't fixed a place, or had I failed to hear him saying where it was to be? Was I wrong there? "No, but this really is very odd. We'll have to come back to it. Don't you notice anything at all?"

"No, I really don't know what you mean. What am I supposed to notice?"

I began to doubt whether I'd been in this room at all; had I mixed everything up somehow? The air seemed to be humming, it all felt unreal; he said nothing.

"But I'd been to your office in town before that, and we hadn't fixed a place for today, or am I wrong? I didn't write anything down before Christmas."

"Are you really sure you don't notice anything here? Look around!"

I became less and less confident; I didn't notice anything about the room. "I really don't know what you mean. What am I supposed to notice?"

He said, with emphasis, "But don't you notice that this furniture is *exactly the same* as in the other room?" At last I saw the light. "Oh, so you've moved?" "*Yes.*" With a smile of relief.

I felt I was being regarded and treated as if I were crazy, and went on the attack again when my confidence returned. "You know, with a little less analytical restraint, you could have given me that information before and spared both of us this last quarter of an hour."

He smiled, with an effort, and we returned to the real subject.

I could well imagine that someone in a worse way than I was might not get over such a situation without developing an anxiety state.

At home, I felt unsure again: Ought I have registered the furniture? I had noticed that the room looked similar, but that could be just his style. If I was concentrating on something very important to me, I didn't necessarily have to take note of my surroundings: The furniture was nothing unusual in itself, chairs upholstered in brandy-colored leather, suitable for superior offices. The Lufthansa branches had them in black. And I hadn't heard about his move, because I lived seventy-five kilometers away.

I did gain something from these conversations, though: It was illuminating to me when he asked, surprised by the speed with which I had once been prescribed psychopharmacological drugs, whether I might possibly have mobilized anxiety in my first analyst. This idea, suggested in an objective and interested tone, did me good.

However, he also seemed to disapprove, so far as I could tell, of my decision to end the analysis; this had developed during our four hours together.

To my surprise, he told me, at the end of our last conversation, that he could not pronounce upon the uncertain question of my stability. All of a sudden, apparently, it seemed such a thing could not be evaluated from mere conversations. I asked—since I didn't know—what, then, had been the point of those conversations, if he couldn't come to some conclusion concerning my stability or otherwise from what I told him? Well, he couldn't be sure; I reacted in a strikingly open and intense way. As I saw it, this wasn't so surprising, since I did after all have some experience of analysis, and so was not putting up the same defense as a novice. But no, he couldn't give an opinion on my ability to withstand stress. I felt quietly despairing; I didn't understand any of this. He then said, in a conciliatory tone, that I would be hearing news. I asked from whom. From the supra-regional committee; he had had the matter put on the agenda for discussion; they owed me that, after all.

I had had no idea of this; in the circumstances, if I had I might possibly have tried to act with more restraint and been less intense in my endeavors to get the subject cleared up. I felt as if I had been lured into a trap. How much of what I had told him here, in confidence and paying a fee, as a kind of supplement to my analysis, was he going to disclose there? Well, of course it was all subject to confidentiality, he told me. I knew that was so in principle, but then what could he say? How far did analysts really observe confidentiality?

He also advised me to apply for temporary leave, since it looked, so far as he could judge the state of things and the atmosphere, as if my training were going to be terminated. I could very probably avert this by putting in such an application, this was his personal view, and he was prepared to make the application for me. He told me this in his capacity as regional chairman of the training committee, and I had no reason to doubt him. As I had always enjoyed congresses, and didn't want to give them up, we agreed on an application for temporary suspension of my training, with permission to continue participating in congresses. This seemed to make sense, in that I would be continuing my work with patients whether or not my training were suspended, and the value of the congresses was for the patients, in the last resort.

So I wrote my application, and he said he would put it in for me.

After the meeting of the committee I waited: Judging by the mild leper status that was accorded me, the subtle way people kept their distance, and an unexpected letter of solidarity, I concluded that the outcome was negative, but I heard nothing. After six weeks I inquired, and was told they were happy to inform me that my application had been put in, and they were sure I would soon hear. My uneasiness increased; after another period of waiting, I did get an answer, the essence of which was that my training was regarded as terminated, since I had not yet taken the intermediate examination, and they had to conclude, from my application, that I had no present intention of doing so. Nothing had been said about further participation in congresses, but it was obviously self-evident (that permission wasn't given).

No one could fairly reproach me with that factor—lack of interest—as an argument, and I would never have supplied it of my own accord. I felt I had been tricked, like a worker cunningly induced by his firm to give in his notice.

Three years later, I heard that what followed my rejection, and the surprising delay in telling me of it, were due simply to a memo. I had heard nothing of this; I had just had my "paranoid" feeling, which corresponded to the facts, and I had not put that on record.

Surely analyzed people couldn't treat me, also an analyzed person, in such a way.

My last few sessions with my analyst were a forcible attempt at communication. They ended in a sense of bitter injury, with the "Westwall" atmosphere at its worst. I had not given up all hope of our coming to terms, perhaps even fathoming the reason for the barrier between us. No hope of that, amidst such tension. He did say some nice things about my clothes: I dressed "ravishly;" and about the analysis: With me, he had never felt tempted to fall asleep. This was a compliment. Obviously he did doze off with other people. I thought it a strange sort of acknowledgement. I had never seriously thought of such a thing, had taken the idea of an analyst falling asleep as a joke. I had broken off sessions myself if I was too tired; if my first analyst was exhausted she said so. But neither she nor I had ever really fallen asleep, and I wouldn't have entertained such a notion of him either. What was the compliment about my clothes supposed to mean? Yes, I liked my black suit myself; it was appropriate to mourning for a father, and I resembled my mother in it. The material was soft and comfortable and didn't scratch. However, the compliment seemed strange, excessive and untypical.

Lack of clarity at the end of analysis seemed unworthy. A friend who had been analyzed stated, as a point admitting no argument, that one should plan termination six months ahead. However, he didn't know my situation, and probably couldn't imagine it as difficult as it was. The well-known analyst had said I was right to stop as soon as possible. I might well have to bury some dreams of analysis. My attempt to communicate now, at the last minute—after I had previously given a well-prepared, if not quite accurate, account of my wish to end the analysis—was no use at all in such an atmosphere.

Life outside was not without its complications. After my decision and the following sessions, I fell sick: Suffocative bronchitis with a bad cough and a night of breathing difficulties put me out of action. I spent over a week hammering away on my typewriter, getting rid of all that was dammed up inside me, and I coughed up a great deal. It was a relief: I saw nothing I could do but write it down. None of my friends turned out able to bear the full weight of my condensed life story, the concentration of the analytical experiences I had thought through and suffered—or not, at least, to an extent that would have been enough for me. They had their own lives, and their own problems, running only partly parallel to mine. It would have been hard for them to cope with so much misery, destruction, uncertainty for the future, so much that called for sympathy and shared indignation. My typewriter listened to me without asking questions or contradicting me. Directly after the ending of the analysis I was sick again, with an even worse cough, difficulty in breathing, and suspected pneumonia. I brought up a great deal of thick, green mucus. My first analyst used to have a persistent cough. At least this removed me from all the tension: I went to stay with friends, then went home, typed. This brought relief. And I was afraid of forgetting things before I had understood them. My brain was too full: I must record all this, clarify it and put it in order before it was gone.

My last sessions of analysis still hurt a great deal. As far as I was concerned, they had been concessions to the usual six months an analysand was always supposed to observe before termination, to deal with detachment and possible defensive motivations for ending the analysis, and so on, and so forth. I hadn't quite buried the hope that we might yet understand each other a little bit, either. At heart I couldn't imagine actually ending my analysis just like this—a failure, nonsense, with me not properly seen or understood, in an emotionally chaotic tangle, a mess. Breaking it off.

I felt engaged in self-defense against that dreadful tension, the sense of being destroyed, the feeling of injury left by every session. Ending the analysis was simply necessary, the lesser evil.

I wanted a diagnosis and asked for one. It came slowly, with difficulty: "Sensitive paranoid personality, narcissistic disturbance." This was partly fashionable and partly outmoded. The idea of paranoia had been a bone of contention between us; I thought that he simply had no empathy for my sensitive perceptions, and that was why he described them as crazy. In the present situation, when he gave me this diagnosis, it seemed to me too little worth argument to be taken really seriously. (How far it ate into me later is another question.)

I thought his interpretation of my "fear of genitality" out-of-date: Plastic analysis, Woolworth analysis, simplistic thinking. There would have been some point in it three and a half years ago. But we were not on that plane now. I felt more like a partner in a marriage of very long standing, where the sexual attraction is past history. How could someone like him inspire me with sexual anxiety? I couldn't even imagine sleeping with him any more.

To be told, all of a sudden, that I was "unanalyzable" scared me at first; then, however, I took the interpretation to be more the result of defensive embarrassment than anything else. Tit for tat: *You* couldn't analyze me—no, you couldn't *let* yourself be analyzed. Or an argument in the sandbox: You're dumb—no, you're dumber. And yet I was not untouched by his pronouncement, as I noticed, and still do, in moments of depression.

If I was "unanalyzable," then my three initial interviews, my first analysis and the time I spent with him had been sheer nonsense. In that case the diagnosis should have been made sooner and this potentially devastating information should not have been handed to me now, as a little time bomb for me to carry away with me. Moreover, progressive doctrine said that everyone, even the most severely psychotic, can be analyzed, it just depends on his finding an analyst who suits him, someone who can understand him. Perhaps "unanalyzable" really was correct—for him. But I felt the generalization was nothing short of malicious. Who was to say for sure that there wasn't someone else who would get on with me better than he did? Wasn't it a shabby trick to discourage me from later attempts at analysis?

If this analysis had failed, did it mean I really had to file away all my dreams? It was taking me all my strength to haul myself out of this analysis anyway, with the help of all possible little aids and props. I wasn't so very confident and strong. Where was I now to get the ability to feel things decidedly and without too many scruples, to stand by a decision? Just now, of course, I was angry, furious, and trying to ignore his interpretations. But the word "unanalyzable" bored away within me, undermining me; he was my training analyst, and he had known me for three and a half years. In my darker, weaker moments I felt it was a curse. "You shall not be happy with anyone." Later analysis wouldn't help me either, and I needn't think it would. In any case, who was going to take me on? Or at least without great reservations and only a moderate amount of confidence??? Was he justified, even if he had noticed my "unanalyzability" long ago, in confronting me with such a fact now, all of a sudden, at a point in time when I wouldn't be able to work through it? Shouldn't he have drawn conclusions from his evaluation of me earlier, in the course of those three and a half years? Was his remark just a kind of emotional boomerang, the effect of our parting—after all, a little earlier he'd been perfectly happy with the way things were going? He had agreed to our ending the analysis. Or had he been trying to spare me, because of my peculiar disturbance, which I had to fade out to such an extent that I didn't see, perceive or understand it?

If he couldn't get along with me then it should have been a matter of importance, and a humanly responsible act, to end this state of affairs early on. Not to go on suffering because of me, giving me guilt feelings, and not to describe me as impossible to treat in general: To acknowledge his limitations, and not make me responsible for them or condemn me on their account.

Even if I couldn't be treated in general, which very likely was not the case, wasn't it of economic significance for me to understand this and take account of it for my future life? He might have thought I'd have to come to terms with it and modify my professional aims accordingly. How was somebody who couldn't be treated herself to treat others? My unanalyzability should not, after all, be taken as personal spite against him, affecting only him as my analyst. At bottom I was the victim, the one affected, carrying a very basic and severe problem about with me. Ought I to be left alone with it? Ought he to tell me such a thing, bluntly, like a man wielding a weapon, by way of explaining the course of my analysis, and that in the third session from the end? Who was at stake in my analysis? Sometimes my brain rebelled. It couldn't be true, an analysis couldn't end like this. Communications of this nature simply had no place in analysis—yah boo, sucks to you! Why? That's why! Wham. And no further comment.

Why did he leave it entirely to me to decide on the ending of the analysis? "When would you like to stop: Today, tomorrow . . . when?" Did he have a plan, did he have a diagnosis? What part of me had he understood? The fact that I apparently couldn't distinguish between him and me, his feelings and mine, was new to me too. And it was all my fault again. If he was right, I was very seriously disturbed.

But maybe he was reckoning on my not taking his interpretations seriously any more? On my seeing them as relative? (I am now [three years later] still not quite sure if I haven't absorbed much of his destructive view of me. I don't much trust myself or my relative mental health, am easily made insecure if someone regards me questioningly, doubtfully, suspiciously, as potentially crazy. And how much of his suspicious, negative technique of interpretation may I have adopted in my dealings with other patients?)

The last session had probably been fixed for too early a date. The "Westwall" mood was at its worst from the start. He came several minutes late, as so often before, giving outside pressures as the reason. We both sat. He kept at a touchy sort of distance; almost by way of therapy, I then drew my chair back. A knowing, derogatory smile: "You see!" The session was torture. He was metaphorically armored and so was I. I heard and felt, once more, what an imposition I had been, what a trial. There was no chance of understanding. Irritation and a sense of injury and tension on both sides; I had that sore, burning feeling in my chest again, wanted to cough, became restless and could hardly bear to stay in the room.

My analysis was over. He would confirm, if asked, that it had been ended "by mutual agreement." He didn't want to put any obstacles in my way. And he would keep my sessions free for me for another six months, in case I was in a bad way.

*   *   *

Directly after the termination of the analysis I had convulsive bronchitis again, and took time off with it. There was increased tension at the hospital too, and I didn't know if I could stay there. My mother and my friends were very supportive; it was nice to be cared for and feel solidarity. When I was rid of my cough and my temperature, I went back to my old room and unburdened myself at my typewriter. My mother and my friends were staunchly on my side, no questions asked. I didn't have to explain much. Probably this was the best way to cope. I needed peace, and time, and then everything would be all right again. I didn't have to defend myself or reckon with constant misunderstanding. I settled in and put down roots at home again, and was glad not everything was ruined and in tatters. Good will wasn't confined to my home itself, either; I found it in the neighborhood as well, a non-verbal, Hessian, animal warmth that did me good.

During the weeks and months after the end of my analysis, I often woke with a very unpleasant feeling, remembering scraps of dreams to do with being in analysis, or "back in analysis." I was left shattered, as if paralyzed, and had difficulty in forcing myself to do routine tasks. As if my backbone and my vitality had dissolved. At first the dreams came once or twice a week, then less frequently. I learned to allow for and accept these horrible feelings on the mornings they came, seeing them as setbacks in the convalescent process. But they were still weird, and threatening. Suppose I couldn't shake off the sense of paralysis one morning, suppose I couldn't pull myself together at all?

I was more withdrawn at work, not as committed as before. An analyst colleague, meaning it as a compliment, said I was better integrated now. I could have come to blows with him on the spot; surely he, a trained analyst, couldn't judge so superficially, by appearances. "Yes, I'm quieter now, more resigned." That defined the front line again.

I noticed a change of attitude on the part of my acquaintances who had been analyzed, and it upset me badly; many of them treated me critically, suspiciously, cautiously, weighed what I said with extra care; the customary basis of trust was gone, a natural sense of belonging, which I only really noticed when I lost it. Suddenly ordinary irony, jokes about analysis over a beer, didn't seem appropriate any more, at least not on my part. People kept aloof, were hostile when I tried to overcome this new strangeness. Slowly, but unmistakably, I was becoming someone to be avoided, a kind of leper to be kept at a distance.

At first I put this change down to oversensitivity on my part, due to my hunger for human contact; without analysis, I wanted more from other people. Or it might be my inclination to paranoid feelings. I thought I was indeed oversensitive, and tried to behave differently, in a more friendly manner, seeming more at ease. I was not very successful. Finally, a woman I knew explained: She had had quite a shock when I mentioned the end of my analysis. It had alarmed her to see how quickly and unhappily analysis could come to an end, and in my place she wouldn't go about telling everyone about it. I saw what she meant. I had already been feeling like a blasphemer among the faithful. However, this stealthy, cool rejection, the faint contempt, the sense of exclusion were painful and unpleasant. Particularly when I didn't understand them, and didn't trust my own feelings.

My work, however, gave me some security. It was to some extent inspiring. I had pushed myself to the limits of my powers, and that had been a good thing. I was not in such a hurry now, without daily analytic sessions, and not so touchy either. However, there were not many people who really agreed with me over the termination of my analysis. Many were horrified, and quick to condemn it as another of my problems. A few believed it had been right, when they saw that I did seem to be altogether better.

I found it hard, myself, to stand by my own convictions. I had forcibly pried myself free, with the help of superiors at work, of friends, of 120 horse-power and a thick skin—well, a thick wolfskin—and of my family background. I had done the thing I seriously contemplated doing three years before, from which I had let myself be dissuaded by interpretations, references to my problems, and so forth. My colleagues and my analytically-minded friends were now quite sure that I ought to go back into analysis after all. It was almost like being tugged into a vortex. And privately, out of the analytic context, I did see some sense in it. I was certainly not of the opinion that I had no neurosis at all. I would have liked to learn and understand things I felt were true about myself. It was just the *kind* of analysis I'd had I thought was so dreadful. I wasn't against analysis in principle.

And now, when I didn't feel well, or parts of therapies hadn't succeeded to my satisfaction—in fact, at the least little thing—all my self-confidence threatened to collapse. Perhaps I really *was* harmful to those around me? Perhaps I really *did* have a very special neurosis in urgent need of treatment? One that made me unendurable? Was it just that people didn't openly let me know? Did my patients pretend to be happy with me from opportunistic motives? If my training analyst had had such difficulty with me—hadn't he been perfectly right? Was I so lacking in insight, so incapable of discernment??? Wouldn't I do better to go back into analysis after all?

I could: My analyst was still keeping the time free for me. Any gentle hint could throw me right off balance, no matter from whom, even people whom I'd seen as ranging from the not very sensitive to those quite unable to judge me at all. They could confront me, once more, with those doubts of myself I kept at bay with such difficulty. I was often on the point of calling my analyst. And I felt sure he would have been kind to me in my wretched condition. What held me back, besides the idea of giving in, was my experience of that wounding "Westwall" mood. Qualitatively, almost nothing had changed there. What sort of disturbance did I have? Ought I to call? Should I? If so many people, and a training analyst such as he was, had so much trouble with me, wasn't there truth in it somewhere? However, my analysis with him had simply been awful. The memory of it restrained me even when I was in a bad way.

I met an analyst who listened to me, believed what I said, and didn't offer any interpretations, although I was eagerly expecting them. He did not seem to have any practiced diagnostic antennae out to pick up proofs of my disturbance from commonplace contacts; he treated me as if I were a normal woman, merely wondering if I wouldn't still like to have some pleasant psychoanalytic experiences. And I did feel cheated of an analysis with some substance in it; I thought it was out of the question for me to be conducting intensive therapy without adequate supervision, and decided to look for someone who would combine that function with working on my own problems. I could no longer imagine going in for analysis for its own, art for art's sake; I'd had enough of that after all these years. If I came upon problems of my own in the course of my work, that would be fine, I'd like to approach it that way.

I had preliminary discussions with five analysts, of both sexes. With a woman, what mattered to me was her feminine identity; with men, the way they got on with women, especially their independence of attitude with regard to me. One of the five, a woman, was nice, pleasant, good-natured, and I might have gone into analysis with her if I'd been in a very bad state, but her own way of feminine self-realization prevented me: I couldn't have identified with her there. The four men were not much older and some of them not much more experienced than I was. Their reactions ranged from neutrality, through mild blushing and the taking of shelter behind a desk, to a one-sided facial tic betraying sheer panic when, with diagnostic intent, I beamed at its owner. With none of them, except perhaps for the man who blushed slightly, did I feel that I couldn't have upset their balance with relative ease. As for the man who had the facial tic, I might well have been letting myself in for a fair amount of sexual guilt feelings as well, on account of my upsetting personality.

And that exhausted my possibilities of being able to go into analysis in an uncomplicated sort of way. In any case, I had been interested for some time in more recent methods of therapy; I took part in several courses, in quite rapid succession, and had some healing experiences which did me good:

1. At a Gestalt therapy course, I met a woman who kept assuring me of the reality and strength of my feelings, and stopped me from denigrating them by considering them crazy, or bringing them down to other people's standards; she gave me the confidence to trust what I felt. I also learned to take my intense physical reactions to the affects of others seriously—their grief, excitement, etc.—and to trust them. I was never alone with my sensations: A feeling of tension in the head, nausea, pressure in the stomach, abdominal cramps, sexual excitement, aggressive and silly moods, crippling weariness, etc. I always felt very precisely and strongly what others were feeling. When one man couldn't go on speaking and fell silent, I almost threw up, as he had once been obliged to do as a child; his feeling had communicated itself to me. It wasn't my own problem, I was just going along with it. And I wasn't the only one; the others there felt the same, which was reassuring. I was sensitive, perhaps more sensitive than many people, but my sensations were all right.

Aggression directed against my perceptions died down during this course. I had perceived unpleasantness sooner and faster than many of the other participants, had expressed some ideas that had been repressed, had been rather ahead of everyone else, but then it turned out I was right, and I felt I was liked. People who mattered to me thought I was "sweet" and physically attractive. I was being sweet, too; there was one man there whom I liked very much. I had his therapeutic well-being at heart; it was more important to me than my own concerns. An analyst present thought me "a mature, loving woman"—an experienced analyst, who had seen my crying, with a runny nose and no make-up, so that my outward appearance couldn't have led him astray. The man I'd met liked my stronger sides. We could fight, and it was all right if I was the stronger; we could do intellectual battle over some subject or other in the group, and he was quite happy if I won. He didn't feel threatened, diminished, belittled.

I was no longer used to just being liked or considered physically attractive, not having to hide my potential; he didn't think I was castrating. Indeed, he laughed at the idea, and at the notion of his fearing me. I had forgotten I could be attractive, and was no longer accustomed simply to being thought of as good-natured. What mattered to me most was the discovery that I was actually capable of feeling intensely and primarily for another person, and that the effect of this was felt by others. Also that I might not after all—or at least not always, not exclusively—be an unloving and egocentric creature. There was sensuality in me, and I could be good-natured.

On the first evening I felt great rage: Against my analysis, my analyst, the Association. I could have screamed, hit out, wielded a blunt instrument, done murder. My feelings condensed into cramps in my guts and a stabbing abdominal pain. A therapeutic attempt to relate my feelings to my father and stepfather, experiencing them in that way, didn't work. My murderous rage would not change direction. It was related to my analysis. I became envious of those who could re-live moments from their early childhood. They were suffering from childhood traumas, and remembered bad experiences with fathers, mothers, siblings; they wanted to murder, throttle, rape and hate people. But I kept coming back to my analysis. Some of the participants in this course were working through traumas and misunderstandings arising from earlier courses. This, in a way, reassured me: It was a parallel to my own analytic traumas. However, neither phenomenon seemed necessary. Courses ought not to provide traumatic experiences as material for further courses, and analyses ought not to feed on their own traumas, on the reworking of misunderstandings that arose during them and so on. There was sweetness in me, other people could like me for myself; I felt my sensitivity was confirmed—and so were the wounds I had suffered in analysis, if not quite such strong ones.

2. I went to a course on Gestalt therapy and TZI (Themenkon-zentrierte Interaktion—theme-concentrated interaction), and a very unpleasant kind of tension, reminiscent of my "Westwall" atmosphere, arose between me and the course director the very first evening. So I had a private conversation with him, trying to find a common denominator, but the tension kept getting worse. I slept poorly, feeling desperate; this couldn't be true. I really did have something in me which gave rise to tension. Next morning, the course director came to me, explained that he thought I was very attractive, this had suddenly struck him yesterday and he hadn't known how to deal with the idea all at once. He was perfectly frank, and soon we were on the same pleasant wavelength, communicating through skin, eyes, voices. I felt as if I were being caressed. His honesty impressed me, as did the risk he was taking, as course director, in admit-ting to such feelings. His frankness had eased the situation without weakening him. He wasn't angry or annoyed with me for the feelings I'd provoked, and he didn't press me. To him, I was an attractive woman, not a tough nut to crack, not a very difficult case, not highly neurotic or castrating. With his gentle sensitivity, he understood my moods and my groping, ques-tioning account of myself; he couldn't feel I had had the distur-bances I described. Later, an aggressive argument with him did me good. I was allowed to stand by my anger, live it out, and the episode ended well. After that, I could rid myself of my annoyance by going for a swim, and I felt strong and good, as if my anger were translated directly into power. Another inci-dent also meant a good deal to me: There was a woman partici-pant there with whom he didn't get on and couldn't communicate; when she wanted to leave, he left the decision up to her. He didn't insist on payment; he recognized the validity of her arguments. His authority might seem to suffer at first, but she emerged from the situation without any traumas. Amidst group pressure, it would have been so easy to offer an interpretation attacking her as an outsider, hurt her and force her to stay.

3. I reacted fast, and violently, in a primal scream group. Where other participants went back to childhood experiences, I

reverted again, and with great vehemence, to the story of my
analysis. I left one session swollen-eyed, my face flushed. An
analyst present was perplexed. This was still a very recent
wound, he said (it was a year and a half after the end of the
analysis), and the scab had had difficulty in forming over it, as
with the burn on my wrist I'd just given myself on an electric
light bulb. I had thought of this man as a possible future analyst for me. He was surprised when I said so. Why, he asked?
I'd be just as well off talking to a colleague or friend with whom
I could have a frank discussion of the difficulties I encountered
in therapy: With a real relationship. I thought so too, at heart,
but I was always inclined to feel uncertain when all around
were pressuring me. (All things considered, the kindest and
neatest solution would have been to take it that I really did
have a neurosis which was very hard to treat: I would then
have counted as a special case, a very unusual specimen, and
my analyst as a capable practitioner who just wasn't up to such
a complicated disturbance as mine. We could all have agreed
on the matter, and I would still have been part of that world.)
The analyst to whom I was now talking thought that the director of this course was unconsciously rejecting me, and no wonder, as he admitted to hating his mother. So that was it!

One participant in the course brought me nearer to understanding another phenomenon: I began by getting on well with
him, we liked each other, were on the same pleasant wavelength, it was all quite easy. And then tension arose, followed
by a distinctly cool, touchy rejection and hostility. I felt helpless: Why must this happen again, just now? He was avoiding
me, or simply failing to react to my questions. Finally, when
slightly tipsy, he said with a knowing smile, "Well, you see,
it's really quite simple: I'll never be up to a woman like
you, and that upsets me, so I prefer to get out." I was grateful
for this explanation, the more so as his assessment of me was
mistaken.

I felt damaged for some time after this course, as if I had
been dealt a wounding body blow. Once again, I decided to let
it all rest, allow myself to heal slowly, and not go poking around
in the sore places left by my analysis. So much vitality was
flowing out of me, and I was the loser.

4. I made a last attempt at therapy, against my better judgment, in a Gestalt and TZI therapy course conducted by a woman. I became yet more confident of my sensibility, but apart from that the course was hell. I very quickly became the focus of many intensely felt projections: Hatred for the younger sister, for the husband's younger mistress, for the girls of the Nazi Bund Deutscher Mädchen,* plain envy of women who were younger and had more freedom, male fury against women with whom they did not score, against women they desired, against their mothers, and so on.

Even if I could understand and interpret the individual cases, relating them to these people's histories, it still hurt, and as the person concerned couldn't draw all the emotional conclusions directly after the interpretation of his projection, thus solving his problem, I really did incur a lot of hostility. If someone punches me on the chin and I am subsequently told he meant to hit someone else, I'm still the one he hurt.

There was one man I was able to help out of an analytically treacherous situation: He had reacted angrily to the course director and then, in a private conversation with her, related his anger to his mother, seeing it as pure transference reaction. Full of guilt feelings, and discouraged, he diagnosed the trouble as his persistent inability to work through his problems with his mother. I saw the situation differently: The course director really had been unusually sharp with him, and his annoyance was understandable and needn't rest on any unresolved hatred of his mother: It was a likely, logical reaction. The treachery, I thought, lay in the fact that she, the director, wouldn't acknowledge her actual role in the incident; she entirely discounted her own irritation and related his strong emotional reaction directly and exclusively to his early childhood. She now considered herself "neutral" in this, which left him the neurotic one in need of therapy. To my mind, she had felt he was neglecting her and had taken her revenge. She had opened up his old wound, and then acted as if he went about bleeding from it all the time.

This is just how I had developed hatred. I know that what I

*A Nazi youth group for girls

consider healing, for myself, may be entirely superficial. However, I have clung to these events; they gave me courage at difficult moments. Perhaps I am inclined to be superficial in my explanations too. Perhaps that English-speaking analyst at the primal scream course, in whose arms I wept and who then referred me to a friend, stood for my father, or for father figures in America, and I now had permission to turn to someone different, younger, of the same age and status as myself. I no longer had to remain "true to my father." In my experience, anyway, it was more important that he thought me normal, healthy, lovable, not to be doubted as a human being. (But I do still feel cheated of the analytic peaks, of their higher mathematics.)

After the end of my analysis, I came to know several men who were not psychologically damaged. I could feel good in their presence, in a way I'd quite forgotten. I don't think I would have fallen victim to such self-doubts if I'd known such men while I was in analysis, if I hadn't at that time been mixing almost exclusively with people who were in analysis themselves, and were also very sensitive and insecure, whose problems with their mothers and other women had been stirred up and had an acute influence on our interaction.

Apropos of equal rights, I was given some telling insights. I had observed edgily to my lover, very much the doctor: "Your hands somehow don't seem connected with your body, hanging in that funny way." The reply came, amused and thoughtful, "No, no, you're wrong. I play an instrument—don't I caress you well enough, then?" I was startled and touched. The interpretation—a case of understanding on a deeper plane—brought us back to an affectionate wavelength from which I'd strayed with my medical observation. I felt much affected, and my body reacted: I stopped discussing the pathology of his gestures in that argumentative, disputative way. I was struck by the part my longing played in the perception; I had rediscovered something I had forgotten about myself and my wishes, and felt much happier than I had in the preceding discussion, with its cool fault-finding—though my own flaw was still present.

On one occasion I went through the wrong door by mistake, and found myself in the room of a woman whom I wasn't seeing much at the moment. A man on his way out of this room laughed, and wondered if I might not want to go in after all. I denied it in a down-to-earth way, and stiffened up inside—nor would I be persuaded to go in, although she would have been glad to see me, and the look in his eyes told me so. My slip embarrassed me. I didn't feel at ease, and my matter-of-fact voice was pitched too high. I went and did what I had to do, in the room I had sought originally; however, the fact that the incident hadn't been cleared up bothered me, and later I realized that I would very much have liked a conversation with that woman. She had often shown me solidarity and understanding which had done me good, although we had little contact in organizational terms, and the time at which I'd made my slip was about the only possible time during the week when I could have seen her in her room, undisturbed. The man just leaving probably understood that, and I might well have acted on his intuition and satisfied one of my present wishes, a desire for a little human warmth.

I found I could rely upon coming up with this cool, firm rejection of something, made in a too matter-of-fact voice and with a faint sense of uneasiness. I was actually calling upon a deeper level of feeling: Something that, perhaps, I didn't quite want to perceive. Sometimes my refusal to acknowledge this was so strong that I couldn't reach it at all. Often, however, new and better feelings then surfaced.

I was sitting at a bar counter with a friend, a man who hadn't been analyzed, and had just been telling him in a rather ill-humored, clumsy way about my future plans, my voice flat and rather unnatural. He obviously took none of this very seriously, and just said, with amusement, "Okay, softy?" It wasn't a form of address I was used to, but he sounded so cheerful that my mood changed. My future professional plans, and so on, were really only a framework to which I was clinging: Desire was my overwhelming feeling.

Now and then I had fits of movie-going, and would see several films in an evening, one after another. If I didn't like one immediately, I'd be out of the theater again in no time. A lover rang me before one such evening, but I'd just decided on the various films I wanted to see. He thought what I was really after was hopping out of one bed and into another: I said, nonsense, and made a vague date to meet him after I'd been to the movies; then I carried out my cultural plans. While I was out, however, I found I felt his excitement; I forgot about the rest of the films, went looking for him, couldn't find him, felt I was being promiscuous, was annoyed at the lack of opportunity for women to satisfy such needs, was glad I wasn't often delivered up to these forthright and undiscriminating desires.

After I had explained at length to an unanalyzed man why I was in a certain place, what I planned to do, and what I needed to get done, he remarked, summing it all up, "So you want to freshen up your love life here?" I thought this far-fetched and didn't react, or not until some time later. But that really was my deeper motivation, and his remark brought about a change in me, in my body and my mood. I thought it was what might be called a true interpretation (except that I've no wish critically to examine all the more vital, joyous, real men by applying analytic criteria). Some of them obviously do live on a more vital and genuine plane anyway.

There were some books that had a salutory effect on me: *Mit dreissig muss man wissen, was man will* [*You must know what you want at thirty*]: Interviews with women who had made careers for themselves. Almost unanimously, they said that a woman working in a masculine profession, or wishing to reach a certain position of power, has to be considerably better qualified than a man in a comparable situation. They had frequent experience of being ignored or disregarded in discussions, of encountering dislike of what they said, of instilling fear into men. I knew about that kind of thing.

It was news to me that one could remain "irreconcilable" in analysis, that such a thing was permissible and might even be a goal (the foreword to *Lehrjahre au der Couch* [*Years of Apprenticeship on the Couch*]). If I rejected someone, or didn't like something, I saw that as my problem, meaning there was something I didn't yet understand. The ideal, as it ran through my analyses, had been the ability to understand and be reconciled to anything. If I vehemently rejected something, for instance, that was evidence of an impulse which I needed to reject in others as well as in me. At heart, I wasn't supposed to make any value judgments or come down firmly on one side or another. I must understand; indignation was neurotic. Or so I understood it emotionally, anyway. Putting up a fight was frowned upon.

Soul Murder: Persecution in the Family: Schatzmann shows that what

is diagnosed in analysis as a system of delusion founded on complicated defense mechanisms on the part of the son (e.g., homo-erotic
drives) can be simply explained, without any kind of alteration, as
real perception of the father's child-rearing mechanism where the
father has in fact been cruelly persecuting his son (by means of mechanical devices, ghastly pieces of apparatus, mechanisms for
checking up on him and so forth). The son's one psychotic mechanism as described in this case was not to perceive his father as the
sole persecutor: It would have been too dreadful to see clearly that
it really and truly *was* his father treating him in such a way. The defense mechanism in the service of survival was simply to dissociate
this persecution and localize it on some outside subject, removed
from the father, in this case God. The son's brother committed suicide; the surviving brother took this way out. What mattered to me
was seeing the way the system of delusions had been taken seriously, just as the patient experienced it: The precision with which
the book's author traced Schreber, the son's "crazy" perceptions,
his good nature, the way he took the patient seriously, his acceptance of him, showed that the patient was absolutely right and had
not even been mistaken in his perceptions. Indeed, the patient perceived the actual world to which he had been exposed very accurately; in his own way he was quite right, and no allowances had
to be made for him. The author's good nature, understanding and
diligence appealed to me.

   Two Accounts of a Journey through Madness: During supportive therapy, a woman diagnosed as psychotic found she could live out her
feelings and needs—involving the smearing of excrement, regres-
sions, etc.—and ultimately became a painter. Her needs and
wishes were taken seriously; she was able to satisfy many frustrated
needs, and she became whole. Her therapist took care to follow his
patient's internal voice, trusted her feelings and plans. The whole
process had a deep validity, and she had directed her own cure. All
the therapist did was help her translate her wishes, plans and ideas
into action; he didn't leave her alone with her risks and fears. Her
activities were not forbidden, even discreetly, however chaotic her
behavior might seem. The therapist did not think of himself as in-
fallible either; he saw his own weaknesses, his occasional immatur-
ity compared to his patient, his inhibitions and inclination to hold
back. He himself was learning, and he changed in the process. He

took her seriously as an independent, clever, intelligent person, but one who hadn't been able to cope with life as well as he had in the circumstances in which she found herself. He did not allow the external aspects of her behavior to put him off. I very much liked the way they had dealt with the situation.

Women and Madness: I was much interested in the accounts of erotic tension in analysis given in this book by women analysands and patients in therapy. They had a familiar ring. So did the analysts' reactions. A second point: Many women were diagnosed as "sick" or "psychotic" if they rebelled and resisted the role forced upon them. It was *then* that they were put on psychopharmacological drugs and given psychiatric treatment if they reacted aggressively. They came home depressive; i.e., resigned. I myself saw women who were in such a condition; they could be quite all right in a different atmosphere, without any drugs at all. Justifiably, they were very angry. Once these women had come off the drugs, they were furious first about the injustice of it, then experienced guilt because of their primitive rage. I thought they were, basically, perfectly healthy, and their rage or depression (seen as aggression turned inwards) was logical. I could hardly discover adequate reasons in their past histories for diagnoses of depression, and even then I could only as a tiny part of the whole. The oppression they were actually suffering predominated, their anger at their treatment and the lack of respect shown them. These women were neither "mad" nor "neurotic," just angry; they emerged from depression fast once they were able to recognize that they had good reasons for their anger, and could minimize their guilt feelings. They blossomed in groups of similar women. Some were—presumably—too weak to be able to change their situation, and these saw little of its reality, or did so with difficulty. In one group a woman who had often had psychiatric treatment said firmly she would never make a suicide attempt again: The man in the case wasn't worth it. Three of the four women in the group had been beaten up so badly they needed hospitalization. I felt much affected by their accounts. These were very sensitive, perceptive, loving women at heart, not the superficial kind. A "patient" said she was a good housewife, a good mother, perfectly presentable—and who had made her that way? It wasn't what she wanted! She spoke with all the anger at her disposal. She needed help for persistent insomnia. I came to the conclusion that I thought her healthy. I'd have been happy to have tea with her, but I couldn't have "treated" her. I could see very good reasons that kept her from sleeping, but little in the way of neurotic failure to work through. I felt rather taken aback: My medical colleagues had found all sorts of reasons to judge her neurotic, but I could see exactly how she felt.

I was struck by two ideas from a lecture given by Bruno Bettelheim:

1. To encounter parental indifference and lack of interest is the worst thing that can happen to a child, and leaves the deepest wounds, since whatever the child does he gets no reaction, merely indifference to anything and everything. On the other hand, if children have parents who do have ideas on child-rearing, however stern and rigid those ideas may be, the children still have a chance of being loved if they conform to their parents' notions.

I thought of my mother, and how she could beam at children when she was pleased with them, when presumably part of her conditions for being pleased had been fulfilled. She certainly wasn't indifferent. And I didn't want to cling to hatred, as most of my analytical acquaintances did.

2. All children—even the most desperately sick—can be reconciled to their parents during therapy, however difficult those parents may be. If they still hate the parents, their therapy has not worked. People I knew who had been analyzed, or were in analysis, never seemed to make their peace, least of all with their mothers.

I felt shattered after watching a television program of interviews with people who had been foundlings or had been lost as children. Many had never discovered their families again, most had never known a parent, many knew nothing or only a very little about their origins (where they came from, their nationality, their background). These people were no more than particularly notable representatives of the wartime generation, to which I myself belonged: Good examples of war children. Others had, at some point, met their fathers again, found relatives believed lost in flight, or evacuation, or air raids; once the separations caused by air raids were over, most of these knew their family circumstances. At least they had photographs of fathers, mothers, other relations; at least they knew stories about the characteristics of those family members whom a child may be supposed to resemble, and with whose help he can root himself in a known tradition. I sensed a gentle, yearning melancholy in these people who had been lost as children, and I could have wept over it. It showed in their loving care and grave sense of responsibility towards their new families, and a vague insecurity about themselves. For instance, one man, now a father, had been able to offer nothing as an indication of his origins but a story about a horse, in a dialect that sounded East Prussian; however, his son had dark hair, so he may more probably have come from the Polish border, or from farther south. Many of them seemed to be unsure and find it unpredictable what might come from them or their bodies. An unmarried woman who had grown up in Russia had found her family in West Germany only a few years ago, and was now living with them. She seemed very affectionate, and treated her parents as something precious. A woman said of her husband that she couldn't always understand him—but then, no one knew where he came from. He looked sad and helpless. I would have liked to embrace every one of these people, build a nest for them; they were all enveloped in that melancholy yearning, and seemed particularly grave and sensitive, though otherwise no different from other people.

It was Toman's book on family constellations that really reconciled me to myself, my weaknesses, my strengths and other qualities. I read it while I was sick at the end of my analysis. I had an ear infection and couldn't hear properly; I was in pain and stayed in bed. The reading partly filled me with enthusiasm, but it shook and upset me too. A great deal of what it said seemed absolutely right, and saddened me as well as confirming my feelings. Despite everything, I seemed to be the typical younger sister of brothers. In the middle of the book I felt increasingly agitated, restless and hurt, as well as understood; I didn't want to read on. However, the second part of the book calmed me down again; it was just that I still had to realize and take full account of much within me. I did have many sensitive spots, weaknesses and strengths. Many of my own

preferences, upon which I'd brooded and which I'd tried to work
out analytically (for instance, the closeness of important men)
showed up in other younger sisters too. They were no more than
the typical attitudes to be expected if you were born in such a position in the family.

As I read the book, I had feelings reminiscent, in miniature, of
what one might expect during a good analysis: A sense of disturbance, insecurity, a more or less objective view of my own personality, showing my weaknesses and strengths, and eventual
reconciliation to it. I could explain much of myself and my problems and capacities in such terms; I need not be surprised or angry.
The author wrote in a truly tolerant tone, free of prejudice, indeed
with amusement; he was an observer, clearly not hostile to anyone
or any type of person. Perhaps this was the ideal of a benevolent,
non-judgmental analysis.

If I had known about these regularly recurring family situations,
the conditions in which I had grown up—I don't believe I would
have questioned myself so drastically.

Possibly, too, an awareness of the poverty of my critical faculties
concerning elder brothers would have preserved me from too much
analytic confidence.

I did not care to read that "she is all that a man conventionally
imagines a woman to be." This had bothered me for a long time.
Even if I hadn't troubled to be particularly clean and was wearing
drab colors, it seemed I always looked well groomed. "Little Miss
Tidy," I'd heard myself called. Friends in Berlin had taken me
along when they wanted to sound out a professor about something,
just because I looked so neat. I had felt offended that I was seldom
checked on the border posts with East Germany; when I had an aggressive woman friend in the car with me, the situation was instantly different.

"Her enjoyment of work and her practical readiness to fling herself into her career are only average"—I didn't like that, either, although it seemed I could change it "for love of an ambitious man."
However, it wasn't impossible for me to work really hard. "She will
do anything for a man she loves, and whom she has good reason
to love."

I'd often deplored the fact that I had too few real interests of my
own, and was over-inclined to go along with what men enjoyed;

recently, I'd been sharply criticized for it by an analyzed friend. ". . . the way in which she tends to adapt to the life and professional interests of one or more men . . . she is more likely to develop cultural and intellectual interests in imitation of her brothers, or men in general, than on her own initiative."

I had developed an interest in politics only by way of an article by one of my brothers; I don't know if I would have absorbed all the arguments otherwise. When I was studying medicine, I had for a while wanted to specialize in endocrinology. I wanted to use hormones to keep women young and vital. One of the considerations that kept me from pursuing this was that I would have been spending all day in a lab with reagents, and when I became more expert and more specialized, I might have discussion partners in Japan, the USA, Finland, but no stimulating men in my immediate environment. I was amazed by the energy and enthusiasm with which a woman friend of mine approached her lifeless reagent jars. I found it hard to feel such impersonal, detached interest. I was afraid of turning numb in a laboratory empty of humanity.

I had always felt guilty about my slapdash way with money. As an assistant physician, I used to keep my account hovering around zero. When the banks gave credit to the amount of three times one's gross salary—no need to apply, you could just overdraw—I then remained about that amount overdrawn. When I had a full assistant's salary, my expenses tacitly increased to the point where I might be overdrawn by three times that full salary. At best my account stood at zero. In fact, this had never worried me much, but other people amazed me: One assistant physician had saved enough to buy a new Volkswagen in two years. Others took out mortgages, life insurance, automatic savings plans, bought shares. Now and then my conscience pricked me, and I felt like a criminal. But I didn't mind lending money either. Somehow or other, I just didn't seem to have any financial sense; what I really wanted was to support a worthy project. After all, entire families could live on a salary like mine—but I still couldn't manage to save with any real regularity. It was comforting to hear that "material possessions mean little to her." "The man she loves is her most precious 'material possession'." I needn't reproach myself quite so much if other younger sisters also were like that.

Another cheering comment was: "If she has particular talents, she will not necessarily develop and make practical use of them." I had heard this again and again, and reproached myself for my lack of initiative. I'd been told I was gifted: As a painter, with language, with my hands—but none of this really mattered much to me. Only later was I hurt and made uneasy by theories about subordination, the lack of competitive spirit, the fear of surpassing my parents and brothers, and thus failing to realize myself fully.

"In her career, she does not particularly care about realizing her own ambitions, or about self-realization. What matters more to her is the ability to do what she enjoys, or work in the company of men she admires."

It was a fact that the proximity of interesting men had always mattered a lot to me. Indeed, male friends had interested me in psychoanalysis. In my last year at school, a friend of my brother's had recommended Freud to me, and when I actually got around to reading him, another male friend suggested it also. I had then discussed Freud with him on the phone. He was inspiring, and so were the people at the hospital to which I then applied for admission.

This alone would probably have sufficed to determine my choice of career. Perhaps it had not been necessary to search for any deep-seated, motivating disturbance. I might have become enthusiastic over proctology, or some other funny specialization, if I'd encountered interesting men in the field, people with intellectual charm.

It clarified my ideas to hear that "her women friends envy her." I had often blamed myself, wondering what aggression I might conceal in my consciously friendly feelings to make other women react that way.

"She fascinates men not just fleetingly . . . but enduringly." Yes, and that had often been a source of conflict. I found it natural to continue relying on former lovers. My analyst had asked me where I got the confidence to feel I could still count on them, even after a long interval. First I had been surprised at his doubts, then I had reduced my expectations. Another analyst had told me, his expression superneutral, "It's easy for you to get a man to like you," as if I employed some special ruse, but that had seen through me!

It had also seemed clear that if someone liked, loved or desired me, my guilt feelings, sexual fears and Oedipal problems obliged me to blot out that fact, leaving it unrealized and unperceived. In fact, it had often surprised me to find that such things happened.

"However, this happens very quickly, or at any rate without much of a splash; she is no femme fatale." An analyst had reproached me for making too little of my conquests, saying that while I met with much response, it wasn't very noticeable; he had interpreted it as my neurosis that I stayed in the background, a "serving maid" figure, and so didn't get adequate social recognition for my success. I understood this intellectually, but it didn't bother me. Now it seemed I was not alone in my indifference (defense, or subordination). The younger sister is less vain than other girls.

I found comments on my intense reactions here too: "Loss can shatter her deeply. She seems to suffer more than anyone else affected . . . she suffers and grieves with all her heart . . . she openly expresses, as it were, what others feel . . . " So I needn't wonder why things affected me so deeply. "At times her suffering can be . . . so great that even the consolation of others does not help her. She wants to follow the beloved dead, not by suicide, but in a quiet denial of life, fading out of the world." I had always respected suicides; I, however, would be more inclined to react with depression, numbness.

Nor was my lack of desire to lead, my minimal professional ambition, mine alone: Younger sisters are more inclined to make such careers as "secretary, doctor's nurse/receptionist, lab technician, admiring companion of an artist, an actress who is the willing instrument of a strongly individual director. I realized that when the younger sister always trots behind her big brothers like a little dog, uncritically admiring, it's bound to leave its mark.

I had been given quite a number of presents in my time, even a very nice car. "Yet she often finds herself more lavishly endowed (with material possessions) than others. Her brothers themselves usually make sure she lacks for nothing." I had seen my attitude as childish, reproaching myself for my poor sense of financial independence, but the fact was there had always been someone in my life from whom I could borrow, who would help me.

I was glad to read: "She can give in without being submissive. She is a good friend, ready to act with devotion when someone she esteems or loves desires it . . . she will do anything for a man she loves and whom she has good reason to love . . . of all types of girl, she is the first to find the right partner. As a woman, she knows what she wants, but she can adapt in every other respect."

"In general, her best choice would be a man who is the elder brother of sisters . . . " In fact, these were almost the only men I knew intimately; at least, my lovers were elder brothers, and almost all had a younger sister. I could have drawn up a map of elder brothers. Former points of conflict were described accurately, as well: "In a man who is the younger brother of sisters, she would miss that sense of leadership and responsibility to which she is accustomed in her own brothers." Yes, I had felt that lack in such a man, as had he, correspondingly, in me. With the eldest brother of a family of brothers, however, the younger sister often finds "to her regret, that he cannot accept her as she is. He wants to change her too much." I had discovered that, several times. Elder brothers held a special fascination for me, but there were many disadvantages to those who had no sisters. "Relatively speaking, about her worst choice would be the youngest brother of a family of brothers, or an only child." I knew that was so, though I'd often been unable to make others see what I meant.

So I was a relatively typical case, of a kind frequently encountered, although supposedly these characteristics become marked only in the absence of early losses and war. However, as both my brothers were so typical of this family situation, we must somehow have grown up comparatively undamaged. My family couldn't be so sick after all.

And my parents' marriage, my mother's uncritical admiration of my father, now seemed credible as well: As the younger sister of a brother and the elder brother of a sister, they made a very good couple.

I was a typical youngest child; others shared my strengths and weaknesses, I was normal, no exception. Thus, I probably wasn't so excessively neurotic and warped after all. At least, not noticeably more so than other people in our society who had grown up in similar circumstances.

It had hurt me that almost everything had been seen from a negative viewpoint, so that I came to regard myself as sick, fixated, entangled in early relationships.

It may well be that sibling relationships haven't been adequately investigated, and that typical roles, in small families in a capitalist society, are obliged to develop as they do, amidst much psychological misery.

But many characteristics do occur quite often in ordinary circumstances, and are no cause to sound an alarm. This might at least have been recognized in my case. No one need express incredulous amazement at an East Frisian's hair color or size, inspecting him closely and wondering if he can really be so tall, or genuinely blond: These characteristics are frequently found in East Frisians. It should be possible, at some point, to perceive one's own type, a type with fairly well-established traits, and to stand up for those qualities in oneself which are basically hard to change, even if this could, with effort, be achieved.

A man who had been conventionally analyzed told me how he puzzled for a long time over an interpretation he didn't understand in one session. When at last, years later, he asked his analyst, she had forgotten about it, and try as she might she couldn't remember. He was left with the unanswered question, and his helpless melancholy.

I might be glad if I did remember interpretations, and they didn't just worm their way deep into me, gnawing away at me, doing me harm.

After Analysis

THE WORST THING WAS, AND IS, MY FUNDAMEN-
tal doubt of almost everything about me: My feelings, my
thoughts, my judgment, my reason. In particular my doubt as to
whether I might not have some hidden, serious sickness after all,
"a deep early disturbance." Was I perhaps "on the borderline of
psychosis;" did some similar suspected diagnosis, never explicitly
imparted to me, apply?

My insecurity was increased by the vague sense, which I noticed
only gradually, of having acquired leper status. My colleagues were
unsure of me, and really did regard me with suspicion. In addition,
there was my genuine insecurity, intensified by my perception of
the doubts and fears of others. At the start of my analysis, in the
first euphoric period during which I still felt great enthusiasm for
many aspects of it, when I met colleagues who were said to have
"run through" one or more analysts until they could find the right
one (someone able "to treat their severe disturbance"), I myself regarded them with scornful suspicion, as if they were crazy. I could
hardly resent such an attitude now. To hint at doubts, or merely at
rather less lofty expectations, is as useless and likely to provoke violent rejection as to point out flaws in the woman of his choice to a
man newly in love. Doubts and uncertainties are awful. Everything
becomes blurred; the insinuations and suspicions of others assume
undue importance. Under that group pressure which emanates
from those who expect analysis to provide major therapy, many
things carry more weight than they would in "normal" circumstances, (i.e., in those not in analysis).

The argument that one can be made insecure only because one
has doubts oneself does not always apply, and frequently is

overused. After all, there are plenty of experiments illustrating the way people can be influenced under pressure from authority, the group, etc. One need only be a little well-disposed and cooperative in analysis, and then one is all too inclined to see personal factors everywhere; after all, that's the point of it. Outer reality—in most cases—takes on a subordinate (and if dominant, then uninteresting) and not really relevant significance.

It is very difficult to describe what it is like to be considered repulsive, to be regarded with suspicion, if not actually as distinctly sick or even "crazy." I can't prepare myself for it; I can reduce the words and jokes to a minimum, but even then they have a noticeable effect. And if I am simply myself and say what I happen to be thinking, that is regarded with suspicion too. Particularly unpleasant was what was left unspoken: I had clearly felt other people's suspicions, but nobody would admit them to me. If they had said, "You're over-depressive—too undifferentiated—you haven't enough empathy—you're too sick in some way, there are certain patients to whom you could do no good"—or something of that nature, I think I could have understood, or at least accepted the logic of it. But the lack of clarity, the failure ever to express a diagnosis, leaving me in great uncertainty, that was the worst of it.

I still fear to give real expression to my rage, despair, sense of pain, unhappiness and hopelessness, since senior analysts might read this, might see an error of judgment somewhere, and interpret it as further proof of my disturbance. I am powerless to combat that kind of thing.

These doubts were not a part of me. I consider them an artificial product. Not that that is any use; that's to say, it does not protect me from fundamental doubt, even when I remember that earlier— at school and college, at my admission interviews, at work under the supervision of highly experienced analysts—nothing really seriously disquieting ever came to light, and the response I met with in patients was such as might please me (I suppose that the consequences of one's troubles would most readily show up in connection with such highly sensitive people as my patients). The doubt is there, as soon as someone uncovers this wound. It is one thing to realize "guilt feelings" in analysis and talk about them; it is another to reduce them in fact. As I write, I have tried again and again to assure myself that I have no cause for shame and guilt, that I have been treated irresponsibly, blindly, affectively, by those with no view of their own limitations. And the thought has repeatedly reassured me. However, my changes of mood show me that I do have considerable potential for vehement guilt feelings within me, ready—at least—to be displaced on other people. I write a letter to a friend, in a mood of spontaneous annoyance; after mailing it I reproach myself, see myself as an unloving bitch, incapable of any constant relationship, egocentric, not capable of reconciliation, maturity, seeing things in the abstract, but instead always lashing out as a result of a sense of personal injury, so that I feel like giving up entirely, and I doubt everything in myself. Such feelings overtake me, and I have a hard time extricating myself. If, in addition, someone happens to express slight criticism of me, I am sure the criticism is right, and feel condemned; and I can feel for those unable to endure their own evil natures. Someone like that really has no right to be a burden on others. Nasty as I really am, all I do is bring discord, strife and hatred. And then I have to set to work to find outside confirmation that I am of real value, something I often feel too resigned to do. Babies have a good effect on me; they can usually get something from me, and they calm me down.

Luckily I had some friends who mattered to me and whose attitude was positive, and without them I don't know how I could have endured such vehement moods, moods that paralyzed and overwhelmed me. I marvel at people who survive such guilt feelings without help of friends.

It is all very well for me to keep telling myself that I was rejected over a period of years, regarded and treated as unlovable, and such things are bound to leave scars: That still doesn't alter my attitude towards myself. A man I knew lost his temper, over the telephone, when he realized the depth of my doubts; I even doubted whether I ought ever to practice my profession again, exposing patients to my evil, unloving nature. Such misgivings are thoroughly discouraging.

Two years after the end of my analysis, I seldom have those anxiety dreams from which I wake resigned and shattered, reminded of a truly terrible time, the mere mention of which could bring me to a state of numb resignation or murderous rage, depending on the situation giving rise to it. The sense of being utterly destroyed, devitalized, of being completely incapable of love and affection, slowly fades and becomes a nightmare, annihilating my vital spirits, my sense of myself, draining me.

That depressive and reproachful current that ran for a while through almost all relationships reminding me even remotely of my analysis has almost dried up. I have often apologized to friends for my suspicious aloofness, but I was able to do so only when I'd understood it and to some extent overcome it, or at least digested it. I still have moods where I am on the alert, ready to fight, on my guard. After such contacts, I am left with a dull sense of inward emptiness which I can fill again only slowly, through some kind of affectionate outside encounter. My warmth is extinguished in the process.

I have become grateful for understanding, but I register it as something unusual when I encounter it. I once dreamed of being in analysis, could remember only vague scraps of my dream, and sat at breakfast feeling very downcast. "You look so stricken," said my companion. I instantly began to weep because I had been understood, without any words, without verbalizing. ("*You* have to make yourself understood," my analyst had said. "How is it that you're misunderstood so easily?")

I am attuned to keeping my reflections, thoughts, ideas and moods to myself, thinking them out *alone,* protecting them from misinterpretation, arming myself, guarding myself. It surprises me when some outside stimulus helps me or contributes to my deeper understanding. I noticed that I'd given up the habit of fruitful discussion. Life used not to be so lonely and difficult. I often, these days, observe myself striking out as a preventive measure, to create space around me. This change in me may be a more efficient way of coping with life, but it isn't particularly lovable.

It hurts me when someone tells me—with or without a slightly reproachful note in their voice—how worn out my former analyst looks. Then I fall into the depths again, wondering if there isn't something very bad, evil, wicked and destructive in me after all. For he is not an obtrusive sort of person, not so very severe or orthodox. How could I do it to a man for whom so many people feel sympathy? That's not how things used to be. Am I really so bad? He is regarded with respect by others, and considered unconventional too. Why is it I keep on feeling I came up against someone cruel and pitiless? How is it that I feel I suffered from my association with him? Is all I feel quite wrong? Wasn't *he* the victim, in the last resort? Did I ruin him to that extent? When I ought to have treated him kindly, gently? Am I the sort of woman who can't let any man alone, and won't rest until she has destroyed him? Particularly a man like that: Friendly, harmless. Views like these are in the air; I keep hearing them. And they activate all my worst fears, especially when conveyed to me in a friendly context, or as a neutral inquiry. At such moments I could weep. Nobody listens to *me*. So now I'm responsible for him and his pallid appearance! Scarcely anyone believes *me,* and I can hardly believe it when someone does take me seriously and listens with understanding rather than a diagnostic air. And it may still be my fault all the same. "How could you pick yourself an analyst like that?" It seems my choice is proof of my secret strategy. "You're an aesthete—he was quite wrong for you." As if there had been any real choice. Anyway, good looks in men had never been particularly important to me; I felt more attracted by intellectual charm. Or so I thought, anyway.

The connection did not simply cease; people talk to me about him; I feel I am held responsible for his general condition; I incur reproach if I say I'm not yet reconciled; he seems to be the proof of my disturbance, my neurotic destructiveness, my malignity.

I sometimes happen to notice how I have accustomed myself to suffering, patience and endurance, bearing things in silence. I went to a play, and after the first ten minutes I felt it was commonplace, badly constructed, and the inconsequent, hectic, poorly acted dialogue left me cold; the atmosphere was repulsive. Formerly, I would simply have walked out. During my schooldays, I wouldn't go to the movies with anyone who wasn't willing to walk out with me if the occasion arose. But now I stayed put, annoyed and critical but still, at first, actively watching, and then feeling resigned and aware of my sick irritability, my extreme sensitivity, that tangle of problems I hadn't managed to resolve in all these years. I tried not to react so violently, not to let things affect me so much, not to take my negative reactions so seriously but to master them, and thus become as healthy, interested, open and capable of enjoyment in my attitude to life as those around me. ("Why are you so vulnerable? What theme did the play touch in you? Why do you want to escape? What intrinsic problem are you avoiding? What are you defending against with your annoyance, boredom and lack of interest? Why does it affect you so much? What prevents you from simply enjoying the play? Others can. What are you defending against? What are you fighting?" "Well, I actually do think this is a commonplace play, fashionably leftish, carrying no real inner conviction, coming to no conclusion, empty, just hubbub, stupid. It really isn't enough to make use of a series of contemporary theatrical tricks. The way they're doing it, naked bodies aren't even erotic." "Ah, you and your high standards—the demands of your superego! Why can't you enjoy the play, why do you have to spoil it for yourself?") And the worst of it is that such thoughts run through my mind almost automatically; it's like shifting gear as you drive a car. I know perfectly well that my reactions are sick and need putting right; I'm different from everybody else.

I can scarcely rebel against such thoughts as these when I don't even notice I'm having them. So there I sit, resigned, on the verge of tears, enduring the performance, which emphasizes the presence of omnipotence of my twisted, neurotic nature. I try at least to settle reasonably comfortably in my seat, to avoid physical discomfort as well.

I was lucky that particular evening. My companion thought the play even more idiotic than I did, and he would have left earlier of his own accord, but was amused to observe my air of painful and resolute endurance.

I have become more sensitive, more cautious about letting anyone get close to me. I find it hard to have anyone in my apartment whom I don't really like a great deal, and by whom I don't really feel accepted or regarded kindly. Denigrating or even inquiring glances hurt me; so much of one's personality is exposed, if one looks around. Cold criticism can spoil so much for me; I just don't have the strength to like my apartment, or a picture, or whatever the object of that criticism was as much afterwards as I did before. When a man who was a comparative stranger to me came to my apartment and then looked critically, intolerantly around him, I felt a horrible atmosphere remaining in the room for hours; I had to recover slowly from his rejection. At such times it takes me a long while to like my surroundings again.

Criticism affects me fundamentally and very seriously. I find it hard to maintain my own standards when I encounter it. I can't simply shake it off by saying, "The man has no taste; never mind." Other people's opinions carry more weight than my own.

My analysts are still there inside me. I wanted to write to a friend whom I couldn't reach directly, but I couldn't find just the right postcard, couldn't decide on one (he was someone to whom I wrote postcards, almost exclusively, trusting the picture on the card to convey the rest of my message). So having narrowed down my choice to eighteen cards, I sent them all in one envelope. I knew my second analyst wouldn't have approved. What was the matter with my ego functions, with reality, the usual way to behave? Was I pressuring my friend, getting too close, being hyperactive, over-whelming and overpowering him? Weren't eighteen cards rather much, rather unusual? Too direct an approach? Was my inner self so fragmented, so incoherent and disintegrated, that I was unable to express myself adequately on a single compact postcard?

Such thoughts are nonsense, of course, since my analyst never uttered them, but I've become autonomous, self-sufficient, and can think in that way without having him sitting there behind the back of my head. It takes strength and courage not to go on like that. My friend just laughed, was pleased, and covered a bare wall with the cards.

I frequently find myself convinced I'm a pain in the neck, and am lucky if people fail or are not perceptive enough to notice. I have been out with friends and spent a pleasant evening, feeling at ease with them, and then, later, I'm not at all sure they felt the same. Had I perhaps been a bother? A nuisance? Were they just afraid to get rid of me? I await their reaction suspiciously, anx-iously. I hesitate just to telephone or tell them directly that I en-joyed my evening with them. If I do get spontaneous, friendly feedback, I breathe a sigh of relief; I *didn't* bother them after all, they *didn't* mind me, I didn't exhaust and drain them emotionally, did them no harm with my unloving, unpleasant core, my conflict-ridden nature, with my absolute egocentricity, my hating, evil, de-structive basic character.

At heart I am always surprised when people just like me, sur-prised to find I'm not entirely a scourge.

It can put others off to see me cautiously scenting the air to find out what effect I've had on them. One friend of mine asked crossly why I was looking like a wounded deer: An evening such as we were spending wasn't all that important, and it troubled him and made him feel burdened with responsibility if his fleeting, not necessarily carefully considered judgment was going to get at all my sore places. Even if I *did* strike him as a silly goose, did that mean the collapse of my entire world? Where was my own judgment? At such moments I feel utterly different from others, destroyed deep down, nebulous, without real substance or any real hope that such a state can ever change, and I feel like retreating in tears.

In some ways I have become more "feminine": Gentler, more understanding of the men I know, less active, committed and political, more anxious. I no longer trust myself to think spontaneously of a politician as a weakminded, irresponsible, impotent fool: The force of my irritation reveals nothing but my own intellectual fantasies of grandeur and my castrating tendencies, my infantile yearning for a responsible father, and so on. I am left perplexed, or helplessly angry, by the robust way in which many people will promote lies, delay their necessary withdrawal, are unashamedly corrupt, but at the same time I think: Am I not really envious of their thick skins? Envious of the firm way that man will tell transparent lies for the sake of his career or for the interests of his party? Am I envious of his lack of shame or scruples? Do I not really admire it; is my anger a defense against my own inclinations?

I have a little autonomous castrating machine on me; I have acquired it, worked for it; it cuts down my affects, ideas and desires to their right size. (Right for my analysts—their analysts—their fathers and mothers???)

After those six years, I have the feeling of having been, humanly speaking, inside a glass case. My previous contacts were more vital, less attenuated, aloof, cautious, disingenuous, planned out. During the breaks in my analysis, I was sometimes able to recapture something of the past; conversations were better and more meaningful then—and that was when I had real needs.

It is strange and unsettling to be totally responsible for myself again, with no excuse at the back of my mind to the effect that my edginess, bad temper, depression, sensitivity or high spirits have to do with my analysis. To be unanswerable entirely to myself: To feel I can and must take myself quite seriously. A woman acquaintance in analysis, at whom I laughed when she mentioned feelings of excitement when she went swimming with her woman friend, replied in all seriousness that it was still too soon for that, they would be coming to it later, it wasn't time for the homosexual element because she hadn't yet got that far. This was a kind of argument I knew well; I wouldn't have expressed it so plainly myself, but I would have acted the same way. Oh no, one mustn't think such things out now, not of one's own accord, without permission, mustn't touch upon them yet. And there was always some excuse not to: My anxieties would soon turn out to have some legitimate cause, for otherwise my analyst would interpret and intervene. But who was really guaranteeing that I had time to postpone consideration of such things? That I'd live so long I could afford to put off important experiences and decisions to some future date? Could I really afford to do so? Isn't it sheer defense to rely on it? How do I know what my world will be like in a year's time? Why shouldn't I entertain a wish to let myself in for something now, venture on it now, at once, when I want to? Isn't saying "too soon" the way to perpetuate and reinforce all my fears, inhibitions and scruples?

In any event, I have learned to hate the act of putting off, almost giving up. It devitalizes me. I've done better with my spontaneous decisions, activities and ideas, and have probably seemed more convincing, too, with the genuine vitality, hunger or longing that prompted them at the time. The chances of something good coming of them were greater, anyway, than if I had reflected on them, made sure they were free of any remaining transference, and then at last, having mulled them over thoroughly, tried putting them into practice with whatever vitality I had left.

I have grown tired of explaining myself, trying to make myself understood to someone who doesn't independently, and with goodwill, see me more or less as I see myself: Doesn't see what I mean and how I am trying to communicate it.

It makes me edgy and impatient, and I soon find I feel resigned. If I meet with surprise, astonishment and rejection, I find it harder than before just to overcome other people's inhibited receptiveness with my own inner conviction. I am allergic even to queries which, from the objective point of view, are fully justified, show interest and don't even denote resistance; they easily make me irritated, they hurt and discourage me, reminding me of my experience of being understood either not at all, or wrongly, or with difficulty, and threatening to confirm it. Something in the way of lightheartedness and trust has gone.

In discussions, I need more strength now, and have to make more effort to cope with and overcome the possibility of being hurt; I am more vulnerable, I become involved more easily in personal animosity, am more readily diverted from a subject to defend and justify myself instead. And once I perceive this happening—generally by comparison with more robust souls—I also feel resigned anger, which does not add to my self-confidence.

Intellectual insight into this process is not direct help. My sensitivity, my sore spots exist; I have forfeited something, much as that fact may irk me.

I am always surprised when people take me seriously, respect my views and opinions, incorporate them into their own way of thinking. As if they were the views of an adult. Some people regard my insecurity with surprise; they see no reason for it. In my normal professional environment, I am not regarded as a little girl.

With analysts, I do have difficulty in presenting myself as a woman of thirty-five. I still seem a child, their nice young colleague, to be found diverting, her company perhaps to be enjoyed, someone whose impulsiveness may amuse them, but not one to be recognized as an equal. My arguments appear funny, witty, amusing, however seriously I mean them. If I try to overcome this effect of hilarity by showing more intensity, then I seem stubborn, fanatical, motivated by personal problems that are easily enough diagnosed, and may be commented upon with a knowing smile. At least, it doesn't usually seem to be any problem for them to do so, smiling, and refusing to take what I say seriously.

In fact I'm always surprised, to be regarded as a grown woman, having learned, or at least learned to feel, that all my thoughts and feelings may be traced back in the main to the first six years of life. Childhood experiences, childhood feelings, childish thoughts—and as such calling forth a sympathetic smile. That would be no bad thing if the children were taken as seriously as they should be. But part of our society's hostility to children has made its way into analysis—mine, at least—as a value judgment, disguised as amusement and the willingness to think someone cute, and be touched by that person's naiveté.

Among analysts, moreover, children's therapists have a lesser image, as do pediatricians among practitioners of organic medicine; one may deduce as much from the fact that they have the lowest incomes and must invest considerably more of themselves in the job, in terms of both time and emotion.

It is hard for me not to carry right on with the reduction of myself to childhood status that I suffered for years.

My warmth—the expression "capacity for love" strikes me as devalued, flat and threadbare—my warmth has suffered, or at least my belief in it has. The greater the tension in a session, the greater mis my mood of defensive belligerence, the more irritated I became and the more likely to go on the offensive/defensive. I isolated myself, armed and defended myself in proportion to the hurt I suffered and my sense of being rejected, misunderstood and misinterpreted. I do not think that is surprising, when I felt I must be constantly on my guard against something that was not good for me, hurt me, damaged and injured me, when I would survive better, if at all, by not letting it get at me, insofar as that was possible. Walking naked among thorns, you will be torn and bleeding; wearing a thick coat you'll get away with surface scratches.

With the strain of defending myself, sealing myself off, coping with my raw wounds—even without the considerable expense of energy involved in stirring up problem areas—I had little ability to take anyone else as seriously as myself: I almost forgot how to think with, feel with and care for another person, giving out warmth. Warmth that I urgently needed for myself, and had almost forgotten about.

In addition, I had feelings of guilt and inadequacy over my own pitiful nature. The classic aim of therapy, after all, was to develop the capacity for love and work, in whatever modified and relative form that aim might be seen; it wasn't to be taken quite literally. But I had discovered that I might not be able to like, love or long for anyone at all in a straightforward way, really and truly and with all my heart.

I had guilt feelings over my human personality, my potential for warmth, my intellectual capabilities, my attractions.

I can explain to myself, intellectually, the trouble I caused in several marriages just by coming upon the scene. After all, many bonds loosen with time; I have a career, have been a working woman, while wives have had children and moderated their career expectations, or were stuck intellectually on the housewife level, either willingly or by force of circumstances. Their husbands are often my colleagues, I am professionally at least on the same level and independent, I have actually done some of the things many women still plan to do, I am a suitable object for the projection of dreams, longings and wishes.

But then I feel inclined to condemn myself for the conflict I stir up, my malign nature that causes trouble, disrupting happy families; for my sexual attraction, which can cause grief or at least inspire dreams, and might destroy or break up families; which is, at any rate, the sort of thing to act as a catalyst to smouldering conflicts and bring them to exploding point.

Obsessive sexualizing—futile, castrating provocation—do you need that kind of reassurance?—a destructive siren—yes, at heart I relate it all to myself. I will admit only in theory any idea that the potential for such conflicts might long have existed, that relationships on the point of explosion were just waiting for a spark, that much might well change in an average ten years of marriage. I have discovered how destructive, injurious and harmful I can be. And I really might have left some unequivocal remarks unmade, refrained from laughter sometimes, appeared less provocative. I could have caused a milder reaction in husband, wife, both of them. But would I alone have sensed something suggestive if the husbands hadn't been putting out signals, if the potential wasn't a reality within them, if they weren't in some way prepared for disruptions, the unplanned and unconventional? I am hurt by reproaches concerning attraction—sexual attraction.

I did have an amusing story to tell at a hospital meeting of that analyst with whom I'd smiled and flirted, and half of whose face was then distorted by a tic expressing pure, unadulterated, naked panic; only directly afterwards, at home, I twice cut my thumb deeply, so that it bled. Guilt feelings are firmly rooted, even if I wasn't really responsible for the man's fears, wasn't his mother, father, sister, aunt, grandmother, confessor, calf-love, or whatever.

I do believe it was my own experience in analysis that gave me such a guilty conscience, adding to my own guilt feelings, plus those inherent in our culture.

*   *   *

I feel insecure about expressing myself in groups. I'm used to one-to-one exchanges, talking, discussing and considering ideas with one other person only. Third and fourth parties disturb and irritate me; I can make intense contact with only one person at a time. And then I get pangs of conscience about the third or other parties, and feel obliged to turn to them in the same way, showing them the same interest as I show to the person in that group who is, at the moment, important as my conversational partner. And it doesn't work: Where the first partner's concerned, I feel a fool for communicating with others in just the same way in his presence, promiscuously, observing no distinction, and I try to share out my attention so that no one feels hurt. Particularly not the person to whom I'm really addressing myself. This makes me uneasy, tense and unnatural. At heart, the others present bother me; I would like to be alone with that one other person, my current partner in conversation, the one I'm addressing; bestowing equal attention all around is a lie. I can make a secret attempt to blot out the others in my mind and feel as if they weren't there, I am alone in the group talking to my partner. But it means much effort, and I am lying to myself anyway and not being kind to the others.

I have almost forgotten how to feel at ease in a group, how to work on something, discuss and consider it in a group. It seems incumbent on me to talk to just one other person at a time. "Have you discussed it with your analyst?" fellow analysands used to ask me. "Why didn't you mention that before?" my analyst asked. "You talk about things a good deal outside anlaysis." "Telling tales outside analysis" seemed about the worst possible act of treachery and breach of trust. Sometimes I feel like a jealously watched wife: Mustn't have any strong commitment to more than one person, more than one point of view, the remarks of more than one individual. Others, obviously, can just talk away, get worked up, angry, enthusiastic when a subject concerns and moves them and they want to discuss it. I sniff the air, cautiously, to make sure I am not being too loud, too intense, aggressive, uncontrolled, am not hurting or neglecting anyone. If I have liked the opinion of one member of the group, and shown it, then nobody else is allowed to count.

I am presupposing a form of jealousy, an intellectual monogamy, which is not real at all and which other people don't in the least expect of me. Exclusively one-to-one conversation seems to me meaningful, permissible and right. I can make good, quick contact with one person, exchange opinions and clear points up with that one person.

But I can't do anything similar in a group, can't fall easily into the group atmosphere and just go along with it, can't let the discussion simply take its own course.

I believe that brooding in the isolated, analytical situation has changed me, making me a partner sensitive to, and apt to concentrate on, the labile state of the other person's well-being. If he is not feeling good, I feel guilty. I have learned that if a relationship isn't a good one then it's because of me and my inner nature. Perhaps my analyst is a jealous, restrictive, anxious husband in his married life; or perhaps it's just the technique, and the fact that we dealt selectively with my problems, and there was no emotional sense of bipolarity, role relationship, shared experience. I have no means of knowing—and would find it hard to come by the information honestly—whether I took on some of my analyst's own difficulties, or was influenced by the setting.

As for that setting and the analytic rules, they soon, in my imagination, came to stand for convention, accepted usage, the way to behave, etc. Interpretations become independent, generalized, and affect one's whole attitude towards life. If it is a bad thing for me to start talking as I am getting on the couch and a little before I'm actually lying on it, then it is probably a bad thing, too, if I don't vote for the usual party, accept the usual, traditional, classic doctrine. His amusement at so much in me that was unconventional and didn't observe the rules of the game arose from a solid basis of convention. If I wholly accept and am conversant with the etiquette of bourgeois table manners, then I can afford to cut up potatoes with my knife for once without attracting attention or being suspected of lower-class origins. It becomes the casual behavior of the upper classes, and says something for my upper-class chic, whereby I know that this way of eating potatoes is acceptable in Alsace. At least, it doesn't indicate that maybe I think correct table manners are baloney; it may be supposed that in the last resort I'd know how to eat potatoes correctly.

* * *

I constantly find myself making excuses for my analysts and the analytic bureaucracy, trying to make myself understand why it was me they picked to treat in such a way. I find it difficult to shake off the inward habit of obligation and gratitude I owe them for the hard time they had of it with me. And yet I didn't end up in such a desolate state out of pure malignity, just to annoy them.

Basically, I was treated no differently from anyone in conservative psychiatry, just more discreetly, on a higher intellectual plane, more subtly. When stronger emotions and criticisms ventured to the surface, and I might well have needed more intense contact for a while, they wouldn't listen anymore; it was all covered up, damped down with psychopharmacological drugs, and my real problems were seen as something sick. My criticisms, which might express themselves in roundabout ways, by means of a song, were not understood.

And I do not feel like showing gratitude and understanding for that.

I do reproach myself; I do that easily and vehemently. I see my own faults, deficiencies, the neurotic mechanisms I bring into play when others see something as neutral, or anyway as normal group behavior.

In a gymnastics course, our group was divided up; four members of it at a time were to do the exercise we had just learned while the rest watched. I became unsure of myself under the others' watchful eyes, forgot part of the exercise and couldn't go on; my movements became stiffer, nothing worked anymore, I felt inferior to the man in front of me and the woman next to me, and was altogether embarrassed by the way I moved. In addition, my inhibitions irked me. Immediately, I reflected: If I couldn't compete with the woman next to me now, and instantly felt inferior to her and just gave up, how was I to manage in real life? If I was worse than usual when watched by others who were testing and observing me, didn't that mean I wasn't up to the competitive struggle for existence of the outside world? Or anyway, that I didn't flourish and improve when I made an effort necessary for success in life? "You're more gifted and sicker than the average," my analyst had told me, hadn't he? Why couldn't I maintain my capabilities when others were watching—specifically, at the moment, that little exercise I'd learned? Why did I allow my capability to be so destroyed?

Why was I so sensitive, indeed hypersensitive, so fragile, so abnormal? ("The sensibility of a schizophrenic," he'd said.) Was I back in the family situation, an incompetent little grey mouse, baby sister in this small foursome doing gymnastics? Was I letting myself be impeded again by ridiculous transferences (the man next to me = my brother, the woman next to me = my mother, the surroundings = paternal high standards = the cruel superego)?

After the five minutes' preliminary exercise I felt quite exhausted by my thoughts. I could have wept. I felt like walking out of the whole course. Nothing had changed: I was in the same neurotic mess as ever. When the man teaching the course wanted us to go on practicing in small groups, several other people complained; one woman said firmly and uninhibitedly that it wasn't a comfortable way to practice and it made her feel self-conscious to have everyone watching; it would be much easier and feel more natural if we all practiced at the same time. And this was the general consensus of opinion—just like that, without any cerebral convolutions. The others didn't reproach themselves, they saw their self-consciousness as quite natural and comprehensible, nothing to alarm them. They weren't bringing up all the misery of this world and their own personal histories in connection with it.

I have become less kind to myself: Less kind, anyway, than I was. If I feel like making myself look pretty, doing my face, trying on crazy clothes in front of the mirror, I have to defend myself against criticism: Is this a narcissistic deficiency? Why do I need reassurance from outside me, so dependent on my outward image? Why is the way I look so important to me, the effect I have on others and on myself in the mirror? Why do I need feedback from the mirror, why can't I like myself on my own? Is there something I have to cover up? Why can't I find the capacity in myself now to be in a good mood, feel well and pretty? Why do I need my prettified reflection in the mirror? Have I any real image of myself within me at all, or do I need reassurance to fill a vacuum? What inner ugliness, dirt and malignity threaten to show through, so that I have to cover them up with cosmetics? Why haven't I any stable, satisfied inner object that always assumes I'm pretty and good and pleasant, so that I don't need the mirror and my clothes, cosmetics, disguises anymore?

If a pair of shoes doesn't fit, if I don't feel at ease in them, can't walk about easily and comfortably, I wonder what's oppressing me and weighing on my mind. Why must I put obstacles in my own way, crippling myself, sending counter-impulses in all directions, the result being awkwardness and discomfort? Why can't I just wear the shoes easily and casually? Why am I so sensitive and easily upset, especially now, in this situation?

Such notions come to me more readily than the simple idea of changing my uncomfortable shoes for a better-fitting pair; I'm afraid of missing out on the possible meaning, the possible surfacing of my problem.

Yet I know perfectly well that the same shoes can have a different effect on me, depending on how I feel; they impede, hurt or allow me to move slowly; yet sometimes it is the emotional factor that has a forceful, and sometimes exclusive effect. However, I automatically go for the negatives, looking for difficulties and obscurities. I hardly have the spontaneous freedom just to take off a pair of shoes that pinch; I'm more inclined to look for the reason why they pinch in myself and take the blame.

*   *   *

A dream, two years after the end of my analysis: I am in a multi-story garage in my car, and I know I've been in there far too long already. I can't find the exit, I go around and around, up and down, finally I do find a way out, in the middle. However, the ramp slopes steeply upward, and my faltering car can't manage the rise. So I have to get out, leaving the car where it is, and continue on foot. But I daren't; it's so steep, such an effort, and moreover other, more powerful cars might come racing out of the garage any minute and run me over, as I'm on foot. There's no proper way for a pedestrian to go up out of here either; it is meant only for powerful cars. I have to keep to the very edge and hope a fast car doesn't come up from behind and run me down. I wait for a moment by the exit, trying to summon up my courage. There's a small, dark man standing at the exit waiting just there, but he's gone a little way out of the car park. He obviously isn't as scared as I am. He moves around the area far more freely than I do; I'm scared of cars coming out all the time. Finally he takes my hand—he has a soft, warm, beautiful hand—and he leads me, drags me, helps me out of the exit. I probably wouldn't have had the strength without him.

*   *   *

Everything is supposed to be communicable through words: The clever use of language compensates for the comparative artificiality of the setting.

It didn't work that way for me. Crying my eyes out on the couch, even when there was a benevolent, empathic, sympathetic silence or conversation, never even began to have the same comforting, fortifying, soothing effect of working through grief as I found in someone's arms, naked, skin against skin. Something quite different, something extra, is communicated by bodily contact: Something firmer, more lasting, more credible. Like a mental corset, a framework of reinforced concrete, from which peace, strength, security and a sense of structure can come.

Perhaps verbalizing works for people who are very aloof, don't like skin contact, have been swaddled from birth and were reared without breastfeeding. I know of more intense contacts— from hearsay, I even know of analysts who can convey, communicate and radiate a great deal without words, but they're the exceptions.

I was moved by the story of a prisoner who had been in solitary confinement; the weekly visit with its thirty minutes' conversation couldn't compare its soothing effect with the weekly bath, whose synthesizing effect, giving her back a sense of her own body, lasted for days. The conversation, on the other hand, seemed unreal, a dim memory, forgotten after a few hours. Something about the whole situation artificial and unnatural.

Progressive opinion said that we don't yet know what really goes on in analysis; what the effective, healing part of the process is. Some thought it lay in the mere conscious experiencing of earlier emotional deficiency, enabling the analysand to begin constructing his life outside in a more satisfactory way; others thought the deficiency was made up in the analytic sessions themselves. In my own analysis it was emotionally clear that we were to deal with making the unconscious conscious, and also with recovering lost ground— within and outside the sessions. Communication was to be confined to language ("Analysis is language; please verbalize;") music and songs had no place in it, although Freud didn't stop thinking while contemplating pictures, paintings, sculptures.

And yet my analyst's tone of voice, his movement, his clothing conveyed a good deal to me; I became an expert on his handshake at meeting and parting, and could read much into it, according to the prevailing mood. In earlier days, during dance lessons, the pressure of a hand could also mean more than many direct contacts did later. It was all a matter of practice; if one wished, one could draw conclusions from it; and uncertainty and insincerity arose from that very fact. I can let words and a tone of voice caress me, if that is what the other person wants; I can also read rejection in them.

The argument that analysis is not principally about recovering lost ground always came up when I complained that I was getting too little out of mine, and was being rejected. At this point, the tacitly recognized idea of recovering lost ground could be dropped; the fault was now all in my insatiable desires and my transference and he was not responsible for that.

Perhaps the distance inherent in the analytic situation positively discourages one from trying to get from it something that wasn't even forthcoming from one's parents, in more hopeful, real and solid circumstances. Perhaps that accounts for the tenuous nature of the relationship.

A positive transference per se is freer of conflict than a negative one; for one thing, it is just the way of least resistance; it's relatively easy to project everything fine, lovable and reliable on to the analyst. And via hostile outside figures (such as parents, siblings, the subjects of earlier relationships) this harmony may also be maintained longer than it might be by physiological means.

I noticed that I made almost no decisions on my own anymore; I took every little thing to analysis with me, and began a process of discussion of it and reflection on it there. Sometimes these matters were not of much importance. I was struck by this in comparing myself with other people, who had achieved more in the same time, made more decisions, didn't tend to discuss and question everything. Compared to them, I felt emotionally dependent. I would have liked to discuss everything I did in advance.

And yet I had had enough of my whining submissiveness and well-intentioned bowing to analytic authority; some time or other I wanted to be in a position to decide for myself, make my own judgments, or anyway ask for help and advice only when I felt it was necessary and I could do no more on my own.

I long to be understood *without* words. Not to have to express myself laboriously, with much expenditure of effort, forever taking care not to be wrongly, negatively interpreted, so that I have to put things right again. I would like to be able to be exhausted, look exhausted; to be allowed to be silent, to withhold things, to have the freedom to keep things to myself, not to have to report, discuss, chew over things I have already worked out and explained to myself, things that aren't of present concern—without having any of that explained as resistance, a malignant, spiteful, castrating withholding of myself. Explained in words of some subtlety, inherent in the system, analytically impeccable, but none the less hurtful.

I would like just to let out half-formed thoughts, immature ideas I haven't followed right through, sentences I haven't entirely formulated; I'd like to let them go, send them out, and watch them settle and collect themselves in peace without coming up against obstacles, without changing and being diverted the wrong way, sent off in directions I didn't intend.

"Free association" at the touch of a button—too bad if you can't produce it. I learned my lesson: I felt the pedagogical force at work a few times when my associations led in unacceptable directions ("far-fetched . . . too soon," he says, or he just hesitates to reconstruct them), associations straying into areas yet to be tackled, i.e., to be corrected, I adjust my inner range, my radius of concern to that consideration. (Even unicellular organisms swim around an obstacle when they have felt it hit them several times.)

If in any doubt, I see myself as dangerous, conflicted, destructive, bad. By now I've come to realize that some men who basically like me very much still feel a need to guard against me and my attractions, so they metaphorically slap me in the face—systematically and with discreet regularity. They regard me critically, looking out for drawbacks, faults, characteristics and conduct which justify them in rejecting me: They quickly resort to political standpoints on which we differ, to remarks about my appearance (clothes, weight, pallor), my professional activities and perspectives, my private life—too trivial or too turbulent—the state of my finances, the style of my apartment, and so on. Then they have something to criticize; at least, that's the emotionally intense aura they give off. Yet they can also be very perceptive in criticizing those very things for which I'm actually reproaching myself in a mild way.

So I come away from such contacts—mostly pleasant enough at first, since there was mutual attraction in principle, beginning after a meal, a coffee, a visit to the movies or some other such occasion—feeling worn down and full of self-doubts, specifically, with the frightening sensation of being quite, quite different, and destructive, and unable to cope with life. Like a wrecker who wants nothing but destruction and a parasitical existence.

Even if I've now learned to understand the struggle of these men against attraction, to understand their feelings and desires, such encounters do probe into sore, tender tissue. It so happens that it is those very men who really do like me, or did like me, who treat me in this way, and then I find I haven't been on my guard at the initial friendly stage. I can tell myself over and over that they are taking it out on me for dreams of their own that I aroused or cut short. But every time I feel destroyed again, my image of myself partially shattered. Their watchful eyes pinpoint areas ripe for improvement; they speak the truth, and we're basically in agreement *there*. I don't, after all, see myself as flawless, only their view can be so pitiless, so one-sided, and the outcome is to the effect that: "You must see for yourself, one (= I) can't love that sort of woman." Nor will they rest unless they have me secretly convinced of the validity of their image of me by the time we part—in mutual agreement on this aspect. Then they look good; they sometimes look really radiant.

I had a friend who'd been analyzed, whom I hadn't seen for some time. When we talked about the old days, I was surprised to find that *I* myself remembered them as very pleasant. However, his sole reference to my conduct at the time, which unfortunately hadn't been anything marvellous, now served him only as the background to his sincerely meant compliment: "There's nothing to criticize *this time*." That had never been my aim, and I left before I burst into tears; he was probably surprised by my feminine vulnerability.

Sometimes I felt as though under some evil influence: Impelled, forced, made to do something that did me no good and was no essential part of me. My better points were not shored up; what is hateful, cunning and crafty in me has. I thought much of that side of me had been artificially stirred up and encouraged. For some time after the end of my analysis, I could well imagine inflicting sadistic torments on my analyst, torturing him, or at any rate hurting him a lot, and enjoying his suffering. I might have reduced him to a nervous wreck with telephone calls; or spiteful or anonymous letters. I might have shot him, smashed him to a pulp, stoned him, chopped him up, crushed him. Then I had further guilt feelings. I didn't know myself capable of such intense vengefulness. I had desired a furious showdown with my stepfather before he died, but I didn't want to get on this kind of twisted wavelength; I didn't like it. However, getting hold of a weapon isn't such a great step from such feelings, and in fact I am surprised that more acts of violence aren't committed. I know one woman patient who actually did get herself a pistol. Perhaps these impulses are translated into auto-aggression, depression, suicidal tendencies.

Why may I not hate? Hate permanently, maybe, forever if that were my proper reaction? Why must I reconcile myself? Analysts react with horror when they find I'm still angry; they think me immature, lacking in insight. "Don't you realize this is transference? Don't you see it's your hatred of your father, who abandoned you and never came back, left you in the lurch? Whom you believe to have treated you badly, negligently, coldly?" This isn't a quotation from anyone, nor even near one; but it might have been put like that. At least I had learned that kind of interpretation and had become an independent practitioner of it.

*   *   *

A DREAM, FEBRUARY, 23, 1978:   Left hand by my left ear; with my thumb, forefinger and middle finger I bring a sturdy little brush out of my ear along with scales of skin: The handle is light in color and stout in shape, the brush brown; the whole thing is sticky, oily, shiny. I am delighted, like a child at Christmas. Then I bring out a worm, like a big maggot, curling; it has undermined my ear, made holes in it, drilled its passageways through it. Like a pale sow bug, strong and sturdy. It leaves me feeling neutral and surprised; it is amazingly healthy, however.

I woke and felt odd; it was like an image straight out of psychiatry; my analysts would have reacted with concern. The ear eaten away by the worm—hand and ear isolated—depersonalization— the layout of the body—brush—penis—penis envy, I mustn't tell any man about this.

Going against the interpretation of dreams I had learned, as if on the advice of some unorthodox practitioner, just letting myself go along with the dream and trusting to find something relevant to myself in it, I came up with:

No need to pay for the brush, it's a gift, I only have to reach for it, it's within me. (Penis, I couldn't help thinking, but it wasn't emotionally right here.)

The brush came out of my ear, shaped like a shell (concha = cunt in Latin America). It was like a baby with brown, shining hair; coming to light now, but it was in there the whole time, in the ear whose cartilaginous structure is undermined and pierced, but I bring out the worm; it is alive, strong, has a firm structure around it, comes to the surface now although it was in there all along. It is rather pale and anemic; a real worm like this one ought to be brown, dark brown like a hazelnut. But it hasn't had any sunlight.

It comes almost of its own accord, I take it out with my left hand. And it curls, and lives, although it is not used to fresh air and light. The white furrows of its segments are like the folds in a picture of a swaddled infant by Wilhelm Busch; however, it can move well, and if I hadn't fetched it out it would soon have come out of its own accord. The ear would have collapsed, and it would have needed to find a new home.

Seen in that way, I liked my dream.

Fragments

A T A CONGRESS I WAS SITTING NEXT TO AN IN-
telligent man I like. I was pleased, because ordinarily I
didn't have much to do with him. When he was looking for something to write with, I gave him a pen; I know what it's like to get
into a secret panic because I want to write something down in order
to capture the thought, but don't have the means of writing with
me. When he was going to give the pen back I said that was alright,
he could keep it, I had several. He looked at me as if I were a dangerous animal; the moment's intimacy was over. After the lecture,
he left the pen on his seat and disappeared into the crowd.

Men don't recognize fear of women: Not their own and not that
felt by others. If a woman seems threatening—in this group at the
congress as elsewhere—that's her own personal problem; she is the
phallic, castrating, menacing creature who puts men to flight. The
sad part of it is, however, that this means men are unable to work
through the problems that afflict them in life and love, are unable
to change them. Little change occurs in those very men who entered analysis reasonably well aware of their problems and fears,
and they feel it; it passes into a sense of resignation concerning life,
their analysis, love. Something really has changed in many of
them, but not on this particular point. It hurts me to see the trouble
they take, with all that effort and analytic work, and they are still
cheated out of working through their fears. But how can they deal
with those fears if their superiors don't see them either; if they
don't even recognize that hostility to women exists, a phenomenon
in the world around them, that many men today are afraid of genuinely independent, loving, competent women; if their fears are always interpreted as mere reaction to the castrating female? Woman

236

seems increasingly dangerous if men learn that their fears are justified. All they can do is go on looking for ever more diminished women who don't arouse such fears in them. However, when such women are loved, they blossom too, and may arouse alarm, and then one is back to the beginning again.

With this particular man I felt it was sad, almost tragic, to see him take such trouble: Cheated of life after so many hours and years of analysis.

If men could at least experience tenderness among themselves, they might feel better balanced, less hungry, less full of basic longings. But what man has had such experiences, and who could afford to admit it openly if he did? Many have never known them in their lives, and dream of them secretly as of something delightful but dreadful. This is understandable if they really have never known such tenderness; by the time they might venture to try it, or the mere idea of it occurs to them, they are analysts and under strict constraints. No training analyst would openly represent himself as homosexual; it was rumored of someone in another group. And in fact it would be an obstacle to a man's career to be thought homosexual; I've known many who felt obliged to make overt demonstrations of heterosexuality.

At a seminar on (male) homosexuality, the chairman insisted with almost passionate emphasis on the castration fears that cause the aberration, or at least on the existential misery suffered by all homosexuals. Only a few participants suggested that it was more than a sickness, and they did so on the quiet, not officially.

If only training analysts could at least admit the idea more freely in the analytical one-to-one situation. But it was just those more sensuous, erotically attractive analysands that I'd seen suffer so much from "years of non-acceptance" by their analysts. As if the analysts had fought down their erections with care and perseverance over the months and years, or at any rate until the attraction was past, or the analysand so worn down and depressed that he had ceased to flourish. Nor would any woman training analyst openly admit to being lesbian, either.

Another factor contributing to my sense of numbness and resignation may have been my lack of success with intensity, seriousness, and effort. I felt I was being cautiously and anxiously obliged to act out below my own level. "You're not as easily stressed as you seem." "Why do you take this as so significant now?" "Why does it affect you so much?" "What early conflict impels you at the moment?" "Take things easier; why do you have to expend such effort?" "The sensibility of a schizophrenic." If I take something seriously, in a discussion or meeting, yes, it is possible that the expression on my face isn't one of detached friendliness; but I don't think it terrible to appear under strain or exhausted. One's powers are there to be used and developed. I find it unsatisfying never to stretch myself to the limits of my powers, even at the risk of collapsing or letting my thoughts reach some extreme conclusion—so long as I could at least come to that conclusion myself, on my own, without having it assailed and inhibited by judgmental standards. "Political liberalism:" Spoken with a smile at my outrage, my immature opinions, the verdict given at a discreet distance.

I came to sense my analyst's limitations and assimilate his advocacy of them. They didn't fit my own potential capabilities.

I questioned everything about my family, probably loosening some constricting bonds in the process. However, I was something of a trial in my explosive vehemence, and I was lucky that my family is not the kind to let itself be totally scared off. I was lucky that I could still count on family protection against disaster in times of need, could find and be able to accept stability and cohesion there. Such a background can give one the courage and freedom to be more venturesome.

I had ground my teeth till there was a groove in them, my dentist told me. Was I under stress? Did I know that if I went on like this I'd break my front teeth? To my indignant protest that it couldn't be so, nobody had ever mentioned the toothgrinding, he said, with a superior smile: Yes, so everyone said, but six months would do it, and the groove was a fresh one. Hadn't anyone heard me grinding my teeth?

Another reason why I must write things down.

I had a crippling sense of loyalty towards both my analysts. But was either of them really loyal to me, did either of them really care about me? I was accepted for analysis apathetically, maybe even with controlled reluctance, and analysis continued in the same spirit well after my second analyst must have known he wouldn't really be able to get anywhere with me. I wasn't even accorded the relatively non-judgmental diagnosis of "counter-transference problems," which doesn't pin the blame on anyone: No, I was the one setting a "counter-transference *trap*," into which I had cunningly lured him with my subtle neurosis, leading him up the garden path. It wasn't *he* who had failed to do his part, to fulfil his function to the best of his ability; *I* had prevented him, I was to blame for his partial incapacity and my own failure to flourish. More guilt feelings for me then, and a yet more vigilant superego observing my remaining spontaneous activities more keenly than ever.

My intellectual quest for understanding and recognition was found unacceptable: Stopped in its tracks, or diverted to a plane which I didn't find enlightening. That, however, was due more to my own resistance, defense, and unwillingness to accept what was good than to the possibility that those particular interpretations and associations might not be right for me, even if they suited the analyst's own emotional background. Thinking things out, reflecting at leisure, trying things playfully, I have often felt influenced by forceful pronouncements. It is discouraging, on coming to a conclusion, to meet with no response to it, or with an inadequately positive response, or to find one must defend it against opposition. And often that can't be done; my reflections were sometimes just tentative suppositions.

I didn't know just how much of a vital, human investment I would have to make in my analysis: Much of my potential commitment, my interest in life and my environment, much of my free energy was turned inward, constricted and paralyzed, transformed into nagging, doubting disquiet, which made me touchier, more vulnerable and more suspicious than I had been before, so that it was hard for me to commit myself to anything objective, and if I did, it was only in a watered-down way. So that human relationships lost substance too and became unimportant; if I fell in love my mood was only mildly radiant; perhaps it was already affected and shaped by those accounts I'd be giving of it later. I had no real need of acquaintances, or anyway much less need than before, since all intimacy was either discussed in one of my sessions, or else kept for discussion in the next session. Analysis wasn't taking its proper course if I discussed matters of importance with other people; that was acting out, subsidiary transference, and so on.

An ideological point threading its way right through my analysis was the insistence on "discussing" all aggressive tensions, disagreements, arguments and sources of annoyance either in groups or with acquaintances or partners, so as to clarify them and eventually understand oneself, once misunderstandings have been cleared away and reciprocal neurotic contributions worked through. This may be theoretically possible, and indeed I would think it desirable.

In practice, however—with my patients and colleagues and among analysts—I have found that it often doesn't work that way, even with the best of intentions on both sides. I have found that there are differences of perception, of one's present capacity to face problems, one's own or those of others; there are forms of resistance of which even analysts aren't aware, and which make basic communication downright impossible—communication, that is, of a kind genuinely based on understanding rather than on the observation of a mutual distance. This may then be ascribed to "incompatability" or disguised in some other way. However, I believe it happens more frequently than is generally supposed, that the degree of freedom present just isn't enough to enable people to get to the common basis of a problem, and you are only making life more difficult if you insist on clarification and discussion. Many relationships continue, free of difficulties, after some detachment; problems can disappear entirely if both parties have found their way back to the right degree of distance from or closeness to each other.

After all, the world is full of situations involving conflict, and one can't be expected to get to the bottom of all of them.

In short: I found new freedom, which made daily life easier, in the possibility (opened up to me again by a nurse on the ward) of quietly preserving a certain detachment in many cases of tension and difficulty in my work and my private life, instead of having to understand and clarify everything, as instructed by my analytical superego. I was able, anyway, to cope with many problems better by observing them and changing my stance—closeness .versus distance—towards them than by discussing them. Penguins turn and peck each other if a proper distance between them is not observed (about 40 centimeters, according to a television film I saw).

In releasing an analysand from an earlier and traumatizing web of relationships, enabling him to have new and more pleasant emotional experiences, the analyst really should be a preferable alternative to the objects of the analysand's previous relationships: A bargain, a good buy, more loving, more reliable, more tolerant and clever, a more inviting object of identification, more empathic than those pathogenic earlier figures. One abandons what is familiar only for something that's clearly better; the exchange must be worthwhile. But for the relative isolation of the analytic situation, I could probably never have felt much enthusiasm for my analysts. I felt inhibited by a certain coolness, the obvious unhappiness about life and love, a low capacity for just finding life good, come what may.

It was hard to make others (other analysands, that is) understand how I felt, or even give them some slight degree of insight into it. Compared to other analysts, mine, seen from outside, was not a stern orthodox figure; indeed, he was regarded as easy-going and unconventional, not convinced of the value of traditional analytic principles and open to newer methods. For instance, he did not, in principle, reject the idea of participation in courses based on other methods (Gestalt therapy, bioenergetics, and so on) during analysis with him. He did not forbid or reprove such activity, but seemed disinterested.

My explanation of his sudden implacability—something not typical of him—would be that his insecurity made him particularly susceptible to the mood of the group, itself to some extent implacable, to current doctrine, to a stern (and perhaps peculiarly German) version of applied psychoanalysis. If I leave aside the circular argument that his manifest unconventionality and his casual attitude were his defenses against the opposite impulse, then it may well be that he just put up less resistance than others to the analytical group superego (along with that sadistic emphasis which had slipped into it), and that in cases of doubt or when he was not sure of something he would fall back on "what is normally done" in such situations, on what is usual in this group. And I suppose that this was what proved so destructive to me, for I had met with that superego elsewhere; it had dogged me, and continued to do so, in my dealings with analyzed colleagues, at congresses and seminars, pervading my leisure activities. Some part of it, therefore, fell upon fertile ground. And that was how the system as a whole functioned.

I realized that I just can't live without earthly gods; without someone of whom I'm very fond. In the first (and pleasant) months of my second analysis I idealized my second analyst, briefly registering all the errors, misunderstandings and omissions of the first one. Then, however, when the going became harder with my second analyst, I revised my opinion, and idealized her again; I thought she was kindness, intelligence, clarity and capacity for love personified, and I thought that for quite a while after the end of my analysis. Only when I had more friends around me again, and was feeling better, could I gradually get her into perspective, slowly and with much emotional difficulty, coming to see her faults and those qualities in her which were not good for me.

It really was extremely hard to admit (to myself, too) that six years of life, of intense identification, emotional activity and introspection had done me no good, had injured me, possibly changed me irreversibly, and that in any case it would take me some years to build myself up again, even if I could do it at all.

I could see, perceive and admit as much only with the support of friends: People who gave me new inspiration. Without the alternative they offered, I think the insight would have been too much for my mental economy.

Now when I meet enthusiastic analysands idealizing their analysts, I am inclined to feel suspicious; perhaps they need to do it, and the figure now standing in the shadows (the earlier analyst) has really been rather gruesome; or they have to erase the bad memory by superimposing their enthusiasm for the new analysis. I for one would have needed more stability than I actually had to perceive flaws at the time, instead of warming uncritically to someone.

If an expensive journey has proved unsatisfactory, it is hard to admit and realize the fact, and all the more so when many years of one's life and a great deal of money are involved. And when one's future career and its financial basis are dependent on the end product of those years, the space available for critical thought becomes even smaller. One may indeed wonder whether it wouldn't be more productive, meaningful and of more future use to support whatever family one may have acquired during that period decently, rather than wondering at length whether one's own analysis is going well, and thus plunging into professional risks. For the shape of one's career is then largely determined, and it really is a great luxury even to have the chance—at that age, after such long training—of stopping to wonder if one really wants to be an analyst, a psychotherapist, or a general practitioner or a specialist. Not many people can afford to do that, certainly not those outside the medical profession, and those inside it have usually inwardly rejected organic medicine during their analytic training. At least, they would presumably be at a disadvantage compared with those who have identified at all points with organic medicine.

However cautious and liberal he makes himself out, the analyst does carry enormous weight; he becomes more essential and of more decisive importance than anyone in an outside relationship. Doubting him would mean questioning the whole analysis, one's entire personal commitment, the point of the expense of time, emotion and money, and not least one's professional identity. It is hard to convey the importance and the absoluteness attained by the analyst's words, judgments and opinions (which one soon learns to divine), or the way other people (friends, acquaintances, relatives) lose importance, credibility and substance by comparison. To doubt the analyst and all institutions that his authority is based on, requires self-confidence, something that I for one very soon lost.

Perhaps psychoanalysis is too dangerous and requires too much general knowledge of basic human fundamentals to be applied at all.

*   *   *

I missed out on any adequate assumption of the parental functions by my analyst: On the assumption of responsibility in situations of crisis, which really might have given me security. I was appalled by his failure to take destructive and autodestructive impulses seriously, his almost bored expressions such as, "You have to see it through." "These things happen." "That's all part of it," or by his weary air of knowing everything already, his refusal to be drawn out of the reserve proper to an analyst determined not to act anything out, or by the relative lack of concern he brought to bear on ideas of suicide. It was the analysand, complete with neurosis, who bore full responsibility for the course of events. If a patient is endangered, and is seriously entertaining thoughts of suicide which may be explained by the analytic process, it ought to be clear that the ego functions should at times be assumed by the analyst, so as to make sure nothing irreversible happens; for instance, the analysand should be treated as an in-patient until this phase is over. It is only that the threshold at which a training analysand ought to be treated in the hospital lies higher than for so-called normal analysands, since both analyst and training analysand in the relationship must overcome considerable reluctance before they even consider the idea. (After all, the most devastating possible rumor that one can set about concerning an analyst, the most efficient way of destroying his reputation, is to say that he was once a psychiatric patient. The allegation marks him once and for all. It says little for our progressive understanding of emotional illness if medical practitioners employ the same techniques of exclusion and discrimination among themselves as is the case in society at large. You can't seriously expect a firm to re-employ a man who has had a psychotic episode but is now free of symptoms again, if you shy away from such people in the ranks of your own profession. That is where understanding ought to begin. It is, of course, sometimes said that the best therapist, with the greatest empathy, and carrying the most conviction, is a cured schizophrenic, but this is a sophisticated flight of fancy rather than anything else. Analysts generally prefer to have their decompensations cured by a diagnosis leaning on organic medicine.)

But it is dangerous if defense on both sides so tinges the analysis that the real threat to the analysand is no longer taken seriously enough: Crises are considered to be likely, and frequent, and no cause for concern. I for one had the impression that suicide and aggressive outbreaks were risked casually, almost taken into the analytic calculations, as if it were all the luck of the draw.

I was supposed to acquire a "stable introjection" in the course of my analysis, something I had missed out on, because of my fatherless state, among other reasons. But in my private and professional life, I have never, or only very exceptionally, been able to find people with that independence of judgment and conduct, the independent power to fight and not to compromise, the steadfastness and resistance to isolation, qualities that could bring about such good, stable introjections. I can't help believing that the extent of emotional independence, the courage of one's own convictions, the resistance to corrupting pressures that are exacted and striven for, are just ideological, or at least are rare exceptions. I think the intensity with which independence is sought is in ratio to its rarity.

The ability to live alone was another bit of ideology in my analysis. What for, I wonder? So as to make me less dependent on others, less vulnerable to the threat of the break-up of a relationship?

To enable me to live on my own and be self-sufficient? But I don't want that, or not as much as I was supposed to. I was not raised that way, I'm not so made that such an isolated condition is the best thing for me. I probably acquired a large amount of group ego from my family and society. At any rate, I'm dependent upon plenty of contacts for my optimum well-being. I can train myself to do with considerably fewer contacts, less conversation, not so many people around me daily; to take everything that moves me to the typewriter and get rid of it there, or just keep it to myself—perhaps imagine a partner, or put the whole of it into a letter. This does work, and can sometimes be satisfying. "Freedom's just another word for nothing left to lose."

But I don't want that; it's achieved at the cost of human contact. I have the urge to communicate what I feel, and if I reduce that urge I am socially crippled. Japanese dwarf pines can live with a minimum of trace elements—but what a life! Anyway, the emotional self-sufficiency to which I was supposed to aspire wasn't enough for me.

After my initial interview with my first analyst I had felt very much the same—depressed and crushed—as I did after a year's analysis; I ought to have taken that mood as an indication of things to come. Since then, in any case, I have taken note of first impressions; I restrain myself from the handy explanation that they're transference mechanisms—which is kinder to myself—and stop to think if I really do like someone. If, with my training, I still react allergically or edgily to certain problems, I now take it as unlikely that I shall feel able to clear the matter up by means of introspection, maybe a few hours' supervision, or further analysis of my own. I have refrained from treating people, with whom I didn't get on (because of my past history) and referred them to other therapists; it was possible to explain this without hurting anyone's feelings very much. After all, a basic right to be liked exists. "If you don't like someone it means you haven't understood him"—I found that an important precept.

I was always in the wrong; I observed the same phenomenon in others I knew whose analysts hadn't succeeded—or so it seemed to me—in liking them; the analysands, suffered from *their own* neuroses, which had made them so "unlovable;" at best they still suffered from the counter-transference mechanisms which they had employed to cause similar negative reactions in their analysts.

Would it really be hurtful, irresponsible and irreversibly traumatizing for an analyst having ascertained that no matter what efforts he made he couldn't manage to like an analysand, simply to say so? Something along the lines of: "I can't get anywhere with you, I don't understand you, you get on my nerves and I can't stand you." Most, if not all, will notice such dislike anyway. In general, neurotic (i.e., nonpsychotic) patients are credited with little sensitivity, perhaps because they don't express themselves more forcibly. One just cannot approach someone who has an obvious psychosis with spurious concern; he will notice, protest, react in his own way to the slightest insincerity of which the therapist may not even be aware. Who is to say that so-called neurotics don't have equally sensitive feelings, even if their reactions aren't so uninhibited? I for one felt a great deal, even if I didn't consciously register much until later; I willingly suppressed many discomforting perceptions about my analyst in favor of the official, unproblematic explanation. Anyway, I believe that their perception on the deeper level is just as sensitive.

As an analysand (and thus patient) I could in the last resort accept it if *one* person, *one* certain human being, i.e., that particular analyst wasn't able to get along with me. He wasn't the whole world to me, he wasn't all humanity, father, mother, family; so his personal judgment would have had nothing absolute about it, wouldn't necessarily have to be the general truth about me. I got on the nerves of *this* particular analyst; he couldn't like me. Very well—or not really very well—but not destructive in any general way. If a private relationship falls apart, that hurts too, but after the acute emotional turmoil there's always renewed hope that I might get on better with somebody else. Some time or other, I'll find a new love. But I do not have to go around from then on stigmatized as unendurable. All may be well with the next man, and what went wrong in the previous relationship was two people's fault.

I have had it with comparisons to organic medicine—but a surgeon who didn't feel fully fit would hardly go on cheerfully operating, for fear of shredding a vital artery. He would look around for someone else who was feeling better that particular day, in that particular situation.

If I get downright inappropriate treatment in organic medicine, and it has harmed me, I can at least count on sympathy and under-standing from those around me; I may perhaps have the fact of that wrong treatment objectively established, though that's diffi-cult. But when mental harm has been done, I'm regarded as crazy; nothing can be proved. I may have taken interpretations in com-pletely the wrong way, and then it's entirely my own fault. It can be said I've seen them quite differently from the way they were meant or formulated. Interpretations, all the same, given with whatever emphasis in whatever actual contexts, are more than their own grammatical content. And it is unfair to ask the layman, the analy-sand or patient, to bear the weight of responsibility for being mis-understood and traumatized. It is, after all, part of the analyst's expertise to consider the situation in which interpretations are given and the effects they will have. If a patient on antibiotics de-velops an altered blood count, nobody considers this is due to his personal malice. It is just a known side-effect to be taken into ac-count, an unpleasant one, to be avoided if possible. With my own analyst, and others too, I often noticed that they were first and fore-most angry with patients who took their interpretations "the wrong way." Things that patients say aren't taken seriously or in any way literally. The analyst can make light of it, appear helpless in the face of neurotic misconception. And yet it is primarily up to the thera-pist to make himself understood; he is there for the patients, after all.

I don't think that it would make much sense, either, to reproach myself with why I didn't end the analysis when I had such doubts, why I went on taking interpretations so seriously even if, in my own opinion, they didn't seem appropriate; why I let myself be so hurt. In the whole context of my training, with acquaintances who had changed in their own analysis, I could hardly have found that possible. All told, I did believe in psychoanalysis and in the point of my own analysis. And I didn't want to step down to the common-place level of those opponents of analysis who would say, "Well, there you are; why go along with such nonsense?"

To play around with thoughts, not following them right through, wasn't approved of. As if I had a police state behind me, within me: Every uncontrolled, dissident and not entirely classifiable im-pulse instantly was denounced, seen as criminal, arrested, investi-gated. And measured against precise, stern, immutable laws. "Yes,

but . . ." "Don't you think that . . ." "But there you are
again . . ." "What makes you react *so* strongly?" (i.e., *too* strongly,
beyond the norm, wrongly, divergently, neurotically, in a way that
must be changed.) Creative impulses find it hard to survive such
treatment. At bottom, the healthiest thing is simply to withdraw
bold, unconsidered, spontaneous impulses, because then I offer less
cause for correction. Even unicellular organisms react to electric
shocks, after a while—according to their capacity to learn, and depending on the strength of the shock.

Everything is ruined by the label "fantasies of grandeur": All
spontaneity, any good mood, any carefree moment, any emotional
confidence and enthusiasm.

My sensitivities, my easily disturbed nature, my inclination to
suffer from tension (perhaps because of my high degree of perceptiveness) were worked out in much isolation, without comparison
to other people who might be in a similar position, and through
whom I might then have found relief from the superego, might at
least have been able to re-adjust. This meant that I appeared to
myself excessively and peculiarly sensitive, vulnerable and unstable; my sensitivity caused me too many guilt feelings ("What [ear-
lier] situation makes this bother you so much now? Why do you
feel it so strongly?"). I fell too deep into emotional depths (a childhood situation similar to the present one can nearly always be
found), and I was over-inclined to regard myself as a special, odd
sort of person with unusual reactions. Given a little more group
contact, the opportunity for comparison with others, insight into
social contexts, such severity would have been unnecessary.

My one point of comparison was with my analyst: His nature,
the extent of his sensitivity. The tendency to think of myself as a notably pathological case may have owed more to the isolating vacuum and my analyst's ascendancy than to my own neurosis. And I
too find it less conducive to conflict to acknowledge my difficult aspects than to handle my present environment in an active way that
might bring about change, and could entail my encountering resistance and unpleasantness in that environment. And I didn't go
to an analytic session in order to make the comparatively commonplace discovery that the noise of an elevator, a shrill telephone bell,
street noises, the sound of many people around the place make con-

centration difficult. More interesting to get back to my past sufferings by way of the cramped living conditions of the postwar period, which made it hard to realize many of one's impulses.

And then one's vitality, one's objectively justified indignation are inhibited, and the analysand, working under stress, becomes almost grateful for the difficult working situation, which has allowed him a valuable glimpse of those problems he hasn't yet worked through. (In hospitals, anyway, those persistently obtrusive activities that make change possible—as when, for instance, someone simply refuses to work under certain conditions—aren't usually instigated by analysands.)

It is probably true that a current situation connects up with an earlier one—and there are people who concentrate better in a noisy, hectic atmosphere—but emotionally, I suppose such a train of thought can only be reconstructed by people in analysis.

I never saw any really convincing heightening of sensibility either in myself or in anyone else whom I knew during and after their analysis; perhaps a little more vision was developed, more ability to classify one's emotions, control them, take them seriously, observe them. Some neurotic restrictions of empathy (through homosexual defense, for instance) can certainly be removed, and one's field of vision widened. But this seemed to me just a cosmetic effect, insignificant compared to what the individual brings with him already. I have seen capabilities in many people completely untrained in psychoanalysis—nurses' aides, social workers, recently qualified doctors—far in excess of those shown by many people who have had lengthy analyses.

I have had quite enough of carrying around the stigma and the personally unresolved problem of an unsuccessful analysis, and the compulsion of having to explain it to everyone who matters to me. Questions arise so frequently, and the subject is so complicated, that I can throw myself into the explanation with enthusiasm a few times, but then the words become automatic, routine, and I get tired of justifying myself all the time. It's so arduous; the questions that come up strike so many sparks in the person with whom I'm talking (many people have had bad experiences and doubts roughly similar to mine in therapy or in their own analysis, and don't like to think of them), and obviously the simplest thing is for people to view me as unusual, personally very unfortunate, problematic, special, exceptional case, because then the danger points where my analysis took a destructive turn are not alarming.

"She is very sick"—or, "He wasn't a good analyst"—"That's no way to conduct an analysis . . ." I feel this sort of response is just a defense against the idea that an analysis can have an unfavorable outcome; that as an effective method of treatment it can also have very damaging side effects.

Arguments against dismissing the course of my analysis as a special case are that I was interviewed before it began by three experienced analysts; I spent some time working with patients in a position of responsibility, and no doubts of me were expressed by my supervisors; and my analyst is not considered particularly underqualified or rigid in his approach.

None the less, when I am with people who have been analyzed I very clearly feel their tendency either to regard me as completely crazy, or to condemn my particular analysis, with those particular analysts.

For some time I saw it that way myself; however, I want to achieve understanding, and that's not easy. Almost everyone I know is personally or professionally involved in some way, and thus partisan. Their offers of explanation were not really satisfactory; I encountered theories either vaguely or decidedly based on my life story, which didn't convince me, or else one-sided, well-meaning partisanship, with indignation directed at my analyst, which was soothing, but didn't solve much intellectually. The remarks of acquaintances who had experienced something similar themselves or heard of such things from others were more helpful, as were the comments of colleagues who had comparable tales to tell of therapies that they themselves had conducted and which had gone wrong. I was on equal terms with them, and not in a dependent situation; they saw me as a partner, and didn't feel obliged (on account of a fee, or for the sake of their status) to offer an all-embracing explanation; what they said was on a lighter level, in a private context. We were not, on either side, under such pressure or expecting as much as one would in an officially fixed consultation. And I had often noticed, during such paid consultations (and the fact that they were paid for established my intellectual inferiority), that I became discontented if no satisfactory explanation seemed to be forthcoming as the end of the session approached (after all, I'd made the journey—paid the money—he was trained, he was experienced; why was I paying good money to tell him things I knew already if he couldn't think of anything to say about them, why was I telling him anything of interest?—I had a customer's right to information). It would have been much the same the other way around, and very likely a latent atmosphere of that kind is not very beneficial or stimulating.

I really did get far more from conversations with friends in private circumstances, on an equal footing, than from professional attempts at explanation. These conversations were more relaxed, freer of the pressure to achieve something and freer from mutual caution, since I myself knew something about my interlocutors, and about their backgrounds, which might influence their judgment. Thanks to that knowledge of their backgrounds, I could defend myself against destructive interpretations; if need be, it was easier to accept something that hurt in a private, affectionate context. And we could give ourselves time to let the ideas flow. Payment of a fee induces a lack of symmetry and a sense of inferiority.

If I should ever find it necessary to go into analysis again, then I would only go to someone who is more relaxed than I. Someone who could not infect me with his own anxieties and inhibitions.

If problems are really worked through then they ought, so far as is possible, to disappear. Both my analysts were relatively lackluster people; why didn't they act more freely, more lightheartedly, why couldn't they just seem radiant on occasion because they thought the world was good, or the day or the evening or the hour? Why are people who have been analyzed not notably more content, happier, more beautiful in their individual ways than those who haven't? Why have so many not realized themselves fully? Is it just because when they entered analysis they were sicker, more inhibited, more neurotic than other people? The argument doesn't seem to hold water.

Personality without any words at all can have a very strong effect on me. There are people who can give me encouragement and inspiration just by their presence, by what they express through their movements, their manner of speech or silence, of simply being there: Creating a stimulating, liberating atmosphere around them, without any interpretations, as if by incubation.

If someone has really worked out his inhibitions and anxieties, this fact should be clearly, convincingly and indubitably communicated: In his body, in his actions, in his whole person. If I myself am afraid of diving off the three-meter board, I may well be able to diagnose fear in someone else, and the cause of it, I may be able to interpret his particular inhibitions, arising from his life history— but I can't give him courage. I could only make a verbal statement, along the lines, perhaps, of saying "I have fears too and can't overcome them, but I do think they're irrational; it would be a fine, courageous thing if you could overcome your own." And then the other person might be able to view his fears in the abstract, and perhaps force himself to overcome them. If I do not tell him about my own problems, but concentrate exclusively on his anxieties in a pseudoneutral way, tracing them back to his problems, he will certainly perceive my anxious uncertainties on a deeper plane, and feel that he really is planning a dangerous, threatening and alarming activity. He will then see this nonverbally communicated and easily absorbed fear as his own, thinking it was just that he didn't previously perceive it in all its intensity. Supposing his superego condemns his fear and caution, it will now have even more work to do; if he only perceives his fear, he will still have a harder time overcoming it. His conflict of ambivalence will swing towards the side of inhibition.

I can come to grips with real people all right, be at odds with them, argue, discuss; all that will come to an end some time, and then it will be over and the wound healed. But what can I do about this? I just don't dare; it's as if he had the Mafia behind him, the official one and the little one at the back of my head, unsettling me, condemning me, against me, disliking me; showing me my evil, quarrelsome, unbearable, unaffectionate, neurotically twisted nature, and so on, and so forth.

Perhaps three months would have been the right length of time for that analysis, the relationship between that analyst and me in that particular situation. Three fruitful months; after that our common potential may have been exhausted. I saw a subject on a course program: "How long do I keep relationships going well? When do they last too long, or not long enough?" I thought that was rather good. Why should every relationship be inexhaustibly fruitful? Many change a great deal, and then run their course, are burned out, can't be revived however hard one tries. Is resistance really always to blame when an analysis proves unfruitful? Can't its lack of success be simply a matter for observation, corresponding to reality? These things happen in normal life. Sometimes cooperation is good and meaningful for both sides; but when a common problem has been dealt with, the relationship may fall apart if there was not a great deal more in it. Not every relationship proves inexhaustible.

What I needed was a strong hand to hold as I ventured upon excursions beset with anxieties, undertook risks, not someone wringing his hands on my account and sapping my courage. Why shouldn't I overstretch myself, say, and fall flat on my face? There is always a chance that I may get somewhere. I generally felt my analyst wanted my reactions slowed down and reduced to standard size.

Other factors may have contributed to my low self-confidence: An indirect potential for identification is missing if one has no father and no family on the father's side. One's mother's (or father's) family and friends approve only of one's similarity to themselves and their families: The traditions and genes that are continued in oneself (there is thought to be a precise awareness of genetic identity in the animal kingdom, among lions, wood grouse, etc.). If I meet relations and friends of my mother's they are looking out for my resemblance to her, and are glad and feel validated if they find it: Their tradition is carried on. The features in which I resemble my father alienate and disturb them, make me unlike them, less familiar. They may have been fond of my father, but he is still a foreign element in the family. They do not care for that, at best they will overlook it in favor of that resemblance to themselves which wins their recognition. This often hurt me; in a way, I was proud of my father's part in me, which would otherwise have been dead, entirely gone, extinguished, but which lived on in me. I can't remember any of my mother's relations ever sounding pleased that I resembled my father; my mother was, very much so, but she was the only one. To the rest of them it was something which just had perforce to be accepted, like a blemish, but couldn't be helped.

I don't think they would have reacted so unambiguously if my father had been around, not to be overlooked, career and all; some of his reflected glory would probably have spilled over into their evaluation of my appearance. Without any family on my father's side, there's no one to be glad I look like him; friends and acquaintances who were fond of him are dying off. I believe it would have been different if I could have withdrawn to a benevolent family on my father's side, or if, for instance, neighbors had looked kindly on my resemblance to him, if I had ever been recognized or addressed because I looked like him. Perhaps I might not have found parts of me so ugly for years on end; I might have found my proper tempo sooner. I was much struck by an analyst's remark that he had always thought of me as coming from East Prussia, and was surprised to hear I'd never lived there; that had been his clear identification of my origins. I was delighted when a friend of my father's said, very firmly, "*You* resemble him more than anyone." I am touched myself when I suddenly see my friends going around in miniature, in the shape of their children; one's feeling for the parents is turned directly on the child. At least, I can seldom avoid feeling that way.

If I can speak of paternal identification at all, it is a rather theoretical activity, based on stories, pictures, on my brothers, who looked much more like him than I did, since after all they were older, and were male. I have his hands, his toes. Hands have been very important to me: When I was studying and we were examining patients I sometimes used to wonder why people with ugly hands ventured to go in for medicine. I was right for a medical career, judging by my hands. I have no means of comparison, but I think it must give one a fuller sense of self-confidence if one can like oneself in one's father.

I don't want to be pruned, like espalier-trained fruit; I don't want the outgoing side of me to be merely threatening, giving cause for correction, giving rise to misgivings. In groups, I have noticed that I react fast and relatively strongly to the group atmosphere. If I seemed about to succumb to anesthesia-like fatigue, others around me would start yawning; if I began fooling around and didn't want to go on with the discussion anymore, the mood around me would also immediately become lighter. I wasn't perceiving things wrongly, in these cases, just strongly.

It's so easy for something of a spitefully exposing, denunciatory, reproving nature to creep into analytic interpretation, or just in one's dealing with others. There is practically no descriptive expression for emotional states that can't also surreptitiously carry a pejorative connotation. "You like listening to music a great deal these days; songs in particular?" So it's obvious that I am isolating myself, want to be alone, have infantile yearnings for the way my mother or father sang to me when I was small. And while that might be so, the real reason for my melancholy was not seen, admitted or allowed. The interpretation unmasked and condemned my need, as if it were on trial, condemned it as something neurotic and retarded.

After a break in my career, I have less contact with the analytic world, and so I see less of some of my acquaintances. I notice with one of them—at heart a good friend—that his attitude, ease of manner and goodwill to me have been eroded and undermined in proportion to the length of time since I last saw him; I think it is because of the analytic atmosphere, his analytic superego, which classifies my unfortunate experience of analysis as something crazy (or anyway highly neurotic). He listens more attentively, pricking up his analytic ears, so to speak, he is suspicious, inwardly on the alert, ready to give me yet another all-embracing, totally explanatory interpretation. This attitude recedes again once I have made pleasant, human contact with him; then I can get him to believe in me once more, but it's an effort. I had a bad analytical experience, I very decidedly did, and such a thing may not be, can't be, must arise from my peculiar pathology, the particular kind of hard case I was. Otherwise, the same thing might happen to him, with his own patients, or as an analysand if he ever undertook further analysis.

If the conversation turns to my analysis or my analyst, he is cautious, keeps his distance. At best, he will say, uneasily, "Are you still chewing all that over?" From his tone, I may conclude that this in itself is sick; this in itself is bound to make a specialist pay attention, and I'd do better to let it go, forget it all, reconcile myself. But I *am* still chewing it over, why not? If childhood traumas stay in the memory so long, with all the emotional weight they carry, why shouldn't traumas arising from my analysis? Why must I forget so fast? Six years of life, to be forgotten in two years. Why should it be so surprising, neurotic and suspect if relatively recent traumas still hurt me? Isn't it a kind of denial to refuse to see that really dreadful things, real damage, harmful side effects can occur in the context of analytical treatment? I know analysts of good repute who admit that they suffered for years from their training analyses and had to recover from the experience, not just get over their own churned up pathology. It is an open secret among those who have been analyzed that, in the course of their analysis, many of them have successively buried their dreams, hopes, desire for change and the liberating of their latent potential (perhaps as a result of interpretations such as "fantasies of grandeur," "demanding attitude," "exaggerated expectations," "analytical fantasies of omnipotence," "insight into reality") and have, to an undue degree, given their analytic disappointments new interpretations. This knowledge, however, expresses itself mostly in irony, comparable to those macabre jokes doctors make. The fact that severe damage can actually be done, giving rise to psychotic episodes, depressive phases, suicidal impulses—and done unnecessarily, no, better not think of that.

The fact that I still think I had a very bad experience of analysis, and I still don't view it with mellow tolerance, I have not filed away those years with a sense of nostalgic reconciliation and identification with them—that upsets people.

With others, I don't experience the same loss of contact and difficulty in winning back liking to the same extent as I do with this particular friend of mine. With them, I can largely build on trust from earlier times; our relationships have not faded so much. They have never been undermined in that suspicious, anxious, temporizing manner. I believe others too become less confident within the system, find their opinions influenced by the group mood. In so-called normal life I can count on a certain extent of human reliability; I seldom have to fling myself so much and so emotionally into the old relationship in order to re-create former intimacy. In the analytic world, however, when I meet a friend I seldom have the feeling that time has stood still and we last saw each other only a short time ago.

What I'm writing is basically nonsense. But I spent the last nine years occupied with it, and I'm not the only one; there are at least some other people who have had similar experiences, if not, perhaps, over such a long period. I took my analysis somewhat more seriously than did many of my acquaintances, didn't consciously hold anything back, maybe I practiced free association more thoroughly than others. And I was blamed for it. "Did you have to tell him that so exactly? Present it in such detail? Couldn't you have kept it to yourself for a while, until you'd taken your final examination? Or couldn't you have tried to clear that point up elsewhere?" Yes, no doubt I could. But what sort of analysis is it if I can't be honest, at least so far as stands within my conscious power? If one must let corruption prevail there too, as elsewhere in one's professional life, I might as well have put aside my dreams from the very start.

It was almost impossible to discuss problems concerning my analytical experience with people who were or had been in analysis, or professionally established in that field. Even under very congenial circumstances, in very easy relationships, people would often listen to me, would be friendly and encourage me to be frank, but secretly their selective attention was directed and focused on my disturbance, still to be diagnosed but to be made clear to me eventually. They listened to what I said, but my remarks served only as raw material for proofs of that disturbance. They did not accept them for what they were, or anyway not in the sense and emotional context in which I meant them, but associated them with my unanalyzable neurosis. Just as a doctor in organic medicine, treating a patient with suspected liver disease, will feel alarm at symptoms of which he would take no notice in a patient with athlete's foot.

Those little affected by analysis, so-called ordinary people, understand me better, listen to me differently, find it easy to accept the way I try to present myself. I don't feel as if I were always being pushed in the same direction.

That mean-minded, loveless way of picking away at everything, finger spitefully pointed! I find more of myself in folk songs, street songs and tunes than in many cool pronouncements. "Don't you think that this might rather point to . . . It's too soon for that as yet; genital defense against pre-genital content; Oedipal choice of object; does this not conceal . . .?" etc., etc. It is rather like cutting up and dissecting a specimen. The tender positive side of me was seldom brought out, that side which I easily feel, for instance, when listening to children's songs; there are parts of me more capable of vitality and feeling than usually came to light in my analytic sessions. (Lines from songs came into my head—"When he heard it he felt horror and grief"—"When you see him tell him I love him, tell him I would like to rest upon his breast"—"fair as milk and blood, deep in her heart she loved a robber.") There must be something other than that analytical language which destroys, intimidates, alarms, pulls everything to bits as it dissects it.

To the orthodox, it is my fault: Why did she look for an analyst like that? Neurotic choice of partner.

I sometimes think, by way of comforting myself, that a bad marriage might have been no less destructive. And anyway I didn't inflict neurosis on any children during that period.

What kind of lying attitude says we must be reconciled to everything? To Hitler, the CIA, the ITT? Why? This ideal had made its way into analysis, as applied to me: I was to understand everything and then view it without passing judgment. Many groups are gangs of assassins, by whatever discreet circumlocution one tries to account for the fact. One may ask what existential and/or neurotic compulsions have caused people to join in and subscribe to such an ideology? But why should I offer nonjudgmental understanding if I'm not responsible for these people as their therapist? I'm not trying to provide therapy for my analysts either, understand and interpret them, I want to get on with living. And they did me damage; for whatever problematic reasons. I want to find my way back to myself, to my capabilities, dreams, and my partially destroyed self-confidence.

But what am I to do with my hate? I could tell myself reasonably enough that I wasn't my first analyst's type. I have heard since of other people who found flaws in her perceptiveness, irritability, and who criticized her. I was supposed to forget her, and many of her interventions. I don't want to identify with her, her values, her way of life. My mother had and still has a fuller life, one that isn't kept on such a low flame. I never saw my first analyst radiant and really happy.

It was the same with my second analyst. It would be brutal to confront him with the full extent of my rage, indignation and bitterness. Much may be explained and excused: He was still relatively young, young for a training analyst; he was just detaching himself from the university hierarchy and from his own training analyst; he had obstacles and difficulties of his own to contend with in his new practice. He wasn't primarily malevolent, just clumsy, and his effect on me was devastating. But not on others, so far as I could tell. Not on others, who had approached analysis with lower expectations, less intellectual hunger, who had, perhaps, sought something other than what I sought in him, for whom he may have meant a contact, an analytical authority, a younger brother figure. Although I did have my doubts about his handling of the themes of sexuality and eroticism in sessions with other women. There was one to whom he had said that at her age she ought to reconcile herself to the lack of available men for her. Wasn't that his own defense against her attractions? My mother fell in love again at the age of sixty-two, and went about with eyes shining, and this particular woman could be very attractive when she liked. What gave him the idea that she had to "reconcile herself?" However, this wasn't my problem, not part of my analysis. It was suspect all the same. I didn't believe advancing age meant sterility, a lack of attractiveness; it wasn't something I observed in my environment, not among people I thought vital and worth imitating.

I wouldn't like to lead such a life as those two analysts. However, they did do me harm, and I can't even defend myself with all my might and hit back. I must be understanding, lenient. Hate should be permissible for a while, though, in myself as in others.

Perhaps I wouldn't have spent so long in analysis without the example of my brothers before me; without my belief that they could do everything better and had more vision than I. As a child I'd believed they could work magic; when I gradually came to realize that they were only leading me on, I still wondered if they couldn't really work magic after all, if they weren't right. They said they had conjured up some special air and shut it away, it was slightly yellowish, and if I looked long enough I'd see it too. If I walked through that air I'd turn to a blistered pulp, they said, so I mustn't. And when I ceased to believe that, did go through the air and wasn't pulped, they said it was because they had let the air out again just in time, to save me.

Interpretations and value judgments, once made, took on independent life in a chronically devastating way. When I had heard them, and they'd struck home, there they were in me, going round and round, able to affect and undermine any new experience. I didn't need to have had a particular situation interpreted; I knew what the interpretations were getting at, what note they should strike, what the assessment should be. If I thought some discussion was mendacious drivel and it made me angry, the first thing I wondered was to whom my rejection originally really applied, etc.

One finds that a process with laws of its own has been set in motion, as with cancer cells swimming about, just waiting for some profitable source of nourishment. Such condemnation, criticism, and erosion can apply to anything in a range of interrelated topics which has once been given a negative interpretation. Off with its head.

I never experienced any convincing projection during my analysis. Or at least, not one that could really be seen as such; those that were comparatively convincing were very commonplace incidents, as for instance if I suspected that my analyst was hungry at midday. "Wouldn't you like to go and have lunch now?" "I think *you're* the one who's feeling hungry, I'm not hungry yet." Even then, yes, I would suppose that I had drawn my supposition from my own empty stomach, but not entirely so. My hunger might make me more sensitive, more attentive to signs of his own developing hypoglycemia, could make it easier for me to put myself in his place, because I was feeling the same.

Otherwise, however, it generally turned out that feelings described as my projections did really exist in him, if only partly so. In a one-to-one relationship, are there any feelings at all that are really experienced by only one partner, and have not appeared in relation or reaction to the other of entanglement with him? When couples come for therapy, it is clear that a feeling is never exclusively limited to one partner only without deep involvement of the other.

Doesn't the analyst react very intensively too? It seemed to me, anyway, in my own therapies.

I was often brought to the end of my tether in those analytic sessions when my perceptions of my analyst's feelings came back to me like a boomerang, rebounding from his smooth and indifferent coolness. It was only bearable if he added mitigating remarks, such as, "Hard as I'm listening to what goes on in myself, I don't notice anything of that kind." That was all right; my perception could survive; perhaps he didn't feel it, but it was right all the same. It was very bad when "It is your anger which you presume to see in me." He meant well by me, only I was so evil, had so much hatred in me, so much horribly unloving, unjustifiably touchy and aggressive potential within me, that I couldn't perceive his benevolent attention; I misjudged it because I was so perverted. Since I had to make use of projection, as a means of relieving my burden, my hatred must be so great and strong that I couldn't bear it alone anymore, and must spread it into my environment. Like a psychotic patient who externalizes her impulses, wishes and feelings, in the form of voices or delusions of reference, to help her save her own threatened equilibrium.

I didn't believe he was as angry as I was at the exact moment, but I did think I could feel his annoyance, which my problems had probably aroused. But the boomerang "projection" was horrible; it claimed my feeling was nonsense, emphasized by the evidence of the projection mechanism ("*I* am not the one who is angry, *you* are angry"—yes, I really was, and so apparently I'd projected it). I prefer to put it that one is "drawing conclusions about others from oneself," it seems more humane and less isolating, and creates some connection between those involved. At bottom, after all, all understanding works by drawing some new conclusion from the familiar, from ourselves, assuming that the other person will react in a similar way in similar situations; this is why it's confusing finding one's way about in a strange culture.

At least I never thought I sensed feelings in others which were entirely imaginary: Sometimes I was wrong, but I could easily abandon such ideas again. (Perhaps these were true projections: Just fantasies and suppositions which could be toyed with and easily revised.)

The experiencing of projections was one of the points of my analysis. If I assume to start with that one reason it failed was because of my relatively high sensitivity, I think that the diagnosis of projection mechanisms did me more harm than it brought me intellectual clarity. More care, caution and consideration ought to have been employed with so confusing and unsettling an interpretation, one leaving me in such general doubt.

With my own patients, in any case, I have become cautious about steering too rapidly towards early childhood factors. I often just know too little about a background that's unfamiliar to me, a patient's situation at work, the usual and recurrent conflicts encountered there. Even if I have read up on the subject for my own information, my empathy remains academic. It would be easy for me, with my own educational background, to diagnose a conflict with the superego, problems with the father figure, in—say—a piece worker; but I can only make assumptions about the real pressure he is under, his bosses, his colleagues and their financial anxieties, the atmosphere at the place of work, his fear of unemployment. Nor should I relate the atmosphere of offices in which many workers share one large room, a situation which invites feelings of persecution (paranoid reactions), directly to a current or previous family situation; nor do I know whether family problems—which are almost universal—play a noteworthy part in sleep disturbances of shift workers. How does one evaluate anxiety states in factory workers when the danger of a life-threatening explosion really does exist? Is there any point at all in referring back to childhood fears? Or am I to compare such a patient with his less anxious colleagues and draw my diagnosis from that comparison? Perhaps his is the healthiest feeling, most based on reality. I found a group therapy session instructive: Two employees of an oil refinery with almost identical anxieties spoke scornfully and with anger of attempts at intra-psychic interpretation by doctors who took no account of the permanent and genuine danger of an explosion in a work situation which anyway lay outside any feeble attempts at safety precautions. Probably their anxiety feelings *also* derived from anger with their superiors and fear of the consequences of protesting. Probably a group of similarly situated people would be more helpful and do more to diminish those fears than the selective working through of, say, a conflict with the patient's father.

Perhaps many so-called psychotic episodes during analysis are just a reaction to the nature of that analysis, an artificial product or an attempt at healing. The official line taken is generally that the analyst stuck it out and endured the analysand's bad experience with him. Yet in the therapy of couples, it is self-evident that if one partner becomes psychotic, both are involved, that the apparently or indeed actually healthy partner has at least contributed his or her mite. In analysis, no one usually takes any notice of the idea that the two people involved are on an equal footing and depend upon each other; the analysand brought his perils with him, and is grateful to have someone look after him in his troublesome condition. In a good analysis, however, there are surely genuine decompensations; but perhaps they occur more rarely than the artificial and unnecessary variety.

An analyst should know and take into account his limitations and uncertainties. He is not, after all, in duty bound to understand everything, entirely, correctly and comprehensively. Even doctors of organic medicine have no such certainty; established methods of treatment turn out, after many years, to be nonsensical, harmful, or in need of modification; there are no really effective ways of treating many diseases. Ought not an analyst to be even more cautious, open and judicious in the use of his methods? How does he know that a patient may not be feeling exactly as he should— feeling what is correct and significant for him?

It may impair one's own self-image and confidence to have to admit that there are many things one doesn't understand, or understands poorly, and one can see no possibility of resolving some problems at all. But the situation becomes very mendacious if one pretends to a certainty that doesn't exist.

If only my analyst could have said to me, justifiably, "I feel that—in my view—my opinion is that—as compared to me, you feel this very differently, very strongly . . ." But not just: "At this point it *is* too strong, too soon, etc. . . ."

My self doubts mingled with all my private relationships; for a while, I valued men only insofar as they regarded me, unquestioningly and convincingly, as "normal" and not crazy. It cheered me and made me feel good if an obviously normal man thought I was healthy and attractive, not crazy, not on the borderline of psychosis, not destructive, not alarming. That was my main criterion. My friends thought that I and a highly normal man, one who was "able to deal well with reality," would make a good couple. He made me feel very happy as we drank coffee together, without a word being spoken, because he simply communicated to me through his pores that he liked the sort of person I was, thought I was a real woman. He had personal problems and wasn't available for me at the time, but that didn't matter; he had given me a satisfying answer to my question, and that was all I wanted.

Sometimes I thought that the worst thing about growing up without a father, so far as I was concerned, was that the fact could be construed in analysis as my Achilles' heel, the evidence of my disturbance (thus deduced logically, mathematically, as in a grammatical declension). Without this argumentation, I might not have remained so credulous; I might have developed criticisms of my own sooner, more violently and more radically, and have removed myself from that cool atmosphere to a more vital, friendlier, more sensuous and loving climate.

I consider it fortunate that I chanced upon an analyst who was technically not very experienced, so that it was basically possible to see through him, and not upon a more shrewd and more subtle one, from whom I'd probably have had more difficulty in breaking free. Outright technical blunders he committed made it possible for me to remember my real self. What he actually said convinced other people—or those willing to listen, anyway; there was no defense against that. "Haven't you taken it the wrong way?" His pronouncements couldn't be seen as my own projections. Things were more difficult, less definite with my first analyst; hers was a more homogeneous nature, less open to attack.

I came to hate the feeling that I was crazy or diverged from the norm because of the way I reacted. If I was worked up over a lecture, thought it stupid and commonplace, I knew that such anger wasn't good, was fuelled by the neurotic part of me. But why must I react the same way as so many others? Why do violent reactions *a priori* seem suspect? There are plenty of real causes for outbursts of rage and hatred around, and mental health surely is not supposed to mean that one overlooks all real misery, unnecessary brutality and intentional cruelty with cheerful equanimity and inner detachment, and a sense of well-being.

Why did I have to have the range of my reactions prescribed for me by my analysts, or at least judged by the standard of theirs? (They did not even claim it was their own, but declared it appropriate in the situation.) I am different from my analysts. I have other ways of reacting, which, however, are largely correct in my immediate environment, where I know people and have friends who feel the same sort of thing. And even if I didn t know such people, who's to say if I am overreacting or just seeing clearly? If I differ from my analyst, that doesn't necessarily mean that my feelings are wrong and inadequate. Majority opinion is not necessarily the truth.

The anger seething inside me became an indication of those conflicts I had not worked through: The more indifferent I was, the healthier I seemed to be.

I can't cling to hatred of my mother for the simple reason that it would destroy me: There is so much similarity between us, or at

least that's how I see it now, we share so many little ways and
habits and turns of speech, our manner of acting in situations of
conflict, the way we laugh and express anger—I really can't be
against all that; there's nothing bad about it.

Later, encouraged by a man who had been analyzed, I thought
of several parallels between my life and my complaints of my analysis: My life story was destroyed, my family situation wrecked, I
was torn out of the context of my relationships: Freezing cold, the
"Westwall" mood, where people could be shot at and killed, dug in
and entrenched, a hunger for caring, for the intellectual inspiring,
the wretchedness of life, the way I atrophied and withered during
that time, the idea of shooting my analyst (no other manner of
death had entered my mind).

I believe this really was the case in my analysis: The connection
with my family really was ruined, unnecessarily and destructively;
it really was a cold situation, barricades up, inhuman, injurious,
enough to make you shoot someone, and I perceived this because it
was reality. And there are real reasons for seeing a parallel with my
life: The war destroyed my family, its menfolk were shot; the uncle
of whom I have early memories died in a cattle truck, his leg shot
off, half frozen and starving; my father was so exhausted with cold
and hunger that he was capable only of crawling, and was shot before the march of many miles through the snow to the camps began; both were starving, frozen and shot, and the last day of my
analysis was also the anniversary of my father's death, thirty-two
years earlier.

A knowing analytical smile is not help to me; that's how it was in
my analysis, the mood and situation shaped themselves that way.
Wounds were re-opened, and may have strengthened, reinforced
and fortified my early experiences. I don't believe that an interpretation of this as a repetition of my early childhood situation would
have got me anywhere if that part of it now present (however it
may be interpreted as transference neurosis) hadn't also been confirmed and admitted. However, this is a futile consideration; the
idea of transference did come up, as did that of a transference trap,
but without any connection being made with the wartime situation,
i.e., it occurred at a very late stage, in the last few sessions.

If I go over an earlier situation again now, it becomes real and
relevant if it is fully acted out.

I keep getting doubts: Ideas I anxiously try to formulate with much expenditure of emotion seem so commonplace, the repetition of very simple analytic principles, which undoubtedly need to be followed. There are many places where one might turn up one's nose: He was not a good analyst—that wasn't a good interpretation—but you mustn't take it like that—that's no way to deal with it, of course—that interpretation made too soon, too late, something was overlooked, no notice was taken of it—you understood the wrong way, etc. And one may turn away with a feeling of superiority. However, these things happened to me, in an analysis which was not in itself unusually poor, which indeed, technically speaking, was a good training analysis. And I know people who have had similar experiences, and who felt crushed for a long time afterwards. But the fact was that those basic principles we weren't following were dismissed from my mind at the time itself—for instance, the principle that analysis is a two-sided situation, for the course of which both partners are to a certain extent responsible; that it would be all right for me to remain intransigent, isolate myself with my opinion, oppose the general consensus (you don't conform to the group, I was told), and that this may even be a positive quality.

For a long time I couldn't/wouldn't read material published about the course of other analyses; it was too painful to see what my own analysis could have been like.

Obviously analysis as practiced lags a good way behind what is thought of in theory and discussion, but that fact should not be denied.

The excessive abuse I lavished on my analyst some years ago, when I accused him of being an anticreative bastard, a womenhater, an asshole, threatened to beat him to a pulp, called him a stupid, narrow-minded, inhibited coward, son of a bitch, lecherous and feeble-minded and so on and so forth, now strikes me as similar to the torrents of abuse uttered during exorcism. The exorcist and the victim unite in condemning the diabolical element in the latter (neurotic, acting out, given to transference); the woman possessed, however, has the advantage of being able to localize the evil outside herself. A woman in analysis must recognize her hatred as her own inmost quality; earlier, it may have arisen in reaction to her environment, but now it is her own, her inner being, and the analytic environment has served only to bring it out and make it clear by means of transference.

I knew, after all, that everyone, myself included, has strong aggressive impulses.

But I don't find it appropriate to agitate someone to the point of bringing out those aggressive dreams and fantasies, making them conscious, working on them, and increasing those guilt feelings that are present in any case. Anyway, I think that on account of our great difficulty in communication and irritated interaction I reacted in an aggressive way which is not really typical of me, at least not as a permanent state of affairs. I consider my aggressive touchiness over a long period something artificial.

(During exorcism, the priest ends up hearing devils speak out of the mouth of the afflicted woman, once he has concentrated on her long enough and lured the evil to the surface.)

I would like to have my brain free again, not stuffed with old history, problems that have not been worked through surfacing at every opportunity, tales I must keep telling, always with the same sense of pressure. It is wearisome to keep telling the story of difficult, intense experiences, and to be constantly dependent upon understanding and confirmation, to long for it and be dissatisfied and dubious if it is not forthcoming. I felt bitter, blocked; I find difficulty in perceiving the present; it seems dim and falsified. I chew over things I haven't been able to swallow, angrily if I am in luck, otherwise with resignation.

If I gained from my analyses the conviction that I was the lowest of the low, impossible to love, is that perhaps what they were trying to convey? Wasn't it, perhaps, counter-transference (i.e., transference of the analysts, of their problems)? Isn't it possible I just took over their feelings? Wasn't it the simplest thing for me to agree with them anyway, at least in my condemnation?

"No, *you* entertain deep feelings of self-hatred and are projecting them on me, you think you feel hatred in me so that you can identify with it better." Projective identification—a self-fulfilling prophecy—the self-hatred of the depressive—the splitting off of parts of the ego—inability to distinguish between myself and others—all this is rooted in my mind.

I don't want to go on being humbly thankful because they

worked with such a hard case as myself, because they did their professional job with me, for the usual fee.

At bottom, this expectation of gratitude is only the idealized notion of practitioners of organic medicine, who see medical achievement in itself as "beyond price."

However, the fact was that it was conveyed to me I ought to be
particularly grateful. And I am not the only one to whom this happened. They kept saying we were "working together," "on an
equal footing," "I'm not analyzing you, we're analyzing you together," "You are analyzing yourself along with me," etc., but that
played no emotional part. The explanation that the special, magi-
cal status of the analyst comes from outside, he is endowed with it
by the patient, was not true of me, at least. I do not develop such
feelings with mechanics, plumbers, salespeople, whom I am paying
for their work.

I think it is perverse for analysts to acquire, so easily and quickly
and for their paid time, the affection earned by parents sitting up at
night when children have whooping cough, nursing them through
flu, going through all kinds of worries.

For money, the analyst becomes a benign figure, all-
compensating, granting what wasn't previously given free, for
one's own sake. But now it's available for money, so it just must
be more valuable. And I myself will do good only for money; if
someone won't pay me enough, too bad. That was how I experienced it, as a corrective to my home background. The illusion of
someone's bothering about me for my own sake can be preserved
only if I under-pay him, if at bottom he really ought to be paid
much, much more for his work on my behalf, if it is far more valuable than what I am paying him. No doubt I'll feel the same with
patients later.

*   *   *

I no longer believe that my analysis was an exception, that I was
extremely sick, impossible to analyze, or that my analyst was a particularly unskillful one, provocative of conflict; rather ,two consciously motivated people found themselves in a sickness-inducing
and destructive situation, and that such a thing is not uncommon.
Acquaintances who have felt that they emerged from analysis "op-

posed in their narcissism," "shattered," "totally uncertain of their feelings," "a wreck," have made me feel this likely.

I see really successful, convincing analytical relationships around me just about as often (or seldom) as good one-to-one relationships, great loves. Most people are lying to the world, and to themselves; as in many marriages, harmonious happiness is often just feigned. Except that more outward pressure weighs upon training analysis, because one's whole career depends on what's officially considered the good course of that analysis. In that respect, a marital conflict may be more easily dealt with in relation to the world outside than a conflict in analysis, which may go really deep and endanger the possibility of further work together. A marital conflict may arouse sympathy, but I have heard unsuccessful analyses mentioned only belatedly and with great caution.

I'd have felt better about it if I hadn't had such high and idealistic expectations, as of a great love (and I wasn't alone in such fantasies, see the man who rallied about an "analytic honeymoon."). If I had been more detached, I could have worked through much with him, and others. I wouldn't have been so disappointed, wouldn't have started doubting myself and my capacity for enjoyment so totally. Marriages of convenience—in this case community interest in training, work and careers—do certainly have liberating advantages on both sides, if you can admit, "It wasn't great but useful, and pleasant enough in the circumstances."

*   *   *

Something very stern has crept into analysis as now practiced, and I would rather not believe it is a primary factor. You will see pictures of Freud hanging at about waist level on the walls of many consulting rooms and institutes, Freud in old age, pictures whose bitter, oppressive, suffering and rigorous severity can only frighten me. (I have difficulty in seeing the wise, paternal, kind, detached element in that picture.) If there were really no other pictures of Freud, well and good—but he looks really pleasant and attractive in photographs taken when he was younger, the kind of man one could love. Then he radiated vigor, courage, vitality. He didn't have cancer then either. Somehow or other, however, those handsome, vital, younger pictures haven't been so popular. (I saw them for the first time when they were shown to me by a young woman analyst who was glad to have a pleasing picture of him at last.) Official representations of him, on announcements of congresses, for instance, always show the stern old man who suffered in the course of his life: Determined, independent, but without much hope. Would he really have liked this aspect of him, at that stage of his life, to be perpetuated? Wouldn't he rather be remembered as a radiant, vital, handsome man, at the height of his physical and intellectual power? I have seen beautiful representations, showing experience, detachment, peace. But when the picture shows someone as sick as that with cancer—and leaving out of account psychological theories of the development of the disease—there is surely something wrong.

Why commemorate a man with a picture in which he looks sick? What kind of attitude to parents and fathers does it show? That surely was not his prime, when he knew love and passion in his life, not just pain and disease, though it's hard for me to imagine such things after looking at his picture in old age.

Is there by any chance something to that malicious criticism by the opponents of psychoanalysis, who compare it—as it is practiced—with the ecclesiastical practice of religion? With Freud in God's place, his picture in the place of the crucifix, his technical writings instead of the Ten Commandments, and with the whole wrath of the superego (otherwise turned on sin) directed against deviation from the dogma; and with that extra weight, induced by one's own history, found everywhere in western society?

(Though the suffering of the crucified Christ does seem to come from outside, with Freud everything comes from within, psychological, somatic, psychosomatic.)

I do not feel freer, happier, less complicated, more confident, more active and stronger than before. If I meet someone the corners of whose mouth resemble my first analyst's, or whose mouth and nose resemble my second analyst's, I still feel a shock, and all the misery of the world comes up from the depths, even when the prevailing atmosphere is pleasant.

I don't see any enormous difference between saying "We are all sinners," and "We are all neurotics;" original sin is with us at birth, neurosis comes only a little later. This is not a great difference to someone of, say, fifteen, beginning to take an interest in religion or psychoanalysis. The head is humbly bowed in a similar way before inner sinfulness and one's own neurosis; except that we are not responsible for original sin, but we did cause our own neuroses.

*   *   *

There may well be a considerable if unacknowledged number of suicides connected with analysis and analytically oriented therapy: Cases where analysis was at least preponderantly the trigger factor, or simply proved the last straw.

What would have happened if I'd given up the struggle? Would anyone have taken the trouble to wonder why, how it happened? Whether something hadn't been going so very well after all? I think it more likely that a fatal outcome would have been diagnosed as the inevitable result of my "early, severe disturbance," of my unanalyzable neurosis and unusually disturbed nature. My analyst would probably have attracted sympathy for the hard time he'd had with me, the trouble I'd given him, and perhaps also for my final culminating act of aggression and malignity. People would certainly have remembered early signs of my danger, would have said it was only to be expected; just bad luck, one of the risks of the game. At most they might have thought it the kind of misfortune that even the most experienced analyst can't always avoid. (At least, the argument in a case of which I knew ran something like that.)

Why must I, during my analysis, heal wounds made in analysis? But why: Why not my real, early emotional troubles? Why did I have to spend a large part of my second analysis healing the wounds left by interpretations of the first as well as those left by the analysis as a whole? Was I really that hard to understand? Why, with my sensitivity, my belief in psychoanalysis and my intensity, must I be given interpretations on which so little thought had been expended? Why must I be grateful for understanding? Isn't that a basic right, a human right anyone may expect in psychoanalysis? Where should it be found if not here? And why do my thoughts run this grovelling way? Why isn't it simply clear and obvious that I should be for the most part correctly understood in my psychoanalysis? Must I really be grateful for that? How is it that small children and the mentally sick understand me easily and accurately? Can't I expect the same from analysts? Why must I struggle for understanding? What's so difficult about me? Why did I have to end up with an analyst who would have such difficulty with me?

The fact is, a claim to omnipotence has slipped into analysis: A claim to be able to explain anything and everything. Secretly, it assumes that it towers head and shoulders above all other sciences. Yes, there are other factors to be considered, sociological, economic and so on, but strictly speaking, these are subordinate. I seldom took anything but the intrapsychic really seriously.

I now think that anyone can be driven to psychosis, depression or suicide by a bad analysis. I think I was just rather lucky; I had something, however small, to cling to at difficult moments. I no longer believe in depression setting in so to speak physiologically in the context of an analysis, or at least not to any great extent. Probably such depression can simply be put down to inadequate, selectively negative, grammatical-mathematical-what-have-you, in short, ugly interpretations. I consider it quite an achievement that I didn't become dependent on drugs or alcohol during that period, and made no conscious suicide attempt. Sometimes mere survival is quite an achievement.

There was never any consideration of whether the interpretations were too superficial. If a baby bites the breast, it isn't being primarily sadistic; it is looking doggedly for enough of something it lacks. If a marked death wish shows up behind one of my slips or dreams, it is abominable to view it with horror and macabre amazement instead of wondering where it comes from: What misery, what fundamental predicament, privation, reaction or injury caused it. I wasn't actually born with it.

This train of thought is really very commonplace and self-evident, and ought not to need mentioning at all in analysis. However, that is what happened to me, and it is no use distancing oneself and saying such things don't occur. They do, and probably quite often.

I learned about my feelings about my body from women's groups. For instance, there's a difference between keeping one's genital area free of odor with deodorants before, during and after one's period, sending one's body fluids and tampons down the toilet without looking at them, or taking note of those personal odors and fluids, which are constantly changing, by using a menstrual sponge which one can wash out oneself. Many memories cling to such odors; when I first became aware after my period of an odor about me such as I'd encountered in my mother, I felt it was something feminine, adult, proper. That was how a real, flourishing woman smelled. I hadn't been to any self-examination groups, but I thought the women who held them had a very friendly and natural attitude to their genital areas, something clearly different from the usual one. My second analyst had informed me—in another context—that a certain amount of cleanliness was simply necessary, from which I concluded that he did not like any very noticeable odor; he certainly didn't feel comfortable about blood. But why should I periodically treat my genital area as something disgusting? Why should I allow my psyche, my understanding of myself, my guilt feelings to echo masculine fears? I haven't met many men who reacted without any anxiety at all to my periods.

I came close to castration fears only once, at the second workshop I attended; I'd forgotten the pill several days running, and my period started as I was sitting on a chair; I hadn't consciously expected it. When I stood up I saw a large bloody stain on the grey upholstery, and was horrified, didn't know what the matter was: "This is it, I'm bleeding to death, I'll die." Such fears are obviously present, deep down, and I suppose that in my vulnerable mood I had more access to them. Men must feel very much threatened by such things. Otherwise, however, I've never really been able to feel castration fears or a sense of inadequacy, exceeding what's described as legitimate penis envy.

At any rate, I am quite sure that my teeming feelings of anxiety and guilt without which, I suppose, almost no woman can grow up in our society, can be dispelled or maximized by the feelings of another person, and to a much greater extent than my analysts would admit to me. My body, anyway, reacts very sensitively, and I can rely on what it tells me. If it doesn't want something, it has its reasons, and vice versa.

I cannot imagine how intense negative transference, the unadulterated repetition of earlier relationships, can occur without causing and consolidating further traumas. I think the process is at the least highly dangerous; a situation is experienced over again, intensively, with all the sensations and guilt feelings entailed. It is supposed to be important to work with the analyst to remove the character of reality from this repeated experience, to understand it, and to make it clear that the present situation is only an artificial one. But who can guarantee that in spite of good, intensive work in the way of interpretation, I shall really be emotionally able to see it in the abstract, keep myself from taking a part of my present feelings as confirmation of the earlier situation? If it is true that one is consciously aware of only a small part of one's experience, then it's unlikely that something repeated in the analytic situation can be entirely grasped in a rational interpretation. I suspect, anyway, that my analyst's antipathy affected me so much because he was uncovering an old wound, even if a fantasized one.

It is common practice, and good, to gently arouse those feelings that aren't currently present or are inhibited, to care for them and treat them with much skill and empathy; excessive reactions are troubling. Considerably less is published about dealing with them than there is about dealing with those feelings which cannot be experienced at all, or only weakly (in the realm of psychoanalysis, that is).

There are clear, sober ideas on what degree and intensity of contact with the original family is analytically healthy. However, the fact that most people in my environment see their parents and siblings on average many times a year, a certain amount of contact by telephone and letter being taken into account too, doesn't prove that this average constitutes the healthiest, most mature and most satisfactory relationship. All one can really do in good conscience is to describe what has turned out to work best in our culture, in our social conditions, without leading to any severe handicaps. It cannot be right to describe all affection or close ties as a pathological case of fixation, etc. Everything in my analysis seemed, in the last resort, excessive.

At any rate, I felt I was being pressured to reject, with hostility, more of my family ties and my past history than I really wanted to. It was like a semi-automatic maelstrom to find rottenness in everything, view it critically and suspiciously, diagnose it as pathogenic if in any doubt. This led me to retreat, hurt and angry. Here I found myself in the company of other analyzed people, whose reactions of furious hatred to their mothers, fathers and the rest of their families occur more frequently and violently, at a lower threshold of irritation, than is the case with people who have not been analyzed. The analyzed seemed to achieve a good-natured, amused tolerance of parental flaws and oddities only later and more rarely.

I no longer think it's just that people who have been analyzed have experienced their conflicts more openly; in my own case I had the impression that there was something artificially constructed and objectively unnecessary in it, perhaps partly due to the criticism I may have been feeling at the time for my first analyst, a fundamentally different person from me. And there is an element of fashion in it too: Everyone wallowing in childhood suffering, believing it must all be turned inside out, cleansed, rejected. It is a kind of sport, locating the sick, ruined, impotent, damaged and hopeless parts of oneself; only the negative is interesting. It means that, being "in the analytic process," I am accepted into the community of analysands, even if my sense of worth is reduced.

The tendency of many analysands to wallow in their personal handicaps can—besides recovering actually depressed feelings— have the effect of coping with the barbaric injustice of life: Blotting it out, decreasing guilt feelings over one's own privileged condition, which everyone who has the chance of going into analysis at all must really experience. Even without much awareness of politics, one can hardly fail to notice that the majority of mankind have more basic existential problems than most analysands: That there is suffering—from hunger, heat, cold, pain, and sickness, and without any hope of relief—without which life is presumably easier to bear. The argument that when you're in a bad way yourself the thought of someone else's worse misery is no comfort has in fact always consoled me, but still remnants of guilty conscience remain. However I might have suffered from my background, I couldn't say every single thing in it was rotten. It was inherently improbable that I had had a worse time than anybody else in the world.

And presumably I was not alone in feeling this way. I think that what makes analysands sometimes seem to be suffering hysterically, in the commonly accepted sense of the expression, is something that goes back to their social consciences, which they are trying to soothe by making much of their individual suffering.

As a middle way between the Prussian precept of determinedly pulling oneself together, or alternatively sinking into one's own extreme misery, a comparison with other people might help get things into proportion. I myself, anyway, had the impression that much private suffering was artificially inflated in the analytic vacuum, that it wasn't only my own repressed feelings showing up, but something additional had come in to reinforce them, something artificial which didn't really belong to me.

Why could I communicate comparatively easily with so-called ordinary people—people who were not analysts, not academics? I always, even abroad and out of my usual setting, found I made human contact more easily than I did with my analytically trained colleagues. I was not, then, regarded with suspicion from the start. Almost everywhere—on trains, in stores, in the street—I saw more that was human, loving, pleasant, humorous than in the tense, cool atmosphere of the room where my analysis took place. Outside, I could laugh at suggestive or outright jokes without having hominess, penis envy and sexual frustration pointed out to me, without anyone's deducing from my good humor that I entertained an unfortunate and imperative desire for coitus with those present. Why was it practically never possible in my analysis to communicate on an adult level? Why were my erotic associations instinctively regarded as "obsessive sexualization," and as such to be corrected? I don't believe that this was peculiar to my own analysis, either, since a great many of my colleagues in analysis reacted in the same way. An association with the genital plane: She wants it, doesn't get enough of it, she'd like to do it with me, I'm supposed to do it with her, ho, ho, ho. And so on. Dealing with this subject is clearly more difficult than dealing with others. Perhaps people are under more pressure here. But I don't translate every angry little thought I have into a punch on the jaw, nor would every little flirtation be enough to lead to coitus or even tend that way. Our relations were never on an equal plane; I often didn't know if he regarded me as deeply disturbed and inhibited, or on the other hand as voracious.

It wasn't always like that. Once when I was in love, but hadn't quite realized it yet, an ordinary person without much education had informed me, "Ah, you're ripe for it now!" without any reproof or horniness or suggestive wishes of his own, just straightforwardly. That was how he saw it, and that is how it was. It was encouraging and liberating.

Many interpretations given me were too much the product of thought, with too little bearing on my real life story.

If I had foreign lovers and found I had a better time with them, that meant I was remaining faithful to my father, observing the in-

cest taboo, and I had unresolved Oedipal problems; I could experience sex only with foreigners and not with anyone resembling
my father. This, at least, was conveyed to me by my general
atmosphere.

And yet my generation of wartime children may be supposed to
have certain notable early impressions and experiences: My father
and uncle were at war when I was born; I did meet my uncle when
he came home on leave, and I had my early memories of him, but
then he was killed. The next important men in my life arrived from
abroad, after 1945: People who had emigrated, soldiers in the occupying forces, men coming home from the war. Much goodwill
towards my parents certainly came my way at the time, and presumably I was grateful for and enjoyed the masculine/paternal attention I received. The occupying soldiers, first Americans,
including blacks, then French, had been parted from their own
families for some time too; anyway, I have very pleasant memories
of them. Soldiers were billeted in the nearby houses, and when we
were playing they often came to watch, lifted up over fences,
dropped hints about the whereabouts of a child playing hide and
seek. Everyone knew that the French liked to sleep with women a
lot; older children went into the bunkers to look. Condoms made
good balloons.

All the agreeable men who lived in our house for a while after the
war, or on coming out of prison camp, came from far away, and
spoke differently too, some of them with a Baltic or Lithuanian
accent. There was a distant, romantic magic about them all, coming as they did from Russia, from prison camp (where we thought
my father was), from the war that still had him in its grip. They
played with me a great deal, and I made them tell me stories of my
father. I certainly was not having a bad time at this period, anyway.

I wouldn't think it at all surprising if I had been subject to certain influences, basically food experiences, at the time. At least, I
wouldn't inevitably consider it pathological for fatherless daughters
of those days to get on particularly well with foreigners.

Also, human values may perhaps be better preserved in the less
industrialized countries. Any immigrant workers' pub has more atmosphere and is more easy-going and nicer to children than its
German counterpart. And I have better memories of the family atmosphere among many Turkish immigrant worker families than of

the families of my Hanseatic, thoroughly analyzed, academic colleagues.

And really, I would think it perfectly natural for any woman who feels there isn't enough human kindness around her, and who has preserved a fair amount of it herself, to value the more sensual kind of man; people who have not been deprived of independence by long training, and/or have grown up in circumstances less distorted by industrialization.

But we never considered the possibility that my past relationships had done me good, helped me, developed me, that my feelings had taken the shape of purposeful action, that I was not so anxious and defensive after all, but might just have been following my yearnings and dreams in a perfectly meaningful way. My relationships were picked to pieces, inquired into, judged by the criterion (upon which not much thought had been expended) of marriage and the family, to which they had failed to lead. (If they had been investigated with a view to finding out how far they had helped me treat my chronic case of athlete's foot, we would have come to similarly negative conclusions.)

In any event, all the people I had found inspiring had more freedom than I did in some area or another: Were less conventional, or had struggled free of convention to better effect.

An article by Sebaastian Haffner meant much to me for some time; in it, he suggested that if we did not have the idea of "great love, marriage, etc." constantly thrust at us, it was unlikely many people would get married of their own volition.

My analyst had taken each of my relationships and worked out the neurotic mechanisms that had driven me into them; the negative motives, injurious to my life and myself, that had guided me. Seen thus, it was not at all hard to find something inadequate in them all, something unsatisfactory and unsuitable to me one way or another. How was it that I had picked a man who was grudging with affection? Well, he had also been attractively forthcoming and intellectually inspiring—as I remembered, but only later.

My analyst never considered the possibility that many relationships are at their best if they don't last long; some relationships do get exhausted, you grow out of them, and they should be ended. No, in accordance with my neurosis I had, yet again, fixed it, managed and arranged things so that I would be hurt. The positive side was simply forgotten; yet I had sometimes felt very content. We concentrated exclusively, however, on the disagreeable, disturbing, obstructive, injurious and cool side of my partners, so that I remembered those aspects more clearly myself. Memory was turned to something dark.

For instance, if we were going to spend a weekend together, men usually finished their work first, and we met when they were through with their routine, not before. I was used to dropping everything; I'd always been shopping first, had the refrigerator full, was all prepared, even if it had been hard work organizing everything. I had laid in good things to eat and drink; they often hadn't. I didn't realize this kind of thing is a common feminine experience until I went to a women's group, and found I was not alone, it wasn't even to be taken as a proof of a lack of respect or love. Men simply see their careers as more central to their existence, without question, without any alternative. I had at the back of my mind the possibility of dropping everything for a man, for children. I had never seriously envisaged the necessity of being breadwinner for a whole family.

I'd had many friendships of which I might well have been glad and proud, but that wasn't relevant. As if interpretations started from the premise, "Everything I've done is shit."

The view of the part played in my development by my family— what remained of my upper middle class, war-damaged, shrunk family—vacillated between "horror" and the idea that I'd been "lucky," but usually came down on the negative side. I was left complaining of the psychic burdens and obstacles with which I had been left.

Again, we scarcely considered the fact that the war, air raids, taking refuge in shelters, extreme financial uncertainty, the fear of starving to death because there simply wasn't any food, such simply elementary threats as these had also played a considerable part. There were times, for instance, when my mother thought it was better not to send us out looking for wartime vegetables such as nettles and dandelions, as one was recommended to do, but told us to go and lie down instead, so as to use up fewer calories. And if my brothers, who were then eleven and eight, hadn't gone in for trafficking on the black market and pinching things from the Americans, our diet wouldn't have been adequate; help couldn't be expected at that time from any other source. For years, we had stocks of stolen American sewing thread, cutlery, canned goods; the record haul was a whole motorbike and an aluminum piece of an airplane body.

Such basic interdependence in the matter of survival probably brings people closer together than I have seen in members of other families, not decimated by the war. It is hardly surprising if there is a stronger instinctive bond, which is probably necessary for survival. That, at least, is the way I would have seen it. I did, at any rate, have security in my background, support in time of need, even if I may have paid a certain price.

The security factor was not taken seriously enough in my analysis; my analyst focused in too one-sided a way on the stunting of my emotional growth. But when I look at the amount of financial anxiety around me today, in mature medical specialists, analysts, etc., when threatened by job loss, I realize I have at any rate never known such anxiety to the same extent, not as a permanent state of affairs. I could at least find support at home.

I feel that destroying my sense of security without offering any really reliable replacement (through analysis, the training analyst, the Association or anything of the kind) was to take a risk which in my case was underestimated.

I might have been able to accept, realize and resolve the negative, constricting factors better if the more positive side had remained present in my mind. Or if at least I had had a substitute for my home in analysis. But if nothing but the dark side is shown, it can become ghastly, inducing despair, and it is too great an emotional strain.

If all else fails, it doesn't matter to me whether my brothers have competed with me, didn't really let me grasp my intellectual potential properly, whether for reasons having to do with their own drives they didn't recognize me as a woman, an attractive partner; whether my mother was maybe repeating her relationship to her younger sister with me, acting as my rival, experiencing the problem of aging, etc.—none of that matters when I can always find support from them.

By comparison, I had very little of anything given me in my analyses.

My readiness to accept interpretations, it will certainly be said, proves that they were justified: Interpretations make their mark

only if they are in some way, at least partially, correct. I believed
that theory for a long time myself, and passed it on to my own
patients. What it doesn't take into account is the way an individual
may be open to psychological influence, which is even more powerful in the analytic situation, depending on its phase. If I happen to
be idealizing my analyst to a high degree, if I like him very much or
I am very much afraid of him, it will be more difficult for me to
take his interpretation as a real offer, fifty-fifty, this may be so or it
may not. If I am in a situation, where I am dependent on relative
unity, for instance in order to avoid decompensation, then it may
be a psychological necessity for me to accept an interpretation,
however wrong it is. Thinking that the analyst may be plain
wrong, has misunderstood, that his thoughts and present conflicts
led him to a different plane, far from my own, and he is now offering me something which doesn't fit me—entertaining such ideas
may be an emotional labor of Hercules, or not possible at all. In
any case, one couldn't describe the situation as an egalitarian one
in itself; even the fact of lying down instead of sitting makes an
enormous difference; if he likes, my analyst can see me, my body,
my face, but I am blind; I would have to turn around to see him,
which was probably against the rules; there would soon be an interpretation and it would take courage. He is trained, he is my
teacher, his technique and the way he deals with me is the most intensive part of my own training. He makes the decision concerning
the end of analysis along with me, yes, but if we differ I am the
weaker party, less competent professionally. Not the one who
makes the decisions, anyway. I have told him a great deal about
my private, tender feelings, he knows everything about them to
which I have access and probably a great deal more. I know him
well myself, by now, but only from what I observe and imagine;
I have not been told any concrete facts. The more intense the
relationship, the more weight his opinion bears. At any rate, I no
longer believe, nor is it my own experience, that an interpretation
can really seem a neutral offer. I regularly had difficulty in rejecting one that didn't seem to apply to me. It took strength and
courage, and a little of the interpretation often still clung to
me. I have seen, in my own therapies, that my interventions,
ideas and thoughts regularly carry more weight than those of my
patients.

I may be told that I am particularly dependent on early objects, find individuation and demarcation of myself particularly hard, am secretly still striving for symbiosis, defend against guilt feelings over my own impulses and wishes for separation, and that is why I accepted so much. One can say so, or then again one can let it alone. But many analysands have similar experiences. "A certain amount of personal hygiene is simply necessary . . ." Why didn't he add, "to me?" Why this standard of so-called sexual health? Why not think what it may mean for me to be liked when unwashed, with my own personal odors and secretions, without my having to disinfect myself? "The cloacal odor that accompanies a beautiful woman." (Balzac)

His associations on the genital plane often missed the mark: He showed lack of understanding, difficulty in understanding, a scornful masculine attitude of amusement, if in any doubt he interpreted things pre-genitally, as indicative of my early disturbance lying behind them. Lightness and wit were put to flight; I think that—in a better basic relationship—one could very easily place oneself on one's analyst's preferred level and stay there.

The rule of discussing nothing, if possible, outside analysis offers the analyst a chance to live out his symbiotic desires and fears to the full. If, on account of his own past history, he should feel slightly discriminated against and disadvantaged by the emergence of third parties, he will come up more readily with interpretations such as acting out, subsidiary transference, than someone who may have resolved his feelings of rivalry, envy and jealousy rather more successfully.

This can be very unwholesome for the analysand, if he is thus confirmed in his existing fears and inhibitions over freeing himself from a one-to-one relationship.

People say the sky is bluer, colors are more intense, life is better since they have been analyzed. I believe them; I know the feeling, only such things aren't new to me. But can they really remember sensations of five to eight years ago, before they went into analysis? Every spring is the loveliest ever. Certainly the chestnuts now blossom more luxuriantly than they used to, more so than they did last (verbalized) year.

Many people feel good after a divorce, too; they develop new interests, talents, friendships, and feel as if they'd been unfrozen. But nobody generally ascribes this to the therapeutic effect of marriage or the former partner.

Almost from the start of the analysis I wondered why training analyses are not supervised, why no one checks up on them (presumably I suspected something wasn't going as well as it should). Objectively, it is hard to see why those very analyses on whose course and nature so much depends just go ahead, and it is actually unusual, or most exceptional, for an analyst ever to discuss one in any other place. After all, it's unlikely that fewer difficulties occur in training analyses than in any other analyses; only the difficulties here, unresolved counter-transference and other problems, carry more weight and in the end more consequences for patients.

I was furious for the longest time that I was never asked how I dealt with my own patients, how my therapies were going, how beneficial or harmful I was to them. My supposed ability to cause conflict, shown in my dealings with colleagues, was much discussed, its dire nature indicated; or I was shown charitable—ecclesiastic concern; he wondered if I was up to the burdens of this career, wasn't I too unstable? By normal standards, the point of medical studies, as of psychoanalytical training, was to treat patients.

A part is also played in the development of faith in the analyst and a tendency to lack confidence by the fact that the average analysand so modifies his environment that he mixes principally, and in a professional sense most fruitfully, with others who are in analysis—the meetings and seminars offered analysands in training tend to bring them together. The people with whom the analysand mixes are on the same wavelength, and will relate misfortune more readily to their own pathology than to real, oppressive factors. Often it is simpler, and causes considerably less conflict, to direct dissatisfaction through grief to anger at the dead, at mothers and siblings in childhood days, rather than to get into arguments and conflict over conditions which are objectively hard to endure.

Many male analysands I knew seemed to me to be suffering unnaturally, as if doing some ecclesiastical penance, with tragic airs that I find most unappealing. Even people who used to be notably sunny might temporarily join their ranks.

I had wished for more empathy, more concern, to be taken more seriously, to have my feelings validated; I wished for less in the way of judgmental efforts to educate me, less measuring of me against the universal standard of others, less striving for the group norm, for conformity. I wished for more that was good-natured and primarily benevolent, to be accepted as I was.

Doing gymnastics at school, in our stretch gym shorts, our developing figures seemed attractive, enviable; it was in the boys' class that jokes about bosoms and bottoms were made. I was lucky, being young for my class, developed later and wasn't exposed to the full weight of prepubescent defense. In our society, there are probably not many men who really think the female genitals beautiful, who don't flinch at any sign of odor, don't feel at heart disgusted, don't approach them only with an effort, and if they cover that up don't have to fight off an urge to retch. In cautious conversation with a woman friend, we both observed how thankful we were to men who were more appreciative, how much we respected them.

Expressions such as "ploughing one's way past that tangle of barbed wire" are at least ironical; "we have to get up the courage to venture in" is honest, but also indicates men's secret panic in facing the knife, axe, circular saw, the devouring vagina which swallows everything up.

Men do seem to feel a permanently acute fear which is far greater than a woman can imagine at all. I have been much struck by the readiness and single-mindedness with which men who've been analyzed make associations with castrations in discussing case histories, while women are struck by quite different aspects of the patient under discussion. Somatically, the fear is well-founded, and perhaps it really is the case that "anatomy is fate," and men therefore are cowards. Moreover, perhaps theories about female castration fears are a grandiose projection ("*Women* have these fears, *we* don't"), because the idea is so hard to bear. During my analysis, anyway, and at other times in moods that went deep, I never felt such powerful anxieties in myself as are obviously permanently present in men of my own age. Commonplace, but understandable enough in itself. During a school sports day, a groan went up from the (male) spectators, and there was a corresponding sigh of relief, when one boy doing several somersaults over the horizontal bar got his shorts caught up in front, but then freed himself, and finished the exercise unharmed. An older, all-boys class refused en masse to exercise on the parallel bars, and it was the same with jumping over the horse or the box too.

In girls' gymnastics, all we had to fear was the hard balls thrown in a certain game; they could hurt developing young breasts, but couldn't really do any great harm. We tended to aim lower down and not throw very hard, but I doubt if the game caused anyone fears of being unable to have and feed children. The girls of my class had no confrontations comparable to the boys' fights, where a knockout blow delivered to the testicles decided victory, and the loser was left writhing and whimpering on the ground.

It is my belief that female self-assurance, which suffers in any event from misogyny, can suffer further from adult relationships with men. I have spent some time thinking over a number of things men have said. Perhaps, with a more frank approach to the homo-erotic in puberty, we could develop greater confidence. If I am able to take another woman's thoughts, feelings and body seriously, and can find them attractive, I can get a better image of myself.

Men who thought me beautiful as I was, just right, adequate, who thought it would be a pity if I lost weight, did me a great deal of good. Anyway I can tell quite accurately, from the way I feel, if someone likes me, or if he's really after a different type, perhaps the slender, boyish sort.

Appreciative men, and a more relaxed attitude toward the homosexual, have at any rate done me more good than searching my soul for situations and unresolved conflicts which have, supposedly, made it hard for me to identify with my mother, suppositions about Oedipal conflicts which I have avoided, so that instead I've assumed a subordinate role, seeing myself as unattractive and ending up by acting and seeming so, etc. More good than complaining of the lack of a father's affection, or the damaging effect of sibling incest taboos. Expressions of approval in a friendly, adult atmosphere—"Your lovely hips"—"You eat well in X"—"Look after your splendid body"—have enabled me at least to suppress potential traumas.

For me, in any event, the present micro-climate is what matters; it is more powerful than those earlier flaws that may be presumed to exist in me.

Afterword

I STARTED WRITING IN 1977, JUST TO BE DONE WITH it all (686 hours, 583, of which were in a training analysis). It took me altogether two years. Writing did not always feel good. Occasionslly it was painful and affected me physically: ear infections, pelvic pain, nausea, nervous cough and stomach problems. My main difficulty, in the process of dealing with this alone, in intellectual solitude, was not to lose confidence in myself, not to think of myself as crazy or stupid. Some, whose professional advice I asked for, kept me at a distance. Others, in the name of friendship, hurt my feelings with psychoanalytic interpretations to an extent that I decided against contact.

Comparisons with other analyses convinced me to consider my experiences as typical and not to devalue them as rare, unfortunate exceptions, as I was consistently and monotonously advised to do.

During the course of my writing I heard of many cases of analysands becoming seriously ill, suffering fatal accidents, even committing suicide. It would be irresponsible to dismiss these events as accidental. It does not make sense to me to declare them to be the unavoidable consequence of the original neurosis.

Looking back on the way I expressed myself in those days, hesitatingly and gropingly, I can see in what ways my analysis damaged me. There is no question that today I would express myself more decisively.
OCTOBER, 1979.

*　　　*　　　*

When my book appeared in 1980 in Germany I still believed that I had had an unusually bad and harmful analysis; that it was at

286

the hands of a particularly rigid sado-analyst; that it was undertaken in strict prussian climate; that it took place in a particularly bureaucratic psychoanalytic society (an "Aryan psychoanalysis")—I hoped and dreamt that greener analytic pastures were to be found elsewhere.

I was wrong. Readers who wrote to me from all over convinced me that the experience of deterioration in psychoanalysis is the rule, not the exception: some people in analysis became "psychotic," some were sent to psychiatric institutions; some became deeply depressed or remained in such a depression; some became addicted to alcohol or drugs; some killed themselves, as did some of my fellow trainees (these were professional colleagues, not "normal" patients). I was actually luckier than most.

Psychoanalysis appears not to differ from country to country: everywhere, very much like the international sound of rock, analysts behave more or less the same; they use the same (minuscule) repertoire of interpretations.[1] They behave with the same political lack of responsibility, making themselves available to whatever government happens to be in power. For example, a Brazilian physician who was undergoing psychoanalytic training was implicated in torture. The governing body of the International Psychoanalytical Association exonerated him on the grounds that he was "merely doing his duty as a soldier," the very same argument most commonly used in the Nürnberg trials and every Nazi trial since.

Analysts behave with no greater responsibility toward their own progeny: after I learned about four separate suicides of colleagues who were in analysis, I became alarmed and wrote to the president of the International and of the German Psychoanalytic Societies. The German president, wrote me to say that this was not "statistically speaking, above average for the general population." The president of the International sent me a short letter bemoaning the "tragedy."

I can no longer believe in the beneficial effects of psychoanalysis. I do not know a single colleague in analysis (the only ones I can judge over the years) who really benefitted from his analysis in the

---

[1]See the many examples given in *Psychotherapy for Better or Worse*, edited by Hans H. Strupp et al., (New York, 1976).

way originally expected (more freedom, a greater capacity for love and work).

Some analysts, of course, possess certain human qualities, like anybody else, which can be helpful in therapy just as they are in everyday life. But these qualities were not created through analysis nor are they even necessarily connected to it. For some people in some life-situations it is better to find somebody who has the time and interest, even when that person gives them only fifty minutes and charges them as well, than to be left with their personal suffering entirely on their own. Also, some people go into therapy in such a bad state that if they don't die they have to get better. So it is entirely possible that some people appear to profit from analysis. All things considered, having both been in therapy and dispensed it for many years, I would now take the position that the climate created by psychoanalysis destroys human relations, and that by and large psychoanalytic treatment does more harm than good.

Dörte von Drigalski
August, 1986.

Notes

PAGE 2

It never occurred to me, at the time, that my condition after the interview might have had something to do with the analyst, that it was possibly not a matter of counter-transference pure and simple—free of any problems of her own, called forth only by the consideration of my projections and role expectations directed at her—but could have been a perfectly ordinary case of interaction between two people of different histories, different likes and dislikes—that I might have touched upon dormant and incompletely surmounted problems in her own life, or someone of my age and potential might act as an irritant to wounds left by her own life story.

One year later, in the last hours of the analysis—I sat in a chair by then—she made a remark the gist of which was: "It was enough to drive anyone to despair—you didn't show any effect at all." I deduced from that remark that my emotional state after the first interview was not my responsibility alone. I must have sensed her condition.

PAGES 5-6

Of course it may be asked, "Why didn't you talk to her about this? Your perception was probably blurred by your problems; you were expecting criticism and that is what you heard." But an analysand usually feels it too difficult to summon up that amount of courage, criticism and active resistance; anyway, my first instinct was to go along with her. Naturally I wanted to please her. Moreover, her remark was along the lines of what she had conveyed to me at my initial interview (whether I could ever feel really angry).

The hurtful notion struck home, anyway, and in a place that was already vulnerable. I will admit that as an example, this is not particularly convincing, but that was the way I heard it; I had expected some response to what had gone before, some kind of benevolent, friendly reaction, and not an objective, professional assessment.

PAGES 8-9

Even so, it usually works better for me to do some more thinking, try things out úntil I feel good, than to force myself into being independent of surface appearances and the norm.

It is important for my self-confidence, anyway, to feel happy with myself and my appearance—at the time, at least. I don't like to wear anything scratchy, constricting, too cold or too hot; it matters for my shoes to be comfortable, for the colors I wear to suit my mood, for material things, or anyway what I express in my clothes, to correspond to my mood at the time, and not convey its diametrical opposite. If clothes are right for my mood, I feel confident; I don't need to spend much time wondering if they are pretty, attractive, right for the occasion. I can stand by my own style then, and am not so easily made insecure by criticism. Liking my reflection in the mirror gives me confidence. And in my really good phases I had no trouble in finding what suited me. For me, it means there's something wrong if I have to search and dither for a long time before I'm dressed in a way that makes me feel reasonably good.

One oughtn't to issue prohibitions before knowing what's behind a thing. Later on, anyway, I came to feel I do best to go along with my dissatisfaction, let it lead me, maybe get to the bottom of it, and then just do what seems relatively most pleasant at the time; there is always some essential part of me, something that is to be taken seriously, behind my dissatisfaction.

It was a strain to force myself to a casual, independent attitude, to forbid myself my own fastidious demands. Yet I didn't really know why an attractive appearance was so important to me.

The prohibition (or what I felt to be a prohibition) on being fashionable and oriented to outer appearances increased the pressure of my superego.

I think, now, that my analyst couldn't really convey to me a casual attitude she didn't have herself. And that it's not by chance that her remark had the effect of a prohibition on me, instead of seeming a who-cares, let-it-go, amused way of distancing the matter.

Her interpretations never quite freed me, either, from the sense of uneasiness her own outward appearance caused me. I think I probably felt that she wasn't really at ease with her own nature, hadn't entirely found her own style, and I had sensed her quiet unhappiness; maybe it was exactly that which I didn't want to take on, or take into myself.

During the analytical treatment of a woman patient who struck me as very beautiful and successful, and was way ahead of me in her self-realization in many fields, I felt her happy relief when (and obviously at last) I was really nicely dressed, in my own style. I was surprised, at the time, by her intense reaction, which I couldn't reconstruct. I still feel bad about keeping silent in the situation, or anyway not broaching the subject.

PAGE 9

There was no discussion of the possibility that my dissatisfaction with myself might be basically positive; e.g., the fact that I yearned for and was seeking esthetic norms and a certain style, but for internal reasons hadn't found them yet.

PAGE 10

It never occurred to my analyst that writing might be something productive for me, a way of working through problems and furthering my analysis; I didn't think of the possibility that her intervention might have landed in my superego as a prohibition.

PAGE 15

At the time it seemed a naive idea, almost impossible to entertain, that my analyst really did feel that way herself, and couldn't do much with my type of person. After all, as an analyst she would have the ability to be clear about her own feelings and keep them from intruding.

In retrospect, I think sibling rivalry may well have been involved as well, but not exclusively in me, very much so, however, in other analysands in relation to me.

Any such notion, however, was to be ignored at the time; it was I with whom we were concerned.

PAGE 16

However, what I found uncomfortable and confusing was the way the possible reality of such a love affair wasn't considered at all; it was almost degraded to the status of a troublesome and annoying side effect. And I sensed that in a good analysis reality must fade into the background, allowing one's own problems to come to the fore. Yet it would have made no difference to my intro-spection, I suppose, if my idea had been taken seriously, as a genu-ine perception; and if the significance of such a liaison for me and my feelings had been considered too, without erasing the factor of reality. I am sure my analyst didn't actually deny the possible real-ity of such a love affair at the time, but exclusive concentration on the intrapsychic element means there is a danger that the analy-sand will sense a prohibition against taking facts seriously: facts that can sometimes be of more import and more uncomfortable than associations arising from one's history.

I do think that some part of unfulfilled sexual desires flows into other activities, such as driving. But did my impulse have to be so automatically nipped in the bud? The interpretation came out pat, just like declining an irregular verb. Or that was the effect on me, anyway. Displacement meant defense, and was bad. For presum-ably sick reasons, I was not living out a feeling (and a very impor-tant feeling) correctly; i.e., sexually and genitally by means of intercourse; instead, I was endeavoring to obtain an inferior substi-tute satisfaction by means of speed.

Of course I did not approve of this; it was neurotic defense, and to be despised.

I was not given the option of thinking that it can be simply pleas-ant, useful and indeed fun, and right for one's own tempo, not to have to dawdle along patiently behind every farm tractor, waiting for curves, but to feel safe driving at high speed. Nor that if one's a stranger in a small town, a fast car facilitates contact with friends living some way off.

I wasn't able to get a good fast car until towards the end of my analysis, when I had definite practical reasons to do so (driving to and from analysis, 150 kilometers, four times a week), and then I could feel all the enjoyment and pleasure and liveliness of it: The physical rightness of a car that reacts well and is powerful and fast enough, that suits one like a new dress, or a piece of jewelry, or a second skin: An additional and comfortable room of one's own.

Not that I think there is any point at all in promoting or intellectually subsidizing something as dangerous as driving a car: People in analysis are particularly likely to have serious accidents. I had one myself, shortly after I began my analysis. It was an accident that—analytically speaking—I had arranged to have, though I was innocent enough from the legal viewpoint. But those reasons prevented me from taking in her intervention.

Soon I just didn't want a fast car anymore, and I regarded the drivers of sports cars with suspicion.

Viewed in the abstract, the fact that any kind of desire or need, any hint of sexual longing, was venturing to show itself, in whatever tortuous and indirect way, might have been welcomed.

It is also possible, of course, that in repeating the pattern of earlier experiences, I took remarks of my analyst's which were actually non-judgmental and maybe even encouraging as negative and prohibitive criticism. However, I don't really believe that; I have learned to listen to my own sensations and trust them. And I know what a positive and pleasant remark sounds like. I can't be forever holding up hypotheses to myself.

The psychological reality, to me, was that much of what happened had a sour, bitter, constricting and inhibiting effect, and was intimidating too. And I don't think that was my fault; any method must take account of such effects and avoid them. Even if the cause were a mistaken interpretation on my part, based on transference, I don't think it's a good thing for me to still be at emotional odds with the situation five years later, still getting worked up about it, trying to rid myself of it, at the expense of considerable effort.

The kind of intervention that could have seemed meaningful to me might have run: "It's nice to see what this man can release in you, but I don't think experiencing it predominantly through speed makes much sense. Are the weekends you spend with him really enough for you?"

Her interpretation had certainly given me insight into the tortuous workings of my unconscious, and credible insight too, but it also fortified my already adequate superego.

PAGE 18

Of my analysis, I can say only that I was made to feel truly vehement misery, great grief and yearning for a father, something I would not unnecessarily inflict on any child. And yet, in the circumstances of the postwar period, I was relatively lucky in the men I knew, because my mother is an attractive woman, and after 1945 a good many men (men from the forces coming home, prisoners of war, former emigrants) came our way, and provided me with a masculine presence around the place; also because I was a pretty child, hungry for paternal attention, and I simply reached out for a good deal of masculine affection. Some of these men wanted to marry my mother and no doubt were kind to me on that account. (A friend of mine once said I sometimes looked like a happy two-year-old; what had been going on when I was two, he asked?)

All the same, even that kind of thing can't be deduced for certain: Life would be different for children born into other social circumstances, without the yearnings of a mother and financial dependence on a father.

We never considered that my feelings might be a matter of sympathy with my mother, that I shared her longing, despair, sense of abandonment; that I shared her individual catastrophe after 1945 and was left a widow at thirty with three children, without husband or brother that I might feel as if this state of affairs must always and in all circumstances hold good, a quasi-biological law. Would it have seemed so vastly important to have a fine, respected and politically impeccable father if people hadn't kept asking about him, when I went to school if not before, and adjusting their ideas accordingly?

If my father's death had not occurred in those particularly terrible times, as my mother, like many mothers, experienced them, I might not have associated the ideas of a full and happy life/paradise/husband/father as I did.

However, I cannot generalize emotionally from that, and a consequence of some significance to me is that I would not like to have a child alone, and indeed I have none.

PAGE 20

My feelings about my father were good, beneficial and heartfelt sensations, going right down to my roots, the very substance of me, fortifying me. I found them real: Different from those feelings called forth artificially and in difficult circumstances. Painful as it always was to end up with a headache, eyes swollen with tears, a sense of bodily tension—still, there was something right about it. This was no vague, watered-down kind of weeping, no artifact; it involved the whole of me, my body, and exhausted me as hard work exhausts one.

Once I had tapped this feeling, it remained with me, almost unchanged in quality and intensity, for almost two years. I am more inclined to ascribe the fact that it then became modified to various outer circumstances and encounters of which I made use in working through it than to the help of my analysis.

PAGE 21

It took me a long time to recover from this interpretation. Much later, when I was no longer in analysis with her, I did slowly free myself to it, with help from certain kind men.

Where is the analysand to find the freedom, strength and independence to realize that such an interpretation is *not* the unshakable, analytically outstanding truth? That is how I, in any event, saw it.

PAGES 21-22

In fact I cannot remember ever speaking of that interpretation again; what I do remember is much weeping, accompanied by a runny nose, swollen eyes and headaches, called forth by thoughts of the war, my father, men coming home, soldiers, uniforms, etc.

I came to doubt it only years later, when my former friend visited me, and a man who hadn't been analyzed looked at me in amazement: My friend had no pep, he thought, and was quite the wrong man for me.

As we had established that my physical experience was not of the right sort, I began to doubt what had been possible in the past, and forgot about it. Now and then her interpretations became fact, too; it was realizing itself.

Perhaps someone else, with a greater ability to question authority and less belief in psychoanalysis and the professional competence of her analyst, might not have accepted an interpretation so unconditionally, or made such uncritical use of it as a way of access to problems that might lie close to hand. Someone with a less rigorous superego or simply with more trust and confidence in her own sensations.

One could also say that the fact I had a relatively strong mother, who wasn't then married, and that at the time I had no man available on whom I could turn my feelings, or at least not one I could see in such an idealized way as my own father, made me particularly anxious, docile and obedient to authority, and thus particularly receptive to any kind of analytic maternal force. It may be that other women would have laughed—"No, really, that can't be so, what an insipid interpretation! I was only telling you that by the way!"—and would have thought they might have changed the story a bit in the telling themselves, to get that interpretation, and that would have been that.

For me, however, such a reaction wasn't possible at the time, and later I suppose I partially repressed the explosive effect and absorbed it into my diffuse sense of suffering.

It took me a long time to feel free of the taint of inferior sensuous experience (as with a corn that becomes painful only when there is outside pressure). Sometimes I realized how deep the interpretation had gone only from my relief and surprise at encountering friendly reactions. An analyst to whom I had just been trying to convey my emotionally mutilated state said forcefully and almost angrily, sweeping my remarks aside, that he wondered what I was after—of course I could get somewhere with men! After that first year of analysis, his automatic reaction was cheering, but a doubt remained: Maybe I had just been deceiving him with my outward appearance. Would his assessment have stood up to closer examination?

A man helping to run a course, to whom I tried explaining my sad fate, began to smile as if I were talking utter nonsense. I cherished the thought of these two masculine reactions, coming as they did from analysts. (The unanalyzed didn't count.)

However, it was three years before I could begin rejecting the interpretation in part, consciously anyway, when the friend who had caused the manifestation of my disturbance came to visit me. (I had long since learned the logic which said that if I did not feel enthusiastic about a man the fault was mine—probably mine, anyway.) I never thought it might have something to do with my partner too; I was convinced of my inadequacy, and then there was always the question of why I had no very close ties.

It struck me as more probable that all and sundry had hitherto been wrong, that I'd deceived men with my outer appearance and my women friends had overlooked something about me, than that my analyst had simply been rather brisk with her interpretation.

PAGES 23-24

Anyway, this seemed more likely, and perhaps easier to believe, than that I should criticize my analyst or the method. At that time, I did not subject any interpretation to serious criticism. I did resist a good deal, but then I supposed my defense proved the interpretation correct. The more correct it was, the more violent my resistance. This was the kind of climate in my environment; with thoughts like these, I could meet with agreement and smiles. Had I been critical, people would presumably have looked blank and referred me back to my analytic sessions.

PAGE 25

The entire situation remained partly spurious. My analyst was trying to help me integrate my aggressive impulses, to convey the fact that they were part of me, understandable reactions, and not primarily evil, and her manner remained friendly. However, it wasn't true that my anger was directed only at those figures from my early life; most probably a large part of my concentrated anger was now directed at her.

Interpretations concerning my relationship with my mother and godmother, memories of situations in which I might well have been justifiably, wholeheartedly angry but could not experience that anger at the time, could now only partially relieve the burden on my superego. I was left with part of my anger, that part that had no definite object or aim, or at least not one that I consciously perceived, that was free-floating and thus all the more incalculable. So much the more reason for me to distrust myself. Presumably I did somehow feel that my anger was directed at her too. If she was now working through my earlier relationships with me, full of understanding, instead of my aggression stemming from the present, real relationship with her—that could mean that this was the better way for me to overlook the murderous impulses in me. At any rate, I now think that a fair amount of the sterility, emotional coolness, and intellectual abstraction in that analysis can be easily explained by the elimination of real, present affects between her and me.

She may have wanted to spare me, and did not take present possibilities into consideration for that reason, but I don't believe that anymore.

PAGE 26

But was I supposed to be able to face forceful sexual and incestuous wishes directed at my brothers all at once, without batting an eye, right at the beginning of analysis, with all the defense I had reasonably and justifiably built up over the years? After all, I wouldn't need to dream or try distancing if the content of my dreams was plain to me, and I had access to it without any guilt feelings and defense.

There may have been something to this interpretation, but it came so early on, powerfully and impatiently and not at my own tempo. Perhaps the incident really did excite me at the time, perhaps his penis and entirely naked body attracted me a great deal: After her emphatic intervention, I couldn't remember anything about it. I deduced, mathematically or grammatically, as it were, that I must have felt powerful sensations which I had been able to control only by means of defense mechanisms, the results of which I was now feeling.

In a different atmosphere, if she had taken more time and been more sympathetic to my hesitation and the gaps and inhibitions of my perception, I might have come closer to this complex. However, the atmosphere was unfavorable to me; I know now that I can experience almost all disgusting odors in a different way—on occasion, at least—in an atmosphere that is friendly to me. Watching Pasolini's "Salo," in which people are fed excrement and eat it by the spoonful, I went out to the toilet almost ready to throw up, but after the end of the film I could imagine it otherwise. I believe that disgust is generally defense against instinctual desires, and I am also sure in my case that something to do with the anus/excrement/cigar smoke was blocked and had neurotic connotations. However, I could not feel or guess at it in an atmosphere so cool and unfavorable to me, sometimes one of aloof annoyance. My awareness of being sick was increased by yet another obscure complex.

PAGES 30-31

I was really satisfied with an achievement only if I had made a tremendous effort, stretching myself to the very limits of my powers, physically, intellectually or both. That was how it had been hitherto, anyway; I was not impressed by anything that came to me easily.

A useful direction for interpretation to take might have been to wonder what superego was forcing me to make such exertions, allowing justification only on exceptional achievements, not on anything entailing less than total effort; such an interpretation would have perceived and allowed the possibility of satisfaction, ever present even if postponed. I could have realized that I was making harsher demands of myself than others perhaps may do, that I develop more guilt feelings over failure and lack of commitment, find it harder to reconcile myself to saying I have done all I could. I might have seen that possibilities for satisfaction existed, though my view of them was distorted. But questions such as, "Why can't you enjoy this at present?—why can't you be satisfied with it?— isn't it enough for you?" helped to build up my superego, condemning my self-condemnation from a higher level.

However, this, taken together with remarks from my analyst such as, "You're not up to as much stress as you seem—less stable than you look," and her admonition, at least on an emotional level, not to make such efforts, not to stretch myself to the limits, did away entirely with one possible way of feeling good about myself, which was then forgotten. It is then likely that one would refrain from actively seeking self-confidence. Women in particular tend to do it.

PAGES 30-31

Boys older than myself, such as my brothers, whom I admired so much in our games, and for their abilities in tobogganing and stealing things, became considerably wilder and more independent in the postwar period, what with time off school, going in for black-market trafficking as the eldest male members of the family, than boys of that age later in more stable circumstances. Some boys of their generation never did reconcile themselves to a bourgeois way of life, went abroad, wouldn't submit to the restrictions of school life. I think that this gave me higher than average standards of the norm in fighting spirit and independence and those qualities I find impressive.

If I don't like a man, it needn't always be because I lack capacity for enjoyment, or show castrating tendencies.

Perhaps I was seeking a more intense life, and felt something was right there; a man who has killed someone in a fight will have done it out of stronger affects than are usually allowed to exist in my own academically trained and thoughtful environment.

PAGE 32

Perhaps an interpretation concerning my father might have meant something to me, but I'm more inclined to think this was a case of identification with my mother, whom I regularly saw filling out application forms, not very efficiently, sitting there rebellious and furious at state bureaucracy. There were plenty of such forms, various different authorities being responsible for war widows and orphans (there was the pensions office, the main welfare center, the orphans' office, etc.). If I had really wanted my mother to deal with my paperwork for me, the wish would have been highly inefficient. I think I simply took over her fury, and also, perhaps her longing for my father who used to do such things for her. In any case, I had no example to follow of peaceable, neutral, confident and assured dealings with bureaucracy. If only she had automatically received a sum sufficient to feed her children as a right, without humiliating and depressing procedures such as the necessity of declaring a missing man to be dead, to appoint a guardian, to answer constant questions about the children's father's career, origins, position in life, and if only life hadn't become so much more difficult in material terms as well.

Anyway, considering all that surfaced in me in the way of dammed up misery, pain and grief, I think it is not a good thing to grow up without a father in such social circumstances. To generalize, however, would be going too far.

PAGE 34

I now think that a preference for me in a mildly depressive state concealed a considerable amount of envy, rivalry, and masculine anxiety. It is not just that I am "closer to myself" when in tears, but the less confident men in my environment do not feel so threatened in their positions, potency, etc., by a quiet little mouse. I am not so close to them then.

PAGES 34-35

It took me a long time to register the fact that barbs laden with jealousy were aimed at my wounds, and to take their presence seriously, not interpreting their effect as primarily due to my depressive state, sensitivity or paranoid perception.

PAGES 35-36

It would have been better to take the dictates of my superego as something positive than to disparage them. At least, I now often find that when I'm feeling wretched there is something important I haven't done, or something else troubling me. In theory, one should have been able to see what standards of achievement I set myself, and if they were really so unattainable and cruelly burdened by the superego. I now think I was constantly working at a level below my powers and potential, and that kind of thing *cannot* lead to satisfaction. I can feel quite happy with myself if I've really made an effort and used my potential, if I haven't held myself back lazily, without commitment, half-heartedly or cautiously. After strenuous night duty I was able to feel self-confidence without anything much to detract from it.

It would have done me good if she had taken my impatience, my efforts at professional precision, my doubts of my present activities as something good, healthy at heart, critical and perceptive of the dubious points in my training, something of use to my further development. It really is a fair question to ask if it was really good and responsible behavior towards patients to let a beginner concern herself with the severely sick, however well-meaning and enthusiastic she might be.

It wasn't recognized that my position in the family had its positive sides as well, helped me and brought me its own advantages.

PAGE 37

Here it might have been possible to clear up our relationship a little, getting at my criticism of her and my desires, which may not all have been so clearly of a pre-genital nature. However, this was not a typical session.

I might also suppose, nastily, that I perceived the destructive process getting to work on me and was looking for an antidote. At any rate, this lover felt very uneasy about the change in me, my depression, my doubts and tears at the beginning of my analysis, and kept saying so. Could all this be right, he wondered? He was worried; it all seemed so vehement and unhappy. Could it be doing me any good? The fact that I aroused such thoughts in him may mean that these were really my own doubts and fears, which I dared not express.

PAGES 38-39

However, it may be that I could no longer afford such ghastly associations. What I had learned through interpretations so far was bad enough; a sunnier, warmer climate might have given me more courage to face the dark side of things, which does have an appealingly eerie, macabre charm of its own.

I am not the only analysand to feel this way; it seems typical of people who have formerly been in analysis to go around all their lives with a load of unresolved, insinuated, surmised problems, vague fears and suspicions. It's easy to make them feel uncertain by hinting at any of that. Nowadays I can often tell if someone has ever been in analysis.

PAGE 39

There may have been something in the theory as a whole. However, the uncomfortable, unpleasant and obstructive part of it, so far as I was concerned, was the way I'd lost my sense of humor and the kind of satisfaction that it had given me. I used to feel very good after weekends at home with my brothers, as if I'd laughed my troubles away and felt cleansed. I enjoyed so-called Jewish jokes. Once I was alone with one of my brothers, I'd opened a can of pineapple and eaten half the contents, taking nearly all the juice. My brother had the other half, and told me he wouldn't have bought the can. "Why not?" "No juice in it." My laughter, our mutual understanding, changed in the course of analysis to lamenting over the aggression lurking within my family. But later I found I missed our ironic form of interaction: It was good for me.

Perhaps I was near the limits of my endurance. If one's whole personality is being nibbled away it can be unendurable to be the butt of ironic jokes. Part of my anger, my fighting back in the context of family relationships, may have been meaningful in the long view. But my stock of people who really liked me was decreasing all the time. Analysis ought to have compensated for this deficiency. At the time I thought it was just because of my neurotic perception that I couldn't realize and appreciate her goodwill, warmth and pleasure in me.

PAGE 42

Might my night of bad dreams not have been seen as a valuable and analytically interesting reaction, a professional tidbit? Why all the empathy, why the whole theory, if strict and clear boundaries are after all to be set to acceptable kinds of experience? If I condemn, anxiously inhibit and cover up borderline situations in myself—how am I going to convey to a patient more acceptance and tolerance and less alarm in dealing with his symptoms? Psychoanalysis has gone radically astray here. Tolerance of reactions that are hard to understand seems only a very little greater than in the rest of society, and after that exactly the same excluding, distancing principles are applied. If those with extreme reactions are rejected and discriminated against in their own ranks, which include people who have themselves been patients, then there is something fundamentally wrong with our attitude towards patients, the people we are trying to understand so well. Why do analysts preserve an awkward silence about their own psychotic episodes and neurotic crises? Why is the proximity of psychosis so likely to arouse panic; why isn't it seen as something interesting, attractive, stimulating? The area, of all others, where analysis should be applied? Something perhaps strange, but beautiful, which one should at some point approach closely?

If analysts only say a little later than the untrained might, "You're crazy, go away and take pills," then there is something very wrong with their conception of themselves.

I had dared to go too far, and was rapped over the knuckles for it. And suppose I had actually had standard psychotic reactions that night? Suppose I'd had delusions, heard voices, thought my dreams were reality—what would there have been in that to incur sudden condemnation, to be denied understanding? If, as an attractive woman, I dreamed of being persecuted, fought against and overpowered in a damaged environment with a predominantly ecclesiastical atmosphere, wasn't the condensed reality an adequate explanation? Was I necessarily having recourse to complicated mechanisms and sexual wishful thinking in my dreams? It was probably the case that I'd mobilized desires which had been sealed off for some time in such an atmosphere. But even if I had done more than dream, if I'd heard voices that night ("You must stay small—stay gray—etc."), would that have been so amazing, would it have been so impossible to feel with me? In isolation almost everyone gets to hear voices after a while, has symptoms which are diagnosed as psychotic in other circumstances. Who decides where the line is drawn, when I am to be discarded as sick, when I must be subdued with drugs? I had no real say in things any more.

Wasn't I being more honest with my feelings in having nightmares than if I'd reacted somatically? I would, of course, have seemed more acceptable and less alarming if I had withdrawn from the struggle a few days before the end of the course with lumbago, flu, a cold or migraine.

What kind of attitude is it towards psychic reactions if even in analysis the conscious working through of problems is considered more disturbing and sick than a retreat to the somatic plane? There may be argument about this in principle, of course, but analysis is concerned with living through problems consciously; where the id was, the ego shall be; that is a settled thing. Basically, the situation does not differ from one in which an employee who feels he can't afford to express criticism or aggression, and reacts with a heart attack or an ulcer. He is considerably better off than the one who reacts with body and mind at once, and whose "nervous breakdown" is returned to respectability only with a solid diagnosis by some mini-substratum of organic medicine. Even in hospitals, where psychosomatic connections are general knowledge, people can seldom afford to go home just because they feel sick of it all—have an actual attack of vomiting and diarrhea, all is well. Criticism is disarmed.

Who says how much *I* can venture, emotionally, if not I myself? And I did see it as a venture; I could have put a quick and easy stop to my dreams with sleeping pills, and indeed thought of doing so, but then I thought that the stress was within the limits of what I could cope with. Why did no one trust me to stand what I thought I could stand? In a discreet, solicitous and patronizing way, I was declared incapable of responsibility for myself; my reaction was described as "too strong" (i.e., I was too weak for it), the fantasies, feelings and insights I had worked out for myself and of which I was proud were declared to be sick (= crazy).

If all this was "too strong" for her, measured against her own experience end feelings, did that automatically mean that I must observe the same limits and ability to withstand fear as she did, or as other analysands did? It could be, after all, that many things appeared to me with my history and background more easily accessible, more playful and natural than to other people, that I could just go down more easily into my own depths?

It could be that for others, such a night might have meant loosening defenses more easily than it did for me.

Probably some of the priests, pastors, churchmen, etc., had shifted some of their condemnation of instinctual desires on to me, thus powerfully strengthening my own sexual guilt feelings. After the workshop I wasn't able to feel anything physical at all any more for a while. And it was surely no chance that one genuinely psychotically decompensated participant, a man connected with the church, was about to get married. He was particularly sensitive to the atmosphere which intensified his current problems.

So I carried that episode about with me for years, with a considerable sense of sickness, shame and uncertainty.

Formal criticism of me and the psychotic drugs that were given to me afterwards prevented proper understanding of the episode.

She didn't ask: "What do you mean by the song? What were you afraid of?" Had we been able to communicate better she might have stumbled upon the text of the song and perhaps might have come to see my criticism of her in the line which ran in German translation "Jedes Wort das legten sie falsch aus"—"They took every word the wrong way." That criticism might also have included my family, but certainly and decidedly it applied to my analyst. Probably it was because of some connection to her that I did not have nightmares until the night before my session and not earlier, circumstances that were very difficult.

PAGE 43

In retrospect the statement is clear: "Who has destroyed my song?" ran the words in their German translation. "They took every word the wrong way, and it won applause." In the original American: "Look what they done to my brain, Ma, they picked it like a chicken bone . . ." I thought then of my brothers, my mother, etc. I now think that I was directing criticism against that kind of analysis, that kind of analytic climate, against my analyst herself, and that was probably why she didn't see what I was trying to express.

PAGES 40-41

The episode lodged within me like an undrained abscess; then it was partly worked through at the beginning of my second analysis. I was thankful to my second analyst for that; it was a good if brief and only partial experience.

Very much later I realized that it was probably the deep-seated hostility to women which had really shaken me; I experienced that clearly and unmistakably at the second workshop I went to.

During my first analysis, I had never felt as strong and vital as I do when I am feeling full of enthusiasm, in love, when my powers and my whole body are stimulated. My increasing awareness of being sick troubled me, made me feel low. I felt oppressed by myself and my environment. My energy was only just enough for everyday life; anything in excess of that, any enthusiasm, were consumed by discontent.

PAGES 46-47

Anyway, my impression that he understood me too superficially and not adequately enough came back after three and a half years of analysis.

PAGE 48

I realized later that he flirted with everyone like this, and sometimes more obviously, that I had sensed real if not very pressing advances, and behaved in a less forthcoming way only as a consequence of my watchful, and probably more boring, behavior towards him after the interpretation. I cannot accept that this was a self-fulfilling prophecy (along the lines of: You went on at him until it was all he could do; or: You shaped the situation which you thought you felt), since he acted the same way with other women before and after I appeared on the scene.

PAGE 49

I now think that my wish to use the informal mode of address corresponded to my perception that the relationship with my analyst wasn't going so well; this happened at the time when the "Westwall" mood first set in. I must have noticed that there was now more distance between us than I liked, more than I had previously been used to, and this may have been my way of trying to recreate greater familiarity. My idea, anyway, was correlated with a wish for more closeness. Perhaps questions would have helped: "Am I too remote? Too distanced? Are you feeling all right?" But there were deeper levels of interpretation here; we stopped short at the prohibition.

PAGES 52-53

He could perhaps have taken obstinacy seriously and appreciated my fighting spirit. Such a fighting spirit is harder to achieve and a better aim of therapy than the docile acceptance of rules. It would have been good if he could have taken my behavior seriously, concluding from it that something was existentially important to me. If, perhaps, he really didn't understand the situation, what I actually meant, what it was all basically about as far as I was concerned, he could have left the problem open. When what was a peaceable and understanding atmosphere suddenly turned into a horrible, walled-in, entrenched and scarcely endurable one, that was something that needed to be understood.

PAGE 68

Now I think: What thoughtless, narrow-minded arrogance of judgment! I can't limit my associations to Schubert, Faust, Greek verse and the other treasures of Western culture. Free association—yes, but in the context of one's own social background, taste, inclinations and limitations. Outside that context nothing is worth hearing or understanding. Etiquette and correct conduct. Like the story of the headmaster lost in the forest, who interrupts a farmer giving directions in dialect—"Please speak clearly and articulate properly."

There was also something wrong with the discussion in that he was—at least in part—not really objecting to the form of the pop song, which wasn't even extremely corny, but was making use of formal criticism to defend against my implicit criticism. I suppose that his affect related to my criticism, that he probably understood it on a deeper plane and was reacting to it. Other people to whom I played the song later—within and outside training or therapeutic analysis—were quick to grasp the sense of the text, anyway. My presumably critical observations weren't even expressed in symbolic form, they could be taken literally, as a precise statement. (As I write, however, I have further doubts as to whether that clear and direct expression, without the use of symbolic disguise, is not yet another way in which I made myself hard to understand; I would like to eradicate these acquired ways of thought from my brain and not replace them.)

"Trash" hit a sore place in me, anyway, and increased my inhibitions: At heart I felt embarrassed, myself, at finding vulgar music so important to me all of a sudden: Pop songs instead of good music, street songs and folksongs instead of Schubert, etc. I thought my musical development lowbrow; I felt retarded. It bothered me that I did not play an instrument, even though I'd been relieved at the time when I didn't have to go to piano lessions any more. At eleven, I had switched over to the common typewriter instead. It took me courage to enjoy pop songs, not just to run them down, but to stand up for what I liked. If people in my professional environment wanted Archiv recordings of the classics for their birthdays, it was culturally shocking for me to spend a similar sum on a record of popular songs. Back to my own misgivings.

I could probably have accepted such a reaction as, "I think this style of music, that tune, that kind of thing is repulsive; I can't stand listening to it"—if he had then gone on to look at the content. With my first analyst, despite her interest and the careful way she listened to the song, it had been a matter of bland incomprehension. Not of annoyance, not of striking back at an old wound, not of a struggle on unequal terms. I may conclude that my second analyst may still have been closer to understanding the meaning of the song. (I should be glad of his difficulty in controlling his affects, which made it possible for me to distance myself and criticize later on.)

Genuine esthetic distaste would have been credible; it might perhaps have amused me; it would have been genuine, consistent, credible and all right, and I think I can judge such things.

But he wasn't really so very refined: Not his room, nor his speech, nor his outward appearance.

PAGES 71-72

Perhaps I was also using these songs to express death wishes against my analyst, and he didn't realize.

Two years later I had such wishes, violent ones; I was well able to imagine shooting him; as I realized only much later, I had ensured that my last analytic session was on the anniversary of my father's death. Probably my feelings at this earlier time were not much less violent. Perhaps my intensity had worried him and he was avoiding the subject. I was attuned to his attitude by now, had had experience of it, so that I wasn't insisting on precise analysis any more, or on his listening.

There are several possible explanations for the way my feelings on the subject of my father remained the same for quite a while: The fact that I'd repressed my grief for so long, keeping it deep within me, so that I now needed time to work it through, the fact that it was a deep biological wound which might not heal at all, and perhaps had better not be opened up, not least the fact that some part of the subject which could be worked through but which was not yet conscious, which was lying just beneath the surface, was neither interpreted nor understood. Something that was trying to get through to consciousness. At any rate, that is what my anger, disappointment and finally resignation at my analyst's failure to listen to my records properly suggest to me.

PAGE 76

I would have been happy with something along the lines of: No, I didn't especially want to come, I expect you sometimes feel the same. It may have to do with the last session, but I don't feel that at the moment. Still, how are you? Or alternately: I don't feel any reluctance in me, and I do think outside factors really did hold me up. But possibly there's something in me I don't myself perceive. However, what does it mean to you? . . .Then my own perceptions wouldn't have been totally excluded. Even if the real part of them had been only tiny, compared to the projective part, and I'd felt it, I would have had to appreciate this approach. It was his business always to perceive certainty and reality precisely, adequately and with the utmost sensitivity, in all their delicate ramifications. Even if I had been projecting, thoroughly and exclusively, I would presumably have been more easily capable of insight if my own feeling had not been roundly declared nonsense first. The effect was often one of being rigorously turned inside out, something obviously necessary with me.

PAGES 81-82

Inwardly, I bowed to his assessment. However, a little anger was left behind, along with diffidence about expressing such daring ideas. There was a radius, a form, a code within which I had to think and feel. And what I had felt now was too basic; I had overreached myself.

PAGE 92

What did he mean by "really?" Hadn't he believed me hitherto—was the situation in our sessions so unreal that only outside reality convinced him—what did he actually think of me and what I said in analysis, if so brief an impression from normal life was stronger than all my attempts to communicate in the preceding sessions? That hurt me; I felt alone and under great strain. Who was guaranteeing that, in such a mood, I wouldn't cause an accident or simply run into a car in my state of confusion and distress and inattention? All this could easily happen, even if my ego functions kept me from overt suicide. Analysis could end in an outright deadly way.

My analyst does not fully understand the hostility that exists towards women, the current repression of them, the way they are devalued. It may be said that this area lies outside his field of perception, outside anything he is able to experience closely, and he can hardly be a master of empathy in this respect. However, it is possible—and it was, with me—for a doubt, a failure to take someone seriously, referring her real perception of the hostility in her environment and towards her back to her early childhood, to have extremely confusing and disconcerting effects, immensely increasing the pressure of suffering.

We did not take into consideration the simple, group dynamics aspect, which other people without any analytic training could see (envy, rivalry, "that happens regularly with this sort of person").

PAGE 96

The man who was around and was important in my life from the ages of three to five, my almost-stepfather, was Jewish; strong, loving men/father figures were just coming back from exile abroad when I was at an impressionable age. In 1945, I thought a dress and a pair of shoes from New York were wonderful. Possibly I defend against tinges of anti-Semitism with philo-Semitism, but in fact my parents' friends, the people who really cared about us, were people who emigrated, and that remained essentially the case, certainly where I was concerned. I don't know how I would have survived the period of my analysis without the unquestioning faith of such friends.

PAGES 106-107

Very much later, I realized that his annoyance might relate to my incorrect street address, which contained the word for "blade," not exactly a welcome idea directly after his operation. My hidden, aggressive potential was being treated on the wrong and punitive plane. I could feel his injured and aggressive reaction, but could make nothing of it on the apparent plane.

PAGE 113

Fifty minutes were certainly no biological necessity, not the only space of time within which the human brain could work analytically. However, they were presumably a unit which had proved useful and meaningful, though it also had its disadvantages. If I couldn't manage to tailor my affect or my memory to that fifty minutes, I could still feel it hours afterwards. In later courses (for instance, in Gestalt therapy) I found the use of open-ended periods of time better and more humane, increasing the intensity of the whole procedure. It also makes me feel cautious if I know I must be functioning clearly and objectively again within the next half hour, I must have my agitation filed away by then, or it will hinder me in my work. If it is not sealed off, if I have only let a little bit of it out, time disintegrates the experience and the memory. Subjects can be made more bearable and less overpowering and troublesome if they are divided into portions, but this can also disturb and impede the entire process of working through something, so that affects express themselves in a more shallow and cautious way. If it had simply been the case that my analyst happened to have planned his day in those units, I would probably have understood. However, I felt I was being ordered about, forced to keep rules whose point I didn't see and to recognize their validity. Later, he once remarked I had treated him in such discussions like a simpleton.

PAGE 114

This problem solved itself later; I don't know just why, but one day I suddenly found I had no more trouble with it. It was a relief to have dictated a letter on the day of a patient's discharge, or earlier; it was less unpleasant to sit down and dictate than to endure my lack of order and guilty conscience, and in the end I found I sometimes liked doing it. I relate my sudden ability to an earlier remark—"But don't you want to go on vacation feeling you've done it?"—when I was going to leave something undone; and also to the infectious example of people who do get things done fast. Anyway, in such an atmosphere the remark had its effect on me; I hadn't clearly realized what a constant oppressive weight of guilt my unwritten letters and general neglect to get things done meant. At the start of a vacation I had often had bad dreams about things left undone, and frequently it took a few weeks before I stopped dreaming of the hospital. I still had some trouble getting myself started, but it was worth it for the relief. The effort was rewarding, the painful element in forcing myself to get down to work was nothing compared to the guilt feelings I might otherwise expect. And I did not stop to reproach myself with the fact that I found starting work hard, or wonder why I did. I simply made an effort, gave myself a push, and it became easier and easier.

One positive aspect of my inhibitions was that it is downright arrogant to try to fit a complete human being into a system of medical diagnosis after a short and relatively superficial acquaintance. And it can also be aggressive to land someone with such a diagnosis and then quickly rid myself of him into the tape recorder. However, I did react faster than usual with people I didn't like; I found their case histories were rapidly out of my room and into the archives.

If I felt great reluctance to dictate material one reason could be that I did better to let the entire complex of thought mature within me for a while, and then, after a certain interval of time, I could do the job relatively easily.

PAGE 120

And even if he had been right there, might this not simply have shown my sensitivity to many interrelations of problems? Why couldn't he consider *that* possibility, instead of setting me right and interpreting my conduct as the result of tension?

PAGE 121

I can make allowances for his concern for me; for my ability to work, my relationships with my colleagues, and for the fact that that was why he so often slowed me down, tried to put the brakes on and lead me to react in the same way as other people. One did indeed function best, fastest and most easily if one remained uninvolved, but surely that was not the aim of therapy. He was measuring me by his own standards and those of others. He was a training analyst, and that was my career aim.

PAGE 123

Only much later did it strike me that it was downright embarrassing for them not to have thought of this before. I had expressed something which had simply been forgotten and repressed in their concern for the child and their helplessness in the face of her basic sickness.

PAGE 136

I still feel annoyed with myself for the trouble I take and my submissiveness when I have tried to "integrate myself," "fit into the group," poking around in myself and wondering what I may have done this time when some tension I can't explain has arisen among the men around a table.

PAGES 138-139

Why couldn't he simply perceive my longings and desires for once? Perhaps I was lacking passive caresses and tenderness meant only for me and my body without giving anything in return? Something simply given me free. But before I could perceive or realize that at all I had been corrected, criticized, put right. He didn't like me that way. I had to act differently.

I had satisfied my appetite for meat and condensed milk while in Switzerland for the second course, and it had agreed with me. Why shouldn't I perceive my hunger for eroticism with no strings attached for once, maybe satisfy it, and then see what would happen?

PAGE 140

The possibility that I might, as an object of projection, have released stereotyped reactions in them was not considered. Yet there are women, and I have to reconcile myself to that, who see me and instantly reject me without coming to know me any better.

PAGE 141

Did I have to try and conform to the ideal of the woman in the film "Ein Schiff Wird Kommen?" Couldn't he understand and recognize that I had felt deeply revolted? Did it absolutely have to be all my problem? Couldn't it also lie in the way this acquaintance of mine, at a mature age, had spared himself sexual experience? Yes, this was my analysis, focusing on my problems, but presumably the man had problems of his own too, which had not left me untouched? Perhaps he had wanted to put me to flight; in his colossal ambivalence. Anyway, my analyst and I became hung up on wondering if I'd be able to initiate a man or not, and I was left the arrogant, egocentric one, with no desire for the inexperienced. A woman who was looking, in an infantile way and without any maternal feeling, for someone else to take the lead, make the first move, provide the activity, childishly refusing to pass on what she knew to others.

PAGES 154-155

It didn't seem as if we could discuss the point that perhaps some things came to light more clearly and openly in relation to a new woman colleague, someone who wasn't yet involved in the interrelationships of dependency.

Since I have come to see the reality of hostility to women, I have found my problems in working with men extremely commonplace and obvious. At the time, however, what with the internal anger I felt against those who had previously done me harm (my brothers) in that they made it harder for me to get along with my colleagues now, I constructed for myself a system of thought that made me no easier to get along with nor more equable. On the other hand, this was a good sturdy kind of anger, and presumably there had been some forceful conflicts with my siblings too, even it I might not remember them as particularly violent and emotional.

Reading List

A. (Jean-Jacques) Abrahams: *Psychoanalytischer Diskurs, Les Temps Modernes*, Paris 1969.

Mary Barnes and Joseph Berke: *Two Accounts of a Journey Through Madness*, London 1971.

Roswitha Burgard: *Wie Frauen Verrückt Gemacht Werden*, Berlin 1978.

Janine Chasseguet-Smirgel (ed.): *Female Sexuality, New Psychoanalytic Views*, Ann Arbor 1970.

Phyllis Chesler: *Women and Madness*, New York 1972.

Bert Engelmann: *Deutschland ohne Juden*, Munich 1979.

Erich Fromm: *The Art of Loving*, London 1978.

Erich Fromm: *The Crisis of Psychoanalysis*, London 1971.

Erich Fromm: *Greatness and Limitation of Freud's Thought*, London 1980.

Muriel Gardiner (ed.): *The Wolf-man and Sigmund Freud*, London 1972.

Janet & Paul Gotkin: *Too Much Anger, Too Many Tears*, New York 1975.

Julius Hackethal: *Auf Messers Schneide*, Reinbek 1976.

Ivan Illich: *Medical Nemesis*, New York 1976.

Gudrun Körner (ed.): *Mit Dreissig Muss Man Wissen, Was Man Will. Gespräche mit Frauen*, Frankfurt 1975.

Tilmann Moser: *"Vorwort" in Lehrjahre auf der Couch; Bruchstücke meiner Psychoanalyse*, Frankfurt 1974.

Paul Parin: *Der Widerspruch im Subjekt*, Frankfurt 1978.

Horst-Eberhard Richter: *Flüchten oder Standhalten*, Reinbek, Hamburg 1974.

Morton Schatzmann: *Soul Murder: Persecution in the Family*, London 1973.

Christel Schöttler: *Vortrag zum Erwerb der Ordentlichen Mitgliedschaft in der DPV, Gehalten am 28.4.78*, Kassel (unpublished).

Daniel Paul Schreber: *Memoirs of my Nervous Illness*, London 1955.

Walter F. Toman: *Family Constellation*, New York 1976.